T0339714

The Gender Equation in Schools

This compelling book takes you inside a teacher's journey to explore the question of gender in education. Jason Ablin uses his background in math teaching, school leadership, and neuroscience to present expert interviews, research, and anecdotes about gender bias in schools and how it impacts our best efforts to educate children. He provides practical takeaways on how teachers and leaders can do better for students. There is also a handy Appendix with step-by-step guides for facilitating faculty-wide conversations around gender; writing learning reports without gender bias; using student assessments to check gendered attitudes about learning; evaluating learning spaces; and creating an inquiry map of your classroom. As a teacher, administrator, DEI director, or homeschooling parent, with the strategies and stories in this book, you'll be ready to embark upon your own journey to balance the gender equation and create greater equity for all of your students.

Jason Ablin (@JasonAblin) has served as a teacher, department chair, principal, and head of school. He holds national certification in leadership coaching and mentoring from the National Association of School Principals and has been supporting and mentoring new leaders throughout the country for over ten years. At American Jewish University and in school-based teacher workshops, he trains teachers to create gender aware classrooms and has taught year-long courses to teams of educators in graduate level seminars regarding the relationship between cognitive neuroscience and education. He is also the founder and director of AJU's Mentor Teacher Certification Program.

Also Available from Routledge Eye On Education
(www.routledge.com/k-12)

Let's Get Real, Second Edition: Exploring Race, Class, and Gender Identities in the Classroom
Martha Caldwell and Oman Frame

Gender and Sexuality Matters in the Classroom: An Educator's Guide
Marni Brown, Baker Rogers, and Martha Caldwell

Identity-Affirming Classrooms: Spaces that Center Humanity
Erica Buchanan-Rivera

10 Perspectives on Equity in Education
Onica Mayers, Jimmy Casas, Jeffrey Zoul

The Gender Equation in Schools

How to Create Equity and Fairness for All Students

Jason Ablin

Routledge
Taylor & Francis Group

NEW YORK AND LONDON

Cover image: © Getty Images

First published 2022
by Routledge
605 Third Avenue, New York, NY 10158

and by Routledge
4 Park Square, Milton Park, Abingdon, Oxon, OX14 4RN

Routledge is an imprint of the Taylor & Francis Group, an informa business

© 2022 Jason Ablin

Sections of Chapter Two are originally from an article by the author published in *HaYidion: The Prizmah Journal*. Gratitude to Dr. Elliott Rabin, Editor, and Prizmah for permissions.

Trademark notice: Product or corporate names may be trademarks or registered trademarks, and are used only for identification and explanation without intent to infringe.

Library of Congress Cataloging-in-Publication Data
Names: Ablin, Jason, author.
Title: The gender equation in schools: how to create equity and fairness for all students / Jason Ablin.
Description: New York, NY: Routledge, 2022. |
Series: Routledge eye on education | Includes bibliographical references.
Identifiers: LCCN 2021056638 (print) | LCCN 2021056637 (ebook) | ISBN 9781032101323 (paperback) | ISBN 9781032107813 (hardback) | ISBN 9781003217022 (ebook) |
Subjects: LCSH: Sex discrimination in education—United States—Prevention. | Educational equalization—United States.
Classification: LCC LC212.82 .A25 2022 (ebook) | LCC LC212.82 (print) | DDC 379.2/60973 23/eng/20220—dc18
LC record available at https://lccn.loc.gov/2021056638

ISBN: 9781032107813 (hbk)
ISBN: 9781032101323 (pbk)
ISBN: 9781003217022 (ebk)

DOI: 10.4324/9781003217022

Typeset in Palatino
by codeMantra

Access the Support Material: www.routledge.com/9781032101323

For Lisa Bellows Ablin, Kayla Danit, and Noa Sarit. You are my everything and my always.

In memory of David Ablin. Big brother, I felt you sitting beside me throughout this entire journey.

Contents

Downloadable version of the Appendix is available at www.routledge.com/9781032101323 to be printed for classroom use

About the Author

With over thirty years in education and educational leadership, Jason Ablin has served as a teacher, department chair, principal, and head of school. He holds national certification in leadership coaching and mentoring from the National Association of School Principals and has been supporting and mentoring new leaders throughout the country for over ten years.

In 2008 in a sabbatical year, he partnered with top developmental psychology and cognitive neuroscience researchers to bring research findings into the classroom and education. He has written for the prestigious journal, *Mind, Brain and Education*, about the research findings of Dr. Mary Helen Immordino-Yang of USC who examined the impact of two boys who received functional hemispherectomies and its impact on their capacity to learn.

As an instructor at American Jewish University's graduate programs for teacher training and master's degrees in education and in school-based teacher workshops, he trains teachers to create gender aware classrooms and has taught year-long courses to teams of educators in graduate level seminars regarding the relationship between cognitive neuroscience and education. He is also the founder and director of AJU's Mentor Teacher Certification Program.

A native of the Lower East Side in New York, with a BA from Vassar College and an MA from New York University, Jason Ablin now lives in Los Angeles for thirty years with his wife, Lisa Bellows Ablin, and daughters, Kayla Danit and Noa Sarit.

Follow Jason on Twitter @JasonAblin and continue the conversation using the hashtag #thegenderequation!

Introduction

I decided to go for it. After twenty-five years in formal education, working as a teacher and administrator in middle and high schools, I decided it was time to challenge some assumptions and see what would happen. In the fall of 2013, I took the position of principal at a well-regarded private Pre-K through eighth grade day school in the middle of Los Angeles. I was ridiculously excited about the opportunity; I had never been a leader in a school with an early childhood and elementary school. I had read reams of papers and research regarding children as young as newborns through ten years old, but I had never seen them in action day in, day out. I was excited to get to know them, to support their growth, and to learn.

Few doctors grew up in a hospital, few lawyers cut their teeth in a courtroom, few senators had their first life experiences in the halls of government. Teaching is the only profession where we distinctly return to the scene of the crime. Teaching is the only profession where you will already have spent, modestly, somewhere between 17,000 to 20,000 hours in the place you will later call your workplace. Yet for teachers, summoning the memories of childhood experiences can be productive, but can also be fraught with complications, reinforcing social trends that need a true revolution such as the issue of gender.

DOI: 10.4324/9781003217022-1

Many of my past students would gladly share that I never felt shy or inhibited about rattling them to push the larger agenda of growth. One of my favorite expressions for new teachers is that our job is to "comfort the afflicted and afflict the comfortable." In a crowded auditorium at the beginning of back-to-school night, at my new school, in September 2013, with over 500 parents in the room, I decided it was time to make everyone uncomfortable.

After introducing myself and expressing how excited I was about the coming year, I announced that I had a homework assignment for everyone in the room. I told the parents that over the course of the year I wanted to hear reports back from them about how it was going. I made pointed eye contact with a number of women in the audience before making my next statement.

> 'Moms, you are now responsible for doing your math homework with your daughters when they need your help. No waiting for Dad to come home, no telling her that you're not good at it, no saying, 'Call a friend.' You need to dive in and support your daughters with their math studies this year. Use the Internet, call someone and ask for help, look at the materials sent home from the teacher to support. And, no telling your female students that you were 'just not good at math in school.'
>
> 'Dads,' I turned my gaze towards several of the men in the audience. 'Your homework is to read to and with your sons. The Internet does not count. It can be newspapers, magazines, preferably books. Pick subjects you both like, do the assigned reading logs that come home from school, go to the library together. Whatever. You're to show your sons that reading matters.'

I paused for emphasis. "I am calling many of you during the year to see how it is going."

The crowd was silent except for a few surprised guffaws. Looking at the women, I saw some nervous smiles. I imagined they were thinking, "How am I going to do this? I hate math. Is he serious?"

The men were harder to read. Many remained expressionless.

Was I successful? I would give myself a fifty percent in touching a nerve or getting parents to respond as I requested. Starting with this first public speech in front of the school's parent constituency, I spent the next five years engaging the mothers of our community in this conversation. I received anxious phone calls asking how to do it right. Success stories, epic failures, mothers who, after their children had graduated and matriculated into high school, were still doing the emotionally grinding work of putting their past insecurities aside to make a difference with their daughters. Teachers reported to me that, for the first time, mothers were asking for videos demonstrating how the math was being taught. The teachers felt pressed to find more supporting materials, but also felt validated and proud. They were experiencing parents who were seeing how tough it was to instruct students in complex subjects like math. The teachers were also having, many for the first time, gender conversations with parents. The mothers were willing to try to transcend their own anxiety about math for the best interests of their children. In other words, they got it. It was humbling and a good reminder what pain and discomfort parents are willing to endure for their children.

One mother, who found that her seventh-grade daughter was quite advanced in math, decided to take a parallel online algebra class. Her daughter, despite her talent in math, would grow nervous before exams, so the mother wanted to set a good example about overcoming stress. "When I came to my first online test for the class," the woman told me,

> I broke down in tears. I couldn't get through the first three problems before I had to stop and shut my laptop. I was at work doing the test during lunch, and all my co-workers thought something terrible had happened. I told them it did. I had to take a math test!!

Mom shared this experience with her daughter and the girl smiled throughout the conversation because she finally felt heard. "I was sitting in an office by myself with nothing really at stake except my ego," the mother recounted. "I had forgotten what it must be like to sit in some classroom with a group of overachieving math students constantly trying to prove that you belong." I had similar conversations with other mothers; nothing that I have said to a room full of parents has mattered so much. In that regard, it felt like a victory and a major breakthrough. At least for the women.

The fathers? Not so much. Just one dad over the next five years engaged me about the task I had placed before them. One.

This didn't entirely surprise me. Now, some of them might have taken on the challenge and just didn't communicate with me about it (how shocking coming from men!). But I believe most dismissed my homework assignment for many reasons, obvious and subtle, which also speak to the profound work that we need to do regarding gender roles in our homes and our schools.

Some said it was the wife's job to take care of schooling, or the teachers at this expensive private school. Some said their boys weren't interested in reading. Some said they spent time with their kids in other ways – playing sports, going to their games. Others said they were too busy, as the breadwinners, working long hours to support their families. And others were just plain afraid.

"I'm afraid that my son will see that I am not a very good reader," confided one father. "English is not my first language, and it was hard for me in school when I came to America and had to learn how to read." Others admitted that they didn't like to read, that there was a contradiction between what they say and what they do.

> I say education is so important, but I never read, I do not take the time to learn new things. That I am a bit stuck, that I would rather wind down in front of a television than pick up a book – perhaps people will think there is something different or wrong about me if I am an avid, passionate reader – that this is not what boys do with their fathers.

I get upset, sad, and feel the pain when some father tells me, with a bizarre sense of pride, that he "got through" school without reading much or ever finishing a book. Statements like these represent a type of compensation in which men engage. As we will see further on, activities like reading can be associated with the feminine, very much challenging masculine constructions of the self. But I am by nature an optimist and hope that some fathers saw the point of what I was trying to communicate and decided to take some action, even if they never came to tell me about it.

Now, some of you may be asking the obvious question and the answer is, yes. Mothers should also be doing math with their sons and fathers should read with their daughters. Families and homes are complex, and throughout a child's development, they need different gender experiences at different times. But gender alignment and modeling, the idea that children look to the parent of same sex for all sorts of cues, gestures, and attitudes to define gender, is very real. We cannot ignore how important it is to dispel the myths that have plagued both our boys and girls whether regarding areas of learning such as math or literacy.

Why the Gender Issue in Schools? Why Now?

It is 1983 and I am a freshman at Vassar College in upstate New York. I am sitting in my American Politics 101 class with Professor Sy Plotkin. He is notable in my life for two reasons. He gave me a "D" on my first college paper and his passion as an educator inspired me to major in Political Science and ultimately go into education.

But something else happened for me in Sy Plotkin's class my first year of college that set me on a personal and professional journey for the next thirty-five years. He was discussing the galvanizing social movements of the 1960s and 1970s and how they shaped our current political system. The civil rights movement, labor, and indigenous peoples to name just a few. What he said next stuck with me ever since. Without dismissing the impact of all these minority movements, Prof. Plotkin said the women's liberation movement was the most important. Not because the others didn't matter. Far from it. But because of the numbers.

"It's simple," he continued, "How can you have over fifty percent of the country and the world's population live under oppressive circumstances, treated unequally, and it not have severe ramifications for our ongoing development as a human race?"

For the first time in my short life, I was overtaken and overwhelmed by an idea. Not just its rightness, but also its clarity, logic, and moral imperative.

And, yes, it did matter for this eighteen-year-old that an older man was making this statement. Gender matters both in terms of the message being delivered and in terms of who is delivering that message.

Not only have too many men not taken the feminist movement seriously, but we refuse to significantly come to terms that we are at the heart of the problem. This is really on our shoulders to fix, within our schools, workplaces, within our families, within our houses of worship and, most importantly, within our hearts. For me to hear a man say these words was more than just coming to terms with a highly rational and thoughtful argument; it was a form of revelation. Plotkin was willing to humble himself and insert into his professional and personal framework this critical realization without apologetics. He knew and hoped he was shaping the minds of his students. I, at least, can account for the power of that moment.

So why is this the beginning, for me, of this story? Why is this the personal origin, at least consciously, of your author's passion about gender in education?

The beginning of the 1980s was an inflection point in the history of American education. It was the start of our country's turning away from the value of education as a central driver for the American Democratic experiment.

When the French intellectual Alexis de Tocqueville visited America in the early nineteenth century, he noted that every town he visited had two institutions, a house of worship and a school.[1] Schools represented the promise and training ground for a free mind and the flourishing of this new democratic experiment. The fight for equal education has been hard fought and continues today, crossing gender, racial, and socio-economic lines. There is no hiding from the fact that African American and

Indigenous people's school systems were specifically established and funded in such a way as to maintain inequalities and disparities. And the battle to create equal opportunities for women was a long and hard fight for justice. But I would contend that the *argument* for an equal education based on universal access is deeply rooted in our country's philosophical soil. Those in power who wish to subvert this reality do so with largely perceived callousness and are regarded as attempting to subvert a fundamental American natural right.

By the late nineteenth and beginning of the twentieth century, this was nothing less than a revolutionary idea. This idea of an American education smashed notions of caste, social class, and institutionalized inequality and gave legs to the idea of the American Dream. American students had access, throughout their schooling years, to both an academic and industrialized education which was denied to other students in other countries beyond the age of thirteen, often based on tests which created elitist systems that favored the privileged or maintained deeply entrenched social and ethnic caste systems. In 1955–1956, nearly eighty percent of American students fifteen to nineteen were enrolled in full time general education, versus a high of thirty percent in most European countries. And there, many more students could only aspire and were relegated to technical training, having been sifted out of the road to a college education by the time they were thirteen.[2]

Regarding gender, while acknowledging that access for women to the entire curriculum was restricted, scholars Claudine Goldin and Lawrence Katz note that by "the end of the 19th century, coeducation existed in all schools and in all grades in most US cities. Rural schools were...uniformly coeducational by 1890."[3] They also record the reaction by educational leaders in Europe to what they observed in American schools as they visited the Chicago Educational Congress of 1893.

'It seems strange,' one of the German delegates from Prussia, 'to see boys and girls not only of thirteen, but even sixteen years of age, sitting together or standing in mixed rows.' The French were even more stunned. 'Of all

the features which characterize American education perhaps the most striking,' noted the female French minister
of public instruction, 'is the co-education of young men
and young women…for it reveals to him a state of mind
and habits which is entirely strange to him.'[4]

More American women received high school diplomas in the
twentieth century than men and more women today receive college degrees than men.[5] As a matter of intended or unintended
consequences, our founding principles fueled the ongoing feminist revolution and the feminist revolution forced this country to
begin to live up to at least parts of its own national mythologies
through equal access to education.

By the 1980s, however, this egalitarian vision and purpose of
that education was morphing quickly. Education was being perceived as merely an economic driver – a means to an end. It was
beginning to lack any real value in and of itself as the country
turned its attention more fully toward post industrialism, ram-
pant consumption, and eventually enormous economic divides.
As that greater purpose and dream began to fade, so did our
educational systems.

California is a great example of where the perceived value
of a child's education and the quality of education seemed to
spiral down together. California was the top-ranked system
in the country, perhaps the world, in the 1960s and 1970s and
within twenty years, by the 1990s ranked as one of the lowest.
The perceptions regarding education and its value are always
wrapped up in what we are willing to pay for. Proposition 13,
which ostensibly froze property taxes in California, guaranteed the inevitable collapse of the system through inadequate
funding.

Ask any public policy expert what single factor con-
tributed most to the decline of California's schools, and
the answer will invariably be the state's retro version of
Brexit: a referendum, passed in 1978 on a wave of populist anger, that was earth-shattering in its impact and has
proven enduringly divisive.[6]

writes journalist Andrew Gumbel. Proposition 13 was not just a tax revolt; it was an assault on poor people and marginalized people of color who were already receiving an inadequate proportion of the state's wealth to educate their children. None of this should come as a surprise as its governor during much of this decline, Ronald Reagan, was associated with disparaging African Americans and portraying them as living off the welfare system.[7] These types of associations, between anti-welfare politics and post industrialism, suggest that education is something the state and the country should not even be paying for.

What is taking place in 2021 is a frightening extension of the breaking of these educational natural rights for our students, and conservative forces are attempting to tighten their grip on what is taught in our schools. Recently, legislative bills in states such as New Hampshire[8] are meant to directly destroy the promise of public education through privatization. State legislation in Texas[9] and Arizona seeks to muzzle teachers on such issues as race and gender, even instituting a $5,000 criminal fine for teachers who speak of issues outside the standard curriculum.[10] These efforts are directly targeted at silencing teachers speaking about their own gender and race experiences in the classroom.

I have been thinking about this issue as a husband, a father, a son, and as an educator of children, big and small. I have gone from seeing gender as one important issue in schools to truly believing it is the critical issue of the day in educational systems globally. We face enormous struggles in human society, environmental catastrophe, extreme violence, authoritarian oppression, race discrimination, but without creating equality and the physical safety, of mind and body, for (as Sy said) over half of the human population, we do not tap into the best of human society to solve these other global dilemmas.

It is also a narrative of constant and unnecessary compromise and narrowing of expectations for our students. As Shauna Pomerantz and Rebecca Raby point out in their study, *Smart Girls: Success, School, and The Myth of Post Feminism*, while females are rocking school and achieving ever high attainment, even in fields which were traditionally aligned with "male" learning, a post-feminist argument leads us down a precipitous set of assumptions.

> With the playing field presumably leveled, complaints of sexism now sound antiquated, whiny and wounded... With gender inequality considered a thing of the past, girls are now seen to have unlimited access to success. But the flip side to this belief is that girls can no longer cry foul when they experience gender inequality: sexism is framed as a personal, rather than social, defect.[11]

It is as if their success in school forces them to compromise their demands for an equitable society when the exact opposite should be true. The point of addressing larger issues of gender in schools is *because* we want the larger society to shift its access to greater equity and fairness. That should be the entire point. We just are not there yet, and work needs to be done.

And I would argue that where females are forced to make these compromises (access to the full educational system in exchange for their political and social silence) many men are just giving up entirely on the entire endeavor of education. The National Center for Education Statistics, while showing significant gains for women in post-secondary degrees from 1970 to 2018, reports that the number for men completing degrees is in rapid decline. Men seeking Associates degrees at two-year junior colleges declined from just under sixty to thirty-five percent, bachelor's degrees from just under sixty to forty percent, master's degrees from sixty to thirty-eight percent and doctorate degrees from a staggering eighty-five percent completion rate to thirty-five percent.[12] The reasons for this massive decline are still up for debate; however, if what we know about the construction of our narrow patterning of masculinity is correct, that men tend to define themselves by what is not feminine, and the larger endeavor of education is perceived as feminine, the answer to this damaging phenomenon may be right in front of us. With men also twenty-eight percent more likely to drop out of high school than women,[13] the practical, and social implications are very real. If we increase graduation rates by a mere five percent, the results are a staggering 18.5-billion-dollar reduction in crime costs[14] and a twenty percent reduction in violent crime nationally.[15]

So, Where Is the Place to Start?

In Ronan Farrow's 2018 *New Yorker* expose on yet another major media figure and corporation mired in allegations of inappropriate and abusive treatment of female employees, he concludes,

> Experts told me that addressing patterns of harassment at a company as large as CBS generally depends on reform at the highest levels. This sort of conduct is tied to over-all climate and oftentimes to how women are seen or valued within an entire organization.

Fatima Goss Graves, the president and CEO of the National Women's Law Center, commented in the same article that "… there's no question that the head of the organization sets the tone for the entire organization."[16]

There are woefully too few women at the helm of politics, in boardrooms and generally in positions of power. Women's sports are not allotted the same resources as men. We have yet to see a female president, or an across-the-board equal pay for women. Sexual violence and harassment are hideously common – a woman is assaulted every seventy-two seconds in the United States and nine out of ten victims of rape are women.[17] Principals and school administrative leadership are predominantly male, teachers are women. We are way late in the game if we are trying to realign adult institutions and re-educate adults, some of whom have been entrenched in these attitudes and behaviors since they were children. The place to put our most sincere efforts and resources is in that all too undervalued and all too critical environment called schools. And the work goes beyond just dignity and respect. This is a global safety concern, ranging from the humiliating and debilitating experience of workplace sexual abuse at all strata to mental and physical abuse to rape to honor killings. We are not truly living in a human society as long as these realities exist. Through work with young children, partnering with parents in the home, we can move the needle on this problem. What decent parent wants their daughter to feel that she cannot be the best version of herself and contribute to society, or perhaps merely existing without fear for her very safety and sanity? What decent parent wants their son to even play the most minor role, even as a bystander, in this denigrating and base behavior?

I am not a formal researcher in this field. Neither am I a thought leader in the field of gender studies. There are extraordinary people who are at the forefront of trying to solve these problems. What I do have to share in this book and add to the framing of a solution is years of careful consideration and observation of what students need to develop into their best selves, intellectually, academically, emotionally, and socially. School is where it all happens.

This book is a reflection on my experiences as an experienced educator who has worked in many capacities in schools and thought deeply regarding the question of gender and how we can best serve our children in the future. *The Gender Equation* is broken down into a series of experiences and reflections where I have had to discard old ways of thinking to be a better educator, father, son, and husband. My professional life has led me to consider this issue with perhaps a greater focus, but my own personal journey has also made this issue vibrate with a special type of urgency which I will also share in these pages. Many of these ideas and concepts, grounded in research, are reflected in stories from the many years of working with students, teachers, other school administrators and parents. The individuals whose stories I tell are amalgams and archetypes; I would never violate the trust of anyone, particularly my students, by speaking about them directly. With that said, their struggles, successes, and self-realizations are authentic. This book provides multiple examples and approaches for teachers and educational leaders to execute and utilize throughout the kindergarten to twelve experience and in any subject taught.

I am very concerned about how we in schools stigmatize and mistreat our girls and boys and all young people who choose to defy traditional binary gender constraints and expectations. From the standpoint of learning, the narrow definition of gender in schools needs radical rethinking, particularly in our growing awareness and expanding understanding of the gender/sex spectrum overall. All aspects of a well-rounded and thoughtful curriculum of learning should be available to all students. Children are experimenting with gender all day long, and we need to give them the space to construct individual notions of gender identity without judgment. Gender identification is not something to be dissected, categorized, marginalized, or fixed; it should be viewed as a normative process of child and adolescent development. The subtle and not so subtle gender constraints we place as stumbling blocks before our students need to go away.

If education has something to do with bettering our world for the next generation, then gender awareness and equity seems to me the fundamental question regarding the future of education. Starting with when our students begin attending school until they leave the formal life of learning, we socialize them into certain gender roles. And in our desire to create greater equity through their formal education, we focus on the wrong things. Having mothers do math homework with their daughters and fathers read with their sons sounds like a small matter. It is not. My earlier experiments with parents were meant to not only allow children to see their parents in an expanded context in terms of gender. They were also designed to make parents more aware of the way they reinforce bias and stereotypes through learning and school expectations. These are old, entrenched patterns of thinking and behavior which reach far beyond creating literate and numerate children. Teachers and administrators and thought leaders will be very familiar with the importance of this argument: That just as learning and knowledge are constructed,[18] gender perceptions and identity are also performed[19] and constructed. School is one central environment where that script gets written, and the drama unfolds over many years. The world of education and gender construction are inextricably linked. This book is meant to provide some clear, simple insights and steps and practical tools which can truly make a difference.

Who Is This Book for and How Do You Use It?

The Gender Equation is designed for a number of audiences. Educational leaders who are interested in starting both a learning conversation and a larger cultural conversation in their schools and districts regarding gender will find several different avenues for engagement. This discussion is getting more complicated, not less. As research begins to emerge on the experiences of LGBTQIA+ kids in our schools, it will be critical that we have *more* conversations and raise *more* awareness. The tools for teachers and administrators for classroom measurement, observation, and reflection in the appendix can become an essential component of staff professional development and training.

Teachers, in traditional or co-educational environments (camps, after school programs, sports clubs), will find the stories and examples of student interaction highly relatable and hopefully speak to what they experience, observe, and feel on a regular basis as professional educators. The data and research provided serve as important reference points for teachers, to heighten awareness of practice and then self-reflection. I hope that my own struggles and stumbling and small victories along the way serve as a source of connection, humor, and inspiration.

Parents need a window into what happens when their kids go to school every morning and the chaotic few hours before kids go back to sleep only give parents glimpses into these critical developmental hours at school. Parents generally want to know how to raise respectful and dignified children who are self-confident and can be who they are without shame or subject to unnecessary stereotyping which impedes their living and learning in healthy ways. Parents and community leaders can use this book to spark conversations that radiate beyond the school walls.

For better or worse, schools are becoming tasked with the mental health needs of our pupils. We are legally and morally responsible for identifying kids with such major mental health concerns that their physical wellbeing may be in jeopardy. Schools are responsible for the safety of every student who comes through their doors. Eliminating the psychological denigration and physical danger for kids who do not fit comfortably into our artificially constructed views of gender norms must become an educational mission. Educational psychologists, inside and outside of schools, can utilize this book to better contextualize and expand awareness of how gender, if addressed correctly as a school culture issue, can support student mental health initiatives.

A Note on How I Write about Children

My students are savvy, obstinate, funny, self-righteous, curious, anxious, and passionate. They are intelligent, careless, empathic, violent, observant, hungry (like, most of the day), think too little of themselves, and think too much of themselves. They want to be heard, interrupt others, support others, come to the rescue, and figure out how to best contribute to the world. They want success for themselves and success for others.

They are not sweet, lovely, kind, or even wonderful.

These simplistic descriptors, which we all fall into using, do not even begin to tell the true story of a student's journey to adulthood. Barrie Thorne, in her seminal work *Gender Play*, writes:

> To learn *from* children, adults have to challenge the deep assumption that they already know what children are 'like,' both because, as former children, adults have been there, and because, as adults they regard children as less complete versions of themselves. When adults seek to learn about and from children, the challenge is to take the closely familiar and to render it strange.[20]

By discovering the unique language and music for each child, we lessen the possibility of reducing them to stereotypes, particularly in the realm of gender. More complex understandings will lead to fewer assumptions. And few are more capable of communicating these honest portrayals than those who have dedicated themselves to educating children, year after year, spending most of their waking hours together. We need teachers and school people to tell the true story of each student, beyond gender discrimination and bias, to impact our schools and therefore beyond in transformative ways.

1

Who's Teaching Whom

Math, Literacy, and Making School for Everyone

I am sitting with my administration in the school where I became principal four years earlier and we are sweating. It is hot in my office, in the middle of August in Los Angeles. The team is sitting around the big oval desk. My whiteboard wall is covered with section numbers and students' names. We are at the end of our usual three-month-long process of student placement and creating the schedule for the new school year. But we are not just sweating because it is hot. We are sweating because there is a course without a teacher, a singlet without an instructor, one lonely class.

If you know anything about school scheduling, the administration usually bows its head in shame and calls in the math department to do this work, who think this process is somehow fun. Most normal people think scheduling is somewhere between planning for the invasion of Normandy and some version of the *Hunger Games* where no one gets out alive. There are mistakes, then mistakes on top of mistakes, specialties like art or music which have been left out, lunch is too long, recess too short, not enough rooms, the rooms are too small, Teacher X will throw a fit if you move *her* room, there aren't enough bathrooms for the early childhood program, why are the PE teachers teaching

DOI: 10.4324/9781003217022-2

non-stop on Wednesday and then not at all on Tuesday, who's going to cover middle school lunch if everyone is scheduled for meetings? It does not stop. And when you are finished and have gotten everything in place, the school admits four more kids into the third grade.

And, as you sit there in mid-August, thinking that you are finally across the finish line, there is nothing more challenging than a single section of fifteen low-confidence students who need a pre-algebra teacher. And you have not a dime to spend on a part-time instructor. These fifteen kids are all female, because we divide students by gender in the classroom starting in middle school. The school, over seventy years old, has always been this way.

"What are we going to do?" my assistant principal Audrey asks. "None of the other teachers are available. We can't redo the entire middle school schedule for one math class, we can't!" I hear the panic in her voice. We all know this is not a bona fide emergency, but the exhaustion of the process is setting in. Patience and nerves are fraying.

(Disclaimer: I will not be spending an inordinate amount of time discussing single sex versus mixed gender educational environments, which is better, which serves the needs of our children more effectively...etc. In some ways, it is beside the point and a distraction from more pressing issues. As I will discuss further on, single sex environments have the same potential for solidifying negative gender stereotypes regarding learning in all girls' schools as well as in all boys' schools. The difference maker is how teachers are trained and how learning environments are structured to support all learners, regardless of gender.)

What makes finding a volunteer more challenging is that this is a classroom of students who score low in math and high on the disruption scale. You might think if you had to choose between teaching an all-boys class and an all-girls class, the answer would be easy...right? No.

The answer to this question is much more complicated. It depends on the group of students, the disposition of the teacher, and the school itself. When we talk about a girls' class that is tough there is always a lot of "drama," and when we talk about a boys' class, they are always "disruptive" and "unruly." Even in the conversation about difficult kids, we cannot help but to genderize the issue. What makes one group of students challenging often has something to do with their history together and who they are as a collective group interacting at these high stakes moments of human development. Gender becomes a convenient, but often misleading default in thinking as a way to understand these situations.

At this school, students are segregated by gender in the classroom, but not anywhere else throughout the day. Watching the switch in behaviors and attitudes toward learning as students walk into classrooms is often instantaneous. It is a case study in gender stereotypes and how quickly, intentionally or not, that switch gets turned on in us.

"I'll take them," I say.

"I knew it, I knew you were going to do this!" Sara, my student dean, laughs. The other administrators are both relieved and nervous. The issue gets taken care of, we don't have to do some all-nighter to rearrange the schedule, and the students get a reliable teacher who can handle them. My admin team is nervous, however, because, if I take the class, it means every day, there is a little less of me being principal around the building. But the decision is made. There is a part of me that is elated to be with kids in the classroom this coming year and another part is terrified and riddled with anxiety.

What we are going to see now is that my perceptions from the get-go of these students, the common measurements, and ways in which we try to assess what students are learning are quite flawed, particularly when it comes to the roadblocks that constructed gendered experiences in learning create. Student attitudes and behaviors help us to understand the connection between self-perception and learning success. Our job as educators is to pay attention and then work to ameliorate these barriers. We need to understand what we are observing to support our students the most, and often it cannot be found through mass testing or even classroom results. My student, Siena, is going to help us understand this phenomenon better.

"Siena, what do you think about the problem on the board?"
She looks up and is silent. We are doing fractions and decimals.
Adding them. Subtracting. Multiplying. And, dividing.

$$2/3 + 4/6 \div 1.5 = n + 1/3$$

"I think I can't do it. I don't know." It is the first thing that comes
out of her mouth when confronted with a math problem. It is
also a kind of a lie that girls often tell themselves. Of course she
knows some of the problem, but the running tape in her head
admits defeat quickly.

Other hands slowly rise around the room. Because the attention is so narrowly focused on Siena, the other girls are not
feeling the tension of response that they often experience and can
just focus on the problem.

"I don't see any other hands," I say. "This is for Siena to
tackle," She sinks, her shoulders roll down.

"Can't you call on someone else?" She smiles faintly, believing it will fend off my focus on her. She is probably imagining
that I am going to do something very typical and back off because she is exhibiting helplessness. But no. This is not going to
happen right now.

"Nope," I say. "It's all yours." The other girls are struggling
now with the silence and Siena's stress. They want to save her!
Even if it means answering a *math* question.

The truth is that while Siena is struggling right now, she is
a student who loves to learn. She has what I call an intellectual
sense. She looks, she absorbs, she consumes. The most exciting
parts of class for her are when everything else falls away and
there is an interesting question being asked or the learning has
taken an unexpected turn. Occasionally, I invite female guest
speakers who have made their careers in a math-related field. I
want the students to meet female models who loved math growing up and who wanted to spend their time thinking about numbers. I invited one woman with a PhD in economics and she put
several problem sets that an economist might study, real-world
applications of the marketplace. Siena's eyes light up when she
sees a seemingly random group of numbers associated with the

cars, their brands, and the model numbers. She points her finger at the board.

"Only that information is important," Siena says. "The price of cars and the size of the cars. The rest, you're not going to care about. Turn it into a formula, with *n* being the increased cost over how much you're willing to pay and then plot the cars on a graph. X axis is cost, *y* is the size of the car. Then you'll know which car is for you." I look at her, stunned.

"Siena, where did that come from?" I ask. My guest smiles and nods her head in approval.

"It makes sense, Mr. Ablin," she answers. "When it's something *real*."

Siena's moment of understanding is shocking in the moment but not surprising. What Siena means is that the learning must be relevant. It should apply to something she can envision, not just a garbled group of digits. I often do speed drills with the students, to work on their computation skills, their time efficiency, and their number sense, defined as their ability to understand patterns and therefore solve the mechanical aspects of a problem with greater ease and confidence. Forty problems in two minutes. Check your answers, then turn the page to side B, do forty more in two minutes. If you see the pattern, the problems are no problem. Siena struggles because she thinks she needs to do every single problem as an individual act of computation instead of pulling back, looking at the pattern and then ripping through these problems. She has poor number sense. And she is far from alone.

When girls are given models of mathematics as a process of computation (we will look at why this is the case in Chapter 6) rather than number sense, this has long term implications for students as they go through their math careers. Siena is not just coming to me this way. This has been the product of the way she was introduced to and asked to learn math for at least the previous eleven years. And the results are not just performance-based; they are developed biological systems. Students in high school who have reached higher and more advanced levels of math expertise show "detectably more efficient connections between the number sense area of the left intraparietal cortex and the frontal lobe."[1] While this still remains correlative information regarding math acquisition and brain development (or vice versa!), the theory is that this has a "spiraling" impact on a student's ability to acquire increasingly more complex concepts and apply them over time to problem sets.[2] In other words, Siena has the 400 horsepower engine. We've just given her tricycle wheels to move the vehicle. How frustrating this must be. It's not that she has a female brain or that, as a female, she learns math a certain way. The educational system, through a complex system of assumptions and triggers, has shaped her abilities and the way her brain functions, limiting her capacity to reach the highest levels of math attainment.

The will is certainly there also. Given interesting problems and work, Siena's eyes look like they are exploding with interest, her smile evolves into a more rounded expression of wonder. She is highly focused and wants to voluntarily engage. The problem on the board that she backs off from tackling is frustrating because it has no real-life application to it. It is too theoretical for the way in which we have shaped her thinking about mathematics. Siena is right when she looks up at it and says she doesn't understand. The digits are arbitrary. She cannot relate.

So, here is what the data looks like in terms of math attainment, here is why the research seems weird to me (as a school person), and here is what the problem really looks like on the ground.

For over seventy years, researchers have focused on the significant gender gap in our educational systems, particularly in math and science. Men regularly out-performed women in these subjects on standardized tests such as the SAT and ACT.[3] They qualify for and enroll in more of the challenging and sophisticated course offerings, creating an even larger gap in graduate programs and then the industries associated with these fields.[4]

The question was: What is the *cause* of this problem? Was this a biological issue – were men just more suited, cognitively, for these fields? Was it shaped by individual choice? These are interesting questions to ask, if you assume that in some strange fairyland our educational systems were providing fair access to women in these fields. The reality is closer to the opposite.

Remember earlier, in the introduction, I mentioned how the great revolution in American society could be found in its schools, which had, by the middle of the twentieth century, established the principle that both sexes deserved an education as a right, not a privilege? This was by no means a clear and easy path. Every step of the way to establish some sort of equity for women in education was met with considerable blowback and resistance. When women were offered educational opportunities, these offerings often reflected bias. Home economics and manners classes substituted for a real education. Separate and unequal, particularly in colleges and universities, was the norm.

With the breakthrough of women into more mainstream educational institutions and with their access to the same classes as men, not only did these discrepancies in data become more transparent but they also become more examined. The interest, level of serious research, and focus in the academic world on differences in performance by gender skyrocketed.

The data in the field is fascinating because, over the past seventy years, as the problem has been exposed and institutions have become more aware of the issue, the gap has been slowly closing.[5] Today males hold only a slight edge in the upper quartiles of math achievement and women occupy firmly upper excellence and the middle of the bell curve in achievement. That's the great news. Not only are men's and women's standardized test scores converging, but what the studies have shown for a very long time is that, on average, women are just much better students than men. Their grades are better than men's on average, including in upper-level, challenging classes. Women kill it as learners. When given access and similar treatment in math and STEM classes, females rise and perform.

The closing of this gap in such a short period of time also seems to toss out, without much question, those who would argue that there is some biological difference between men and women that can explain performance differences. If that were the case, there would be virtually no change in the research data over time. Another piece of evidence suggesting that we are dealing with issues of bias, access, and equity is that there are a number of countries and cultures, such as Asian countries, where this gap just does not exist. Women are expected to perform at as high a level as men and therefore do so. The fact that the math gap does not exist systemically across cultures suggests we have a particular problem that needs to be addressed here, in the United States, where the gap has been one of the largest.[6] There does look as if there are slight differences cognitively in spatial analysis abilities, with men holding a slim advantage, and women outscoring men in computational problems. However, we will see how this may be a self-fulfilling issue that we also may be able to remedy, for both genders.

Now, this is when things start to get weird. And by weird, I mean both in terms of what the data is telling us consistently and with how we are currently interpreting the problem.

The data does consistently show that when you turn the results of standardized tests and school results into a bell curve, men consistently occupy the high end of the bell curve. (When they are good at math, they are *really* good at math.) Women hold the middle to high end of the bell curve and men hold the bottom end of the bell curve. (When men are bad at math, they are *really* bad). Girls also seem to hold their own or in fact do better than boys in math from approximately ages two to thirteen but then in high school males pull ahead. This gap does not magically appear. The foundation for this gap is women's and men's differing levels of belief in their own abilities in math. And those beliefs are established from the first days of their formal education, from as early as kindergarten.[7] There are no clear answers to why this is the case. And while we should be super proud of ourselves that women are showing critical improvement in these primary and core areas of learning, we should be equally concerned about our boys. And this is what the data is showing me as an educator and someone who works in the field.

Before I get to this part, let me pile another weird on top of weird. When I look at these research studies, I am constantly scratching my head. And this is not regarding one or two studies; this is reams of research done consistently over many years from many different sources by many reliable and incredibly talented academics. The major theme in this research is the comparison between test scores and actual school performance. The reason that this is most likely the case is that this is the available data that academics have access to. So, this is what they are using. And I also know that when reading the thoughtful research in this area, these academics will acknowledge that they are comparing two very distinct schooling experiences. Comparing taking a test versus doing school is like comparing apples and oranges. However, when I read these comparisons, I don't think apples and oranges, I think apples and spaceships. On some level, I do not even understand how these two experiences are in the same sentence. I am going to give an analogy to explain.

Let's say you met a good friend on the street. You have not seen her for a while because she was on vacation. So, you ask, "How was the trip?!"

Let's say your friend decided to tell you about a specific ten minutes of the trip and that it was really an amazing, incredible highlight. Or maybe she chose to share a low point, ten minutes that were so horrible that she hopes that nothing like that ever happens again in her life. What would your conclusion be? Would you want to go on that trip? Would it either persuade you or dissuade you from going on a similar trip? Of course it wouldn't. You would want *more* information!

The same can be said for testing. Standardized testing is a tiny, fractional moment in time in the life of a young learner. What does it tell us about them? How is it really going to measure their true capacities and abilities? Many colleges and universities are realizing the same thing and are giving other accomplishments much higher regard when it comes to the admission process, with more than 1,600 accredited colleges[8] no longer requiring them at all. In other words, admissions officers are seeing tests for what they are, a small moment in time which does not begin to tell a significant story about a person besides their ability to wake up in a decent mood, sit in a room for three to four hours, and coherently choose answers to questions that may be booby-trapped with biases and discriminatory patterns that we have not even thought of yet.

So, test scores are flawed. What about school performance? Unfortunately, taking how students perform in school as a benchmark for their abilities has problems as well. Back to the analogy of your friend and her trip. If in answering the question, "How was your trip?" your friend decided that she was going to tell you every piece of minutiae from the planning, to the arguments with her partner about what to do, to packing, to the plane ride, to the airport at the destination ... at some point, you would yell, "Stop!! That's too much information!! I have no idea what is important or relevant to know to answer the question." When I hear researchers talking about the results of students in schools and trying to draw meaningful data, I furrow my eyebrows in confusion.

From this educator's perspective, schools are incredibly complex environments: They are biology, chemistry, and physical science all mashed together in a single building. They are living organisms that are in constant flux and change. And, while I got into education because I love the messy human complexity of it, sometimes I wish that schools were more like a factories or businesses trying to produce widgets. In fact, they are the opposite.

Over the course of a single day, students ride a roller coaster of emotional, social, and learning experiences. Then they do it again the next day and it looks entirely different. One day a child walks into school after having a fight with her siblings at breakfast. Another child comes in and his mother has just returned the night before from a weeklong business trip. And throw into the mix the moods and attitudes and experiences of the educators. Children come in one way and, for a whole host of reasons which we try to compartmentalize and characterize and quantify, they come out another. For example, schooling has as much to do with parenting as parenting does with community and as community does with schooling. Try just sorting out the day-to-day performance of students of the equation objectively. Schools are semipermeable membranes, constantly negotiating and navigating what comes in and what goes out. To tell me that you are picking and choosing from this experience called "school," certain experiences to measure some area of a child's learning and try to draw conclusions about why they are successful or not seems odd at best.

The results of these extensive studies suggest that there is still much to be done in terms of girls and gender discrimination and bias and at least equal concerns with what is happening with boys. While girls are showing gains and there are significant efforts to improve both the stature and access of girls in STEM related fields, a significant self-selecting process occurs by the time girls arrive at middle school. Girls like Siena move through their early education and elementary years and then their experiences become highly pressurized as they hit the societal and economic realities of early adolescence. A simple example is that in studies in early education programs (two to five-year-olds) school classes, teachers (ninety-five percent of whom are women) are twice as likely to interrupt girls when they speak and are twice as likely to allow boys to interrupt them. It is also commonly found that girls receive simply less teacher attention and direct support than do boys over the course of their primary and secondary schooling.[9] These are striking examples of how small behaviors add up over time to lay the groundwork for how girls will be treated versus boys. The result is what the psychologist and researcher at Simon Fraser University Doreen Kimura calls "self-selection."[10] Simply put, you are going to feel certain ways about yourself and be driven to participate in certain activities and even engage professionally in certain fields because of the positive reinforcement you receive in that area. Kimura argues that there are actual biological foundations for this reality, and we will see the arguments on both sides of this equation.

But the bottom line is these are powerful forces that, if not addressed in schools specifically and consistently, through teacher training and carefully structured observation, just perpetuate old biases. Even with women achieving at higher levels in universities and entering more science and math professions, many women still end up feeling they are not as competent and successful in these areas.[11] It's certainly the most damning evidence that some of the most accomplished people in their field still feel the stinging effects of bias. The gender gap in positions and pay remains significant.

For males, the story has two dramatic components based on the data. First, boys occupying the bottom half of the math curve, both in terms of standardized test scores and their performance in schools, suggest that we are sending a very dangerous message to boys: School is either for you or it is not. Anecdotally, I can tell you that this is exactly the language that is used predominantly with boys when teachers, administrators, and parents get around a table and start talking about a male student who is struggling in school. "School is not for everyone," is one. Another: "He does better when he is working with his hands." And of course, like the aforementioned dads: "He doesn't like to read. He says it bores him." What is interesting is that rarely, rarely do I hear this type of language used to describe girls who are struggling with school. Boys can either do school or they can't. We seem to either peg boys as academic rock stars or instead initiate conversations about trade school. This has much more to do with attempting to maintain a very narrow definition of masculinity than working to solve a student's learning issues.

The other piece of data that comes from studying these research papers on math and achievement has nothing to do with math, and for some strange reason, does not seem to be raising alarms. Across the board, not only in the United States, but in all the OECD countries studied, boys lag significantly behind in terms of literacy. The difference is so significant that you really need two separate bell curves to describe the phenomenon.[12] And, in one study, when even adjusted for socio-economic differences in districts and schools, boys were equally likely to fall far behind in terms of literacy.[13] The differences begin early and get reinforced regularly throughout boys' schooling. While a percentage of boys do catch up by the time they finish high school, many do not. The performance gap in test scores is mirrored by teachers' expectations.

In my school, we performed a sweep of end-of-year student learning portfolios, which were loaded with literacy projects and assignments. (The fact that there was very little math on display in the portfolios is an issue we will look at later when we discuss teacher biases toward learning.) Teachers were just not recognizing how the boys were being allowed to produce subpar work in these areas. There is a type of marginal literacy that was considered acceptable with our boys but not with girls. As we broke down the portfolios statistically by gender, we saw clearly that the males consistently wrote less than their female counterparts.

They were given tacit permission to rush through the work. They handed in writing with incomplete sentences that were off topic and often incoherent, and their writing was less sophisticated when examining word choice. Teachers indicated that they did not "have the time" to get the students to do the work over. What they were also saying is that they did not wish to get into battles with boys who refused to take this work seriously. There was almost an assumption that the boys would never enjoy the work, so why push them to do it?

I believe that both issues for boys also fall into another category of discrimination. If school is merely seen as a means to an end, as a driver for economic concerns, for a consumer culture, and men are still seen and experienced as needing to be the primary breadwinners, then school either matters or it does not! Men who do well in school, particularly in STEM, find themselves empowered to reach economic security and success through one of these safe and often lucrative fields: Business, financial services, engineering, medicine. School fulfills its utilitarian purpose, supporting traditional gender roles. In fact, women would be perceived as a threat to this system if they take one of the coveted spots from a male counterpart. While fields like medicine have seen a revolution in gender over the past thirty-five years, engineering, finance, and high-tech lag behind. The pay gap is still a moral abomination, and these fields do little to support a safe and conducive environment for its striving women. These forms of discrimination do not begin in the workplace. They begin in our schools, homes, and communities. They end up shaping the world around us and none of us are better off for it.

If boys cannot "succeed" at school, we must switch our gears quickly with them. Instead of fixing the problem of school for boys, we dismiss these critical foundational years as "not for them." If boys cannot read, write, and barely do the math, the perceived acceptable solution is to find them a different career path. The importance of their education itself matters little. And, another overarching, perhaps ironic working principle with boys is that we shouldn't push them too hard. Because…they are so fragile? Rather, let them opt out than feel like basic assumptions about their masculinity are being challenged.

The constant, and I would argue, worsening problems of attempting to run a decent, respectful, tolerant, democratic society are ingrained deeply through gender bias and discrimination. No tweaking of HR procedures, congressional committees, or #moments is going to lead to prolonged change in the adult world if we do not address the needs of children.

But let's talk about solutions. Let's see how Siena, through teacher approach, could have a breakthrough in learning math and, more importantly, in her confidence.

Siena is sitting in the silence that I have created. The other girls desperately want to "save" her at this torturous moment. I want the tension to rise to a reasonable level without getting out of hand. I want everyone to deal with a certain level of discomfort without it becoming oppressive. Finally, I turn to the problem and say something that is taking a bit of a risk. I hope I will not regret it.

"You know, when I was working on this problem last night, I was also having a difficult time with it." I said.

"When I looked at it again," I added, "I realized that there were *parts* of it I knew. When I started on the parts I knew, I was able to piece together the rest."

"I know parts," she says. "Can I tell you the parts I do know?"

"Absolutely." I answer.

She walks through the problem, and the rest of it falls into place. What is clear is that Siena needed empathy at this moment, but to have her breakthrough she needed more. She needed, "I don't know" to mean something different than what it had previously meant to her. Instead of defaulting to a gendered response, she needed a door open to what she *did* know.

Now, I have a confession to make to the reader. I am not very good at math. In fact, growing up I was on the far, far left end of that bell curve. And, from a content standpoint, it was not a very good idea for me to select myself as the teacher for these girls struggling with this subject. Some administrators might even call it educational malpractice! If you had told me when I was thirteen that I was going to be teaching a math class, I would have thought you were insane or inebriated. I spent a large part of my junior high school and high school years sweating through my math requirements.

For many years I had math instructors whose teaching style triggered anxiety. They were condescending and didn't take the time to sit down with this struggling student and help solve the terror. This was how my math education went. My teachers and I played the gender game. The teachers just thought I wasn't very good at math, and I claimed not to care very much. The reality was if I had a big math test the next day, that meant no sleep the night before. Studying? I didn't even know where to begin. It felt so hopeless. Standardized tests? The SATs? The worst. It felt like being asked for two hours to read a foreign language. Would I even ask for help? Of course not. That was too dangerous. Unlike Siena, I wouldn't dare say that I couldn't do it. In my silence, I was able to maintain the perfect male mythology, "I can do it if I want to, I just don't want to. It's not for me." The truth was that I couldn't do it; I had many missing skills from years of playing duck and cover. Opening up and being vulnerable about my fears and anxieties was just simply not going to happen.

My only saving moment in math came in tenth grade geometry, where I had the good fortune of having Bob Schwartz for a teacher. He played guitar and during free periods he would teach students how to play, too. I don't think I saw him in the courtyard or the gym once the entire time I knew him. He was a good five inches shorter than me, but he towers over my memories of school. He was positive and encouraging. When you got a part of a problem correct in class, it was as if you had discovered the cure for cancer. His eyes would light up, he would stare you down and scream, "Yes, that's right!!" He had a laugh that always seemed outsized for the moment. Mistakes or errors were opportunities for future understanding. Geometry proofs were a form of poetry. I loved language. He encouraged me to see them as a form of elegant expression. Did my newfound love of math have anything to do with Geometry? No. I think it had to do with Bob. He was kind, empathic, and deeply committed. You walked into his classroom and that was all that mattered. It was a truly safe place for all of us who thought so little of ourselves learning mathematics, wherever you see yourself on the gender spectrum.

Many years later, in 2007, I had the great fortune to take a sabbatical year to work with a gifted and thoughtful researcher at the University of Southern California, Dr. Mary Helen Immordino-Yang, exploring the relationship between cognitive neuroscience and education. (She will be making a more detailed appearance later in the book.) She researches the relationship between cognitive neuroscience and education. The nascent work scholars like Dr. Immordino-Yang are doing is truly groundbreaking and, I believe, will eventually lead to a revolution in the way we educate children. That was also the year I had to pour over complex research papers and learn the history of the field. It meant reading tons of data analysis and statistics. It meant knowing the math. At the age of forty-three, I had to reach back and start gaining the confidence to believe I could understand the data. The philosophy, the scientific theory, the educational application were all interesting, but the truth was in the data. And if I was truly going to understand the field, it meant understanding the math and its conclusions.

So, I reached out. I reached out to Mary Helen. I reached out to friends. I reached out to math teachers. And, I reached out to Bob Schwartz, in my heart, because he was the one teacher who convinced me that I could do this, that I was capable.

Often, when we educate children, we believe that their teacher needs to be an expert to teach them well. This is a fallacy. Different children need different types of teachers. When I sat in that administration office and saw that leftover class, I knew that those girls for pre-algebra needed one teacher and that was me. Could I figure out the pre-algebra curriculum? Of course, I could. But more importantly, these kids needed an ally. Siena needed someone who was not going to just call on the next student because she could not understand it. She needed someone who was going to pause, give her time to think, and see past the years and years of established gender bias floating through her system that had convinced her that she could not do it. She needed support and someone who believed in her. I understood, from the vast and substantial research, where these issues emanated from and what they needed as students, very little of which had to do with coefficients or variable expressions. And, I mostly understood their insecurities, and I would get to know them much better as the year progressed.

In 2010, I met Dr. David Rose, a lecturer at Harvard Graduate School of Education and a leading researcher on children with learning differences. One of the many brilliant insights he shared with me was that we normally see and perceive that it is the child who has the learning issue or difference. He then lifted a book off his lectern and said it is the materials that have the learning disorder. A book, with its specific set of symbols to decipher and a limited capacity to communicate its meaning and information through only one sense, that of sight, provides an especially narrow and sometimes unattainable method of learning for many children.

The same is true for gender. Siena needs someone to pause, allow her to struggle, empathize, and show her a road toward success which begins to rewrite the tape in her head. Males need us to make them feel comfortable with the "I don't know" and not perceive it as some threat. Our schools are challenged from a gender perspective. Our goal needs to be to place students with the right teachers with the right training with the right school leadership and with the support of parents to shape a fair, equitable, dignified, and healthy environment so that our children can prosper regardless of their gender expression or sexual orientation. In the next chapter, I will introduce the reader to two students who capture specific gender mindsets given to them by adults that get in the way of their learning. We will see how students can be impeded from their learning before they even walk into the classroom.

(See Appendix A for four essential faculty conversations and exercises to begin the process.)

2

Natural versus Acquired Aptitude
Of Precious Eggs and Kept Princes

Toby stumbles through her days, and I do not mean figuratively.

She stumbles into classrooms, down the hall, into the cafeteria, through soccer practice, and occasionally down a stairwell during fire drills. She is not trying to get a laugh or create a distraction; it's just that her torso and her legs seem to have different agendas. Her feet look twice the size necessary for her body. I can't imagine her even sleeping without stumbling, unconscious, right out of bed. In other words, she is a middle schooler.

> "Toby!" one of her friends exclaims as she launches across the threshold of class, hitting two desks before regaining her balance. "We're going to have to take you to the hospital one day."

"Are you okay?" I ask calmly, knowing the answer. How many times have I posed this question to Toby as I approached her, sprawled out in the middle of a floor or having fallen out of her chair in the cafeteria while eating lunch.

Out of the forest of hair, a huge smile erupts, not because she has avoided breaking a limb for the fifth time today, but because in her raised hand is a note. It is from her previous teacher explaining why Toby is late for class. The smile is one of triumph.

DOI: 10.4324/9781003217022-3

Since the beginning of the year in our pre-algebra class, she has been late to class on a regular basis. But not today. Today, she has shown up. Note in hand, a reason for being late. She may not be on time, but this is a small moment of pride and accomplishment that she does not feel on a regular basis. In contrast, for most of her day, she feels inadequate at school. I take the note from her hand, showing no approval or disapproval on my face. As a teacher, there are times you need to be like Switzerland, a neutral observer.

"Well done," I say in as monotone a voice as possible. "Now please take a seat. We have *a lot* to cover today." She rolls her eyes, slips into her desk and for the next forty-two minutes, she climbs on a different kind of roller coaster ride. This one is largely in her head and heart.

I have been working one-on-one with Toby at lunch, as she is struggling mightily to prepare for a test in our seventh grade pre-algebra class. She is not grasping what to do with the variable when it sits on both sides of an equation. We are moving towards the end of the school year and the curriculum is getting more challenging, as in more conceptual. Toby knows that she needs to isolate the variable, but her computational skills are weak. She refuses to write out the steps when she does a problem, and therefore does not know what comes next. There is no simple numerical value at the end of the equation to anchor her thinking. She looks up at me for the answer, then I tell her, "You know this, you got this, we just did a problem exactly like it."

Most of her classmates are well ahead of her regarding the social, emotional, and developmental changes that overwhelm middle school students. I watch, not only in class but in the hallways of our school, as she misses social cues. Her friendships are like loose paper flying in the wind. Most of the other girls in her grade are starting to just tolerate her and treat her more like the class puppy than a peer with adolescent credentials. She has a good sense of humor and likes to laugh but she is not as funny as she thinks she is. Trying hard to "stay current" with youth culture and music, television, Toby throws around rap lyrics she does not quite understand, but she always seems a bit behind. Before making some comment or reference to her peers, her eyes

betray a type of insecurity, not truly knowing if what she is saying is really "cool" or not.

As I am sitting next to her on this day, I have started to become frustrated regarding her lack of ability and her attitude
of defeat, so I have inadvertently leaned in. I know I should be
more sensitive to her struggles and, by extension, her lack of motivation. But I am having a very human reaction to her not trying
given the fact that I am spending so much time out of class trying
to support her. I notice that her eyes are beginning to open wide –
she is experiencing me now not just as an existential threat but
as a physical one as well. I am six feet tall, 190 pounds with forty-
five-inch shoulders.

I used to both be unaware of the impact of male physical
presence and therefore, deny its effects. This was both out of
my ignorance and not wanting to really deal with the world I
inhabited. Boys Toby's age can already be close to or even my
height by seventh grade. But girls? Toby is about five feet tall
and weighs at best ninety pounds. I berate myself for making
this mistake for the millionth time in my career and then slowly
push my chair away. I lean back and wait for her eyes to relax,
which they eventually do.

She then puts down her pencil, stretching both hands behind
her head. "Mr. Ablin, I'm just not good at this stuff. I just can't
do it. Other people are good at math. Not me." Toby struggles
with a way of looking at her educational abilities which is more
prevalent with girls – her perception of aptitude.

For Toby, school is mainly defined by the four-minute passing periods between classes where she gets to practice her social
skills. The classes themselves feel like a necessary annoyance for
her. As a principal, I have had numerous conversations with her
parents. At first it was about her behavior toward other students
and teachers. Because of a lack of social skills and because she
was in work avoidance mode for most of the time, every day
there was another conflict or moment when she was blowing up
her classroom. Now, most of the conversations were about her
underperforming academically or in the case of math, down-
right failing. She had done so little "school" while at school that

it was catching up to her and making for a genuinely miserable experience.

"She feels terrible about herself because, at this point," I say to her parents. "School is a puzzle she feels she cannot solve. Her feelings about herself are spiraling down. It will be hard at first to get her more on track, but she will not crumple up and blow away. She is stronger than we give her credit for."

There was a several second pause before the father spoke up. "Why don't you like Toby? It seems that you don't really like her." Diedre, her mom, was more to the point. "I'm terrible at math. Her two sisters are terrible at math and her brother excels. It's just how girls and boys are different. She'll be fine." Fast fact: Teachers and school administrators know this well, but outsiders to schools may not – some parents are not ready to engage in these matters or simply do not know how. There are well-meaning parents with good intentions who try hard but remain ineffective. Then there are argumentative parents who might come into your office and be combative but ultimately get the job done at home with their kids. And some parents are just as puzzled about school as their children. Early in my career, this used to really frustrate me. Now, I would rather just focus my energies and time where it will have the greatest impact, supporting the student. So, from here on out, it's just me and Toby.

The main problem is that when Toby fails a test or is in danger of failing an entire class, her parents come in to protect the egg. Words like: "self-esteem," "wrecked," and "destroyed" get thrown around. She is going to fall apart. She will feel bad about herself. And guess what? The egg will break. Toby is a precious egg.

Here, I begin to unpack the question of the larger environment (not biology) as the driving force behind gender differentiation and discrimination. Toby is recognizable by many in our schools. She struggles because she has been told, in many subtle and not subtle ways, that her learning is all about some innate ability which either you have or you don't, and this is what her failure is based on. When the tests come back, or she is in danger of failing a class, her parents come in, put multiple layers of insulation and protection underneath her because, otherwise, she will smash into a thousand pieces.

To be fair to Toby, aptitude is not a singular concept. The Temple University Professor of Educational Psychology, James Byrnes, breaks down aptitude into two categories. The first, natural aptitude, suggests that certain students and learners take to certain areas of interest and show an ability to "pick things up quickly".[1] The resulting barriers in some areas of learning appear to be, for many students, "hard to modify constraints". We are quick to associate the differences between those who learn skills quickly and those that do not as a biological constraint. This is opposed to *acquired* aptitude which Byrnes equates with the development of expertise, built up over time by a regular and steady diet of practice, application, interest, and I would add, a long-term belief in one's ability to succeed. Numerous studies have also indicated that when measuring their failures, females are much more likely to attribute their inability to succeed on natural ability. Peter Kloosterman, Professor of Mathematics Education at Indiana University, in his analysis of studies on Performance Following Failure (PFF) and perceived aptitude, suggests that, at least from a correlative standpoint, for females this is a cycle that develops early and continues to cycle with their learning, particularly in relationship to their math education. One extensive study of seventh grade females showed greater learned helplessness even within the same assessment as problems became harder. The females just did not believe that they were able to overcome what they perceived as their innate inability to perform well, while the males in the same study did.[2]

And there is much we do in schools to support this version of reality. Schools should be much more interested in developing a mindset based on acquired aptitude, but we tend to use language and promote a version of natural aptitude instead. There are always big smiles and amazement from teachers, in all subjects when students just seem to "get it" during a lesson. The Eureka Moment. Musicians and athletes at our schools perform brilliantly as if touched by the hand of God. We tend to focus on the performance or the moment of great insight rather than point out all the hard work that most students had to exert to get to that point, thus establishing an air of natural rather than acquired aptitude. Teacher language does not always help either. When we discuss students, teachers will often use language such as, "she just doesn't get it". This framing of learning seems to hit girls much harder. What we need to examine more carefully is the difference between the way we shape this narrative for girls versus boys. The differences in outlook (for girls, precious eggs and for boys, kept princes) have real ramifications as they get older and eventually transition into the adult world.

You can imagine what females like Toby feel like, day in and day out. They are told that they shouldn't even bother trying to succeed and acquire some of the tools necessary to achieve future success. Because of this sense of learned helplessness, these young women will, over the course of their entire lives, need others to make decisions for them. Rely on others who say they know what is best for them, make the right choices, know what to feel. Toby feels that there is something inherently inadequate about her. She constructs a personal narrative that failure by her own resources is almost guaranteed. This narrative starts to become self-fulfilling and spirals over time, as the adults around Toby begin to reinforce, consciously or not, her role, her lowly place. Her teachers will also fall into a cycle of defeat and then give into the immediate needs and circumstances of running a classroom.

Parents are essential in this process of partnering in rewriting these narratives. It can be done. With even a benign, do-no-harm level of support from parents, I have seen teachers perform miracles with a student's sense of self-worth. But when there is direct opposition to this work via a powerful counter-narrative of student helplessness, teachers become complicit in this process. Toby is left with constant feelings of inadequacy, perpetuated by the adults she encounters both at home and school.

This story of the precious egg is obviously a very old one. It is firmly embedded into the fairytales and myths of our culture (and many others) regarding what girls and women can do, are allowed to do and are unable to do. They can help the dwarfs clean up their home and feel happy and joyful, but the prince must eventually arrive to save her from the endless sleep, from a state of perpetual fragility and vulnerability. The male is the source of her eventual safety and salvation. On our playgrounds and yards and gyms, a bruise or injury to girls is blown up to tragic proportions. Instead of a rub on the back and teachers sending them out again to contend with the emotional and physical minefield of recess, the young girl's cry *must* be attended to, she must be wrapped up in blankets of care because she is on the verge of shattering. Hugs are great, I love them, but I have seen way too many teachers hold on to young girls as if they are made of porcelain, even keeping them by their side until the crying stops. Heaven forbid they are excluded from a group, or the coach does not play her for an entire game. With girls, we are crushing their souls and making them feel unsafe. When this happens with boys, we are tough with them in order to "build character".

Powerful research regarding the time our children are infants and onward supports this aspect of gender/sex identification and development. Dr. Anne Fausto-Sterling's extensive research on the earliest days of an infant's life demonstrates early patterns of development regarding how mothers hold, handle, and speak to males versus females. Mothers are much more confident, less fearful, and less tentative holding male infants. "… mothers of 3-month-old infants engage in motor social play with sons for longer durations than daughters, that they help sons sit more frequently than daughters, and they shift son's positions more frequently and for longer time periods than daughters."[3] Obviously, the opposite is true for girls. In contrast to researchers who posit that gender identity is pre-prescribed before birth, Fausto-Sterling provides a convincing picture of gendered "learning" passed on from parent to child from the moment a child emerges from the womb. Gender/sex becomes "embodied" in cognitive systems in such powerful ways that Toby's feeling of fragility and how others perceive of her as capable of breaking begin in infancy.[4]

Toby forms part of an elaborate and deep system that lets her know that she is to stay within its boundaries and never really challenge the assumptions made for her. Every day, Toby faces a thousand micro decisions and indications that make her feel unsafe from a gender perspective. She will pay a dear price with teachers, with parents, and other adults if she refuses to go along with the narrative of learned helplessness.

We have not encouraged Toby to know that she will be okay if she begins to believe in herself and take the risk of success based on acquired aptitude. She believes she is incapable, not capable to build learning capacity.

I also wish I could report that girls have an easier road for those who are academically inspired and achieve. The evidence suggests a very different story. Even for girls who do well in school, which they do at a higher rate than boys (not always for the right reasons), assessment and test anxiety is much more prevalent than with their male counterparts.[5] While we mentioned in Chapter 1 how the results of testing can be misleading, students' emotional and psychological reactions can provide fruitful information. Girls are placed into a higher level of distress by school and home, with expectations and narratives that run counter to one another. While females are finding great success at all levels of schooling (seventy percent of school valedictorians are women) the traditional social tropes have not faded. The need to "look good" not only adds to the pressures of school success but being able to fit in socially means a constant struggle between traditional constructs of femininity and being perceived as assuming traditional male qualities such as assertive, competitive, and outspoken.[6] These high achievers are placed in a double bind. Yes, you are capable and can achieve, but what will be the emotional and psychological fallout for this neatly constructed gender identity which continues to question your ability to be strong and resilient? Will this be a moment of pride and success, or will this be the moment I fall apart, as I have been told women do?

Angela Duckworth, a brilliant researcher in developmental psychology at the University of Pennsylvania, was presented with quite a problem about fourteen years ago. Why were so many of the highly qualified, physically and mentally gifted, painstakingly selected cadets at West Point dropping out and not making it through even the first year of their training? If you know anyone who has gone through this process of selection to the elite officer training programs in this country, West Point, The Naval Academy, or the Air Force Academy, you also know that the process is as arduous as it gets. The country invests between a million to a million and a half dollars each for the training and education of these cadets and future leaders in our military.[7] I have had three students go through this process, one at each of the three academies. They each walked into high school in ninth grade with the goal of acceptance to one of these academies as their singular purpose. Two had already gone to special middle school physical training and leadership programs to begin the process and bolster their applications. There are multiple physical exams given over time, they need stellar academic reports, high marks on all aptitude exams, multiple interviews with the applicant (and their families), security background checks, and recommendations from US senators and congressmen from their states and districts. You need multiple recommendations of both character and fidelity to country.

So, the fact that West Point was having issues getting these ultra-carefully selected cadets even through the first year of training was a mystery, and one that needed to be solved. I can imagine that engaging a scholar such as Duckworth to find a solution to this problem was seen by those in charge as a type of security and defense-of-the-nation crisis.

Duckworth's research not only dramatically altered the acceptance criteria for West Point but also started a significant revolution across the educational landscape. Working off earlier work by the pioneering researcher in positive psychology, Professor Martin Seligman of the University of Pennsylvania, Duckworth identified mental traits that were more often found in highly successful individuals.[8] Most importantly, these habits of mind were present in individuals who, faced with a particular challenge or obstacle, could overcome it and not just give up. Throughout her research she refers to this quality as grit, or the "Passion and perseverance for long-term goals."

Grit differs from motivation.[9] Individuals are motivated to attempt and try new tasks, assignments, projects, hobbies for a whole host of reasons. Motivation is also very much of a neutral term; we can be as motivated to do something for negative reasons as much as positive ones. Children will do their chores, potentially enticed by a reward or the receipt of their allowance by the end of the week or because if they don't, they will not be able to go out with their friends that night. Children in schools are motivated to perform for a whole host of reasons that are complex and are sometimes known to the individual and, depending on the age, can be highly unconsciously driven. (I feel that an important part of any excellent educator or parent is to make children aware of their motivations. This constant cycle of self-reflection helps children and young adults understand what their real passion is in the world and develop a deep sense of purpose.)

The problem with motivation, as Duckworth found, is that it is necessary but not sufficient. Motivation is often critical for getting us started, but if we want to see things through to the end, we need what Duckworth defines as resilience. We need to learn that when a task or endeavor becomes puzzling or difficult – because it will take time, patience, and persistence – our initial resources of motivation are not enough. A deep wellspring of confidence and stick-to-it-ness are necessary to reach success and grow.[10] Duckworth outlines other qualities in successful people (my favorite being gratitude).

This terminology and language give educators a more concrete and specific vernacular to talk about how children function in our classrooms and where they need to grow. Duckworth has also begun to partner with schools and educators to deepen her research and provide tools for *how* we can better develop these attributes in our students which is much more critical information for us in helping nurture them.[11]

The reason I raise Duckworth's profound contributions to the field of parenting and educating kids, is because resilience defines quite clearly what Toby – and so many other female students I have taught – lacks. I have seen Toby become motivated on rare occasions. She will flare up like a candle for one or two days, really wanting to succeed, for all sorts of reasons. She wants to please her teachers; she wants to not feel so out of sync with the rest of her peers in terms of academics. She is motivated to learn new things and she wants this to be a bit easier for herself in the future. And, I believe deeply, she wants to stop feeling so badly about herself. She wants to feel proud for the right reasons. This is not a young woman who struggles with learning issues. She has excellent verbal skills; she is full of energy. Nothing indicates that she cannot figure out what to do when there is a variable on both sides of the equation.

I would argue the main reason Toby is so profoundly challenged in the mental habits of resilience is because of gender bias. If you have come to see yourself as fragile, breakable at the slightest touch (our precious egg), that any type of obstacle or challenge is going to do real harm, then the prospects of pushing through and persevering are threatening and could be damaging; it becomes a matter of safety. Even Toby's parents continue to use language such as "little" and "easily hurt" to describe her and anything that might feel like an affront to her. Toby may seem lazy or uninterested at times, but I believe real fear, based on her perceptions of herself in the gender role she has so consistently been assigned, perhaps from early infancy, and which has been regularly reinforced throughout the years, is at the root of her struggles.

And then there's Adam. Adam is a rooster. He struts through the hallways of my school announcing his presence loud and clear whenever he can. He is not like some of the rowdier boys in the school who throw each other into the lockers or steal each other's backpacks and hide them in the stairwell. Adam does not fall into the goofy or naughty category where so many young boys and adolescents find themselves. When I walk into a classroom where Adam is, his back is noticeably straight; he sits up with seeming attentiveness and some form of self-worth. His shoulders are squared, and he looks like he has blocks in his shirt sitting on his shoulders. He is not tall, but his solid frame gives him the appearance of height. The Australian Sociologist R.W. Connell writes,

> The physical sense of maleness is not a simple thing. It involves size and shape, habits of posture and movement, particular physical skills, the lack of others, the image of

one's own body, the way it is presented to other people and the ways they respond to it...[12]

He can have more sophisticated conversations with an adult than he might with other boys his age. He has a biting sense of humor, already sees irony all around him, and is willing to share his insights with you.

With all of Adam's good intentions and outward appearances of confidence, he is quite weak in school. He struggles to complete assignments, and he is often unclear about what to do and how to do it when a teacher is giving directions. In other words, he needs a lot of support inside and outside the classroom and is often not willing to ask for it.

He has a particularly tough time in math and Adam has one bad habit that sends him to my office on a regular basis. He talks back. This year, his math teacher, Mr. D., is getting the brunt of Adam's mouth. If you remember from the previous chapter, not being good in math for boys can be double the trouble. Their struggles are not just in the academic realm but in the gender dilemma as well. They are *supposed* to be good at it. Math *defines* them as men. This attitude is a mixture of James Byrne's natural aptitude with a confining definition of masculinity in regard to learning. Struggling in math places young boys and adolescents in a binary bind. They must deal with both the insecurities and failures of the academic subject and the perceived failure of masculinity. Adam is asking himself, for social and environmental reasons, "Is there something wrong with me because I can't do this? My friends all seem really confident in math." Adam will also be endlessly seeking cues and reassurances from other boys and men around him that he is doing masculinity correctly. It is what sociologist and gender scholar, Michael Kimmel, calls the homosociality of males in American life.[13] Men are constantly needing to reinforce and not "lose" their manhood in front of their other male friends. Math class is a central place this occurs.

Adam's teacher, Mr. D, is also not helping Adam's cause. He rushes through problem sets, he does not check for understanding, and Adam feels too embarrassed to ask for help. The teacher assumes Adam gets the problems because he doesn't raise his hand. The other boys also make faces at students, particularly other boys, who slow down the class with "stupid" questions. Mr. D. does not do enough to silence this male-on-male humiliation. Adam, therefore, does not see his teacher as an ally.

He takes these feelings out, all his anxiety and the need to male posture, on his male math teacher.

"You are the worst teacher in this school," Adam says calmly but with a knowing laugh no more than ten minutes into class. Mr. D has simply asked Adam to solve the first warm-up problem. What Adam does not know is that I have just happened to have positioned myself near the door to his classroom this morning and am listening intently to the conversation. Mr. D's classroom management skills lack assertiveness and purpose, so I am regularly observing the crucial first ten minutes of class to give him feedback. He is the only one who knows that I am there. The students are oblivious to my presence. "Everyone knows you can't teach and I'm failing because of it."

Mr. D. replies with a rising tone of agitation. "Adam, please take a seat." Things are going downhill quickly this morning. "Please take out your homework so we can go over the problems from last night."

"I didn't do the fucking…"

I do not let Adam finish his statement before making myself magically appear by moving toward the front. The other boys in the class are everything from sitting still like petrified objects to peering back at Adam to see his reaction to quickly pulling out their materials without making eye contact. Adam does not even wait for me to say anything more. He just picks up his materials and starts heading down to my office.

His mother is called and comes to school. It is now me, Adam, and her sitting around a conference table. She has had to leave work in the middle of the day. She is not angry or even irritated; she just looks exhausted. Both parents work, barely make enough to pay their bills, and their children are given a huge scholarship to attend the school.

"Adam, you need help and support which Mr. D. has offered to you a number of times, and you don't show up to these sessions. And you refuse to put real effort into this."

"I can do the math," Adam says as if it is biblical truth.

"Then show me." I take out paper and write the problem I saw written as the warm-up for the day on Mr. D's white board that morning. Adam picks up the pen, adjusts his glasses. He starts the first step of the problem, scratches over a number, picks his head up and stares into the sky as if he is either thinking or praying. Neither will do him much good – he cannot do this problem. His mother quickly interjects.

"Mr. Ablin, you know he is quite capable. He can do this work, I'm sure." Adam is now turning red. She tries to touch his face to comfort him. Bad move. He jerks back his head and looks mortified. "Everything is going to be great, sweetie. Don't worry. Your dad and I think you're going to be something special."

Adam's mom is just articulating what many boys and adolescents experience as a fundamental gender dilemma – that they are somehow going on to greater things, to conquer the world. Boys are destined. Hard work and determination are an afterthought because there is something already pre-ordained about being born with a penis. And, referring to Fausto-Sterling's research, boys may have a sense of confidence from infancy merely by the way they are handled that permeates into realms it should not. They are inheritors of the kingdom and because of it which seems to be almost automatically linked to success in their DNA. They are kept princes.

They are kept because, once removed from the surroundings that support these masculine mythologies, most of these boys will eventually discover that this is not the way the real world works. Outside of the bubble of all this predestination, is failure, falling down, and being around people who are as good or much better at things. In other words, the ground begins to move very quickly from underneath them. And boys do many, many things over the course of a day at school to try as hard as they can to keep this ego construct intact. They act out in class, they are less likely to follow rules, they draw everyone's attention to them in all sorts of positive and negative ways. In David and Myra Sadker's far-ranging research on hundreds of American classrooms, they discovered pervasive patterns of boys calling out in classrooms, dominating classroom discussions, and willfully acting out to elicit responses and reactions.[14] They receive more than three times the amount of attention from teachers in classrooms when measured in studies.[15] And this paradigm of the classroom is obviously not good for them, and it certainly is on the back and to the detriment of their female counterparts.

So, Adam under the gazing eyes of the perpetrator of this mythology is struggling with two burdens. Problem One: He cannot do the math. If he admits it, if he makes himself vulnerable and open to addressing problem number one, problem two emerges, that what he has been told about male superiority is a myth. Parents and teachers need to ban the dead-end language of "smart and gifted" particularly when it comes to boys. It creates what Stanford Psychologist Carol Dweck calls a static mindset.[16] It reinforces a type of gender bias that remains with them for a lifetime. Dweck also asserts that women and underrepresented minority groups suffer even greater impact from this fixed mindset. They are,

> especially likely to hold ideas about the nature of intelligence (fixed, innate rather than developed by effort and strategies) that depress their achievements. They tend to attribute success and failure to things that are within themselves, and not under their control.[17]

Boys, in this case, tend to associate success with *natural* aptitude and their failure with lack of effort. As with Toby, females do the opposite. Studies show that females mostly align their success with effort. Boys will typically make comments such as "I could do it, I just didn't try" both indicating their attitudes toward what they perceive will make them successful at school and that which protects a constructed manhood of bravado and innate capacity. It is an unfair burden that limits them from seeking help when they need it and giving them a sense of grandiosity, which is false and ultimately debilitating.

Do I think Adam can do the math? Absolutely. But he must *do* the math. Boys need a much greater emphasis on what they accomplish (or don't) as the measurement of who they are and the identity they create. There is nothing written in some big book somewhere that boys need to be accomplished in math to lead a meaningful life. In fact, by maintaining and supporting the myth of the kept prince, we perpetuate all sorts of other kinds of potential harm and havoc in our societies because of the deferential and overly admiring/posturing toward boys. Where does male anger, rage, and aggression come from? Why are men less likely to take care of their physical health than women? What are the origins of male superiority? Well, if you are told you are superior all the time for no reason, then the results are clear and self-fulfilling.

What are the results of all this predestination for our boys? Largely, it is confusion and isolation, and frustration. As it was for Adam, exposure of this myth is frightening and scary. A boy's sense of reality is so conflicted that frustration mounts. And, for many young men, it means veering away from all sorts of potential interests because they may meet obstacles and challenges that are not overcome with ease and a sense of pre-ordained aptitude or certainty. Remember Duckworth and those resilience and grit skills? How critical are they for student success and a sense of accomplishment? For boys, the danger is not of shattering into a million pieces. The danger is that the narrative of potent male identity, built up so carefully but falsely over the years, is a fraud. If so exposed, then, "Who am I? How do I define myself? How can I be so exposed and called out for not being what I was meant to be?" No one ever told Adam that he was going to have to work his tail off to do well or even just adequately in math. Quite the opposite. For boys, you need to fake the natural aptitude game.

For young males, masculinity is an exhausting enterprise that constantly needs to be re-established and regained, "... an exaggerated set of activities that keep others from seeing through us and a frenzied effort to keep at bay those fears within ourselves..." states Kimmel.[18] In one study, male students were asked to identify ways in which they could "lose" their masculinity and they were able to immediately respond with answers such as perceptions from peers, economic loss...etc., but they were hard pressed to come up with answers to how women might lose their femininity.[19] It is no wonder that Adam spends so much time aggressively lashing out at his math teacher. He is working hard to compensate for a cornerstone marker of masculinity which challenges him every single day.

Boys need to be guided and nurtured by the evidence they provide, their accomplishments or failures based on what they produce, not what we think they should produce. I witness this all the time in schools. Teachers are much more likely to say to boys than girls, "you are more capable than what you are showing me." Who says? Why are boys presumed to be able or capable of doing anything in school or in life for that matter without demonstrating it? Instead, teachers need to say, "you rushed through this and it shows. Try it again."

This is also why, I believe, boys love being on sports teams. Beyond the sense of belonging and physical release that encourage so many boys to engage in sports for other reasons. When working with coaches, boys experience the opposite of what they do on a regular basis. Coaches measure their players in minute successes and failures, and what you see is what you get. There are few presumptions, at the outset, about whether boys will be successful or not. Sure, some kids are bigger or faster or have more refined motor skills, but for many coaches a positive attitude, determination and grit are much more accurate indicators of success. Boys are held accountable for what they do. There are few, if any, free passes.

If you miss a practice, you are in the doghouse and do not get to play. If you work hard and show teamwork and improvement, you receive accolades and a certain status for your efforts. Many boys love being able to prove themselves. Because of the previous messaging which they receive, the hard work that leads to success feels more honest and authentic and tangible. Coaches also find themselves in a considerably different authority position than teachers. The culture of athletics has benchmarks and expectations which boys and families (mostly) accept when it comes to student participation. The mythology of the all-powerful and all-knowing coach who will guide a young boy or team to a winning season supports and encourages boys to see their own success as measured by hard work and demonstrated ability.

And parents? The supportive ones let their boys fall down, demand that they show up at practices on time and consistently, and if they are going to sit on the bench all season, it is a good lesson in character and realistic expectations. The challenging parents, of which there are more and more of these days, are constantly looking to reinforce the myth of inherited greatness. They want their child to be the exception because their boy certainly must be somehow exceptional. The rules do not apply to him because, look at him, isn't he already wonderful and worthy and talented? Why aren't they getting playing time or starting? So what if he missed a practice? And the toughest, what do you mean he didn't make the team?

In these circumstances, boys find themselves torn in a thousand directions, not wanting to be disrespectful to their parents, wanting to fit in on a team and be accepted, and not wanting to challenge the myth that they are special, chosen, always worthy.

And what does that boy feel when he makes the team, and he shouldn't have? What does he experience when he is put in a game which he is not ready for, and the coach has clearly put him in to please the parents? The results are a false sense of personhood, of self. By defining his male identity by the myth of the kept prince, we steal his dignity and replace it with a facade, ready to crumble at the first real test or obstacle. When we put him in a gendered box in school, at home, and throughout his environment, we do not allow him to build a set of tools to bring his real aspirations to life, no matter what they may be.

The reason that we must understand our precious egg and our kept prince is that it comes from two different ends of a spectrum of expected behavior which is largely built on gender bias and stereotypes. For girls, it is the helpless, fragile porcelain figurine that needs saving and protection from any challenge. For boys, it is the portrayal of him as inherently great, capable of anything, beyond measure and beyond reality. How the critical skills of resilience are developed in our young people needs to be more studied and refined given the various ways in which we shape the identities of girls and boys. Schools would be a fruitful place to engage with this type of research. Teachers can also do more to take control of their classrooms, exert more confidence, and not let outside influences interfere with their work with our Tobys and Adams. I would love to say that I found ways of improving the learning for Toby in my classroom and Adam in school as seemed so apparent with Siena from Chapter 1. Not so. Often, changing attitudes and self-beliefs takes years of undoing gender-based influences. We can certainly begin by not wrapping our girls in bubble wrap and by not holding our boys in such high regard where they cannot even see the ground underneath their feet. None of this serves our students and children and therefore future adults. We should take some of the wisdom of coaches: Let them scrape their knees, get upset, work hard enough where we can see them sweat and then bear witness to their true growth as a cause of celebration.

Constructive suggestions for schools around our precious eggs, our kept princes, and everyone in between.

♦ Get rid of the language of brilliant, smart, and intelligent (even gifted!) from our professional vocabulary. If you have students who are showing a propensity for deep learning, encourage it and look for creative ways to stimulate their interests.

♦ Conversely, drop dead end language with students about their struggles. "She's just not good at math, not everyone is" or "no matter how many times I show him how to read a poem, he just does not seem to get it" are not constructive. Language feeds into gender triggers which directly inhibit learning.

♦ Make effort and hard work a measurable, primary, educational value in your school. How do you assess, chart, and reflect with students regarding developing persistent effort?

♦ Teach children, from an early age, the differences between natural aptitude and acquired aptitude or expertise. Make it transparent. Emphasize that which is acquired through hard work and effort. I have met many people who have achieved amazing things, some of them were labeled as brilliant when they were young, some were not. All of them talk about the hard work it took to achieve what they did.

◆ Whether in a history class, science and math lesson, or English seminar, explain to the students how long it took for these seemingly brilliant figures to come up with their theories, medical breakthroughs, and solutions. How long did it take the author to write that world-renowned novel? How many drafts? Find videos of famous figures talking about process and time and hard work. Have the Eureka Moment become the untrue false myth that it is.

◆ When speakers come to school such as civic leaders, executives, scientists, or artists, ask them to talk about the long hours of hard work, the failures along the way, and ultimately the satisfaction that comes from putting in the sustained time. They will be glad to accommodate. Speakers often want to know how to inspire so it makes a difference in the lives of your students.

(See Appendix B for a simple, straightforward set of questions to gather data on student attitudes regarding learning. Do your students think they have intrinsic or acquired aptitude?)

3

Learning from the Anomalies

Jessie, a student in my math class, has been in the school from the days of Mommy-and-Me classes. She used to come with her father. Unusual, but not as much these days. Starting in kindergarten, signs appeared that something was different about Jessie. There always seemed to be some drama-storm going on with her. Never a dull moment. Stomping was an infamous trait until she was in fifth grade. In later years, early departures from the classroom became her next modus operandi. In the middle of recess, she would pick herself up and head to some place she was not supposed to be, finding someone to engage in conversation, either adults or other students. She had such nonchalance that adults would just chat with her without asking.

Eventually she figured out how to exit the building undetected by the security guard and would just leave, heading over to the Starbucks across the street. Keeping children physically safe is a bottom-line obligation and social agreement between schools and their communities. Students such as Jessie make that understanding very real almost every day.

She also argues with, well, everyone. It is sometimes impossible to get any work out of her, mainly because she cannot remember from moment to moment what is being asked of her. She cannot find any of her papers or handouts, and she can rarely figure out what the homework was. She breaks down in tears in the classroom on a regular basis and everyone, including her

DOI: 10.4324/9781003217022-4

parents, are walking on eggshells around her, wondering what mood she is in.

She is also assertive. She talks back to teachers, does not seem to give a damn about what other people think of her, and has visions of grandeur and superiority. Jessie is often unaware of her own volatility. She refuses, as feminist writer Rebecca Solnit puts it, to get "erased." "Every woman who appears wrestles with the forces that would have her disappear."[1] We at the school have summoned her parents for more meetings than I can count. With the school psychologists, with the teachers, with me, with outside counselors. Her parents practically have a permanent parking spot in our garage with their name on it. They know they have a difficult daughter. And when you meet the mother, you glean why Jessie thinks about the world the way she does.

"I don't understand what the issue is," she states with a certain degree of sincerity. When Jessie has done something more obviously out of line, such as hiding a computer bag belonging to one of her teachers in another classroom, her mother is more on board with the school. She does not ask us why we can't handle her daughter, nor does she even suggest that Jessie is an easy kid at home. This is not her question. She is asking us a fundamental question which schools do not have a ready packaged answer for.

Given that we have had Jessie in school for almost nine years, and we know she is different, the mother's question is this: "Why haven't we been able to make adjustments? Why are we still having the same conversation time and again? If you don't want her in the school anymore, just tell us. We know she is a handful."

This one line particularly irked me: "We love the school but I'm surprised that all you smart people have not figured this out yet...her out yet." Her words sound snarky and disrespectful toward educators. But they ring uncomfortably true.

In my classroom, Jessie holds it together, but barely. By the end of class, her face is turning beet red. She knows I will not let her leave the room because I know she will never return, so that is the rule – for her. Over the course of the day, Jessie can spend hours wandering the hallways, pinning some seventh-grade boy up to a locker and talking his head off, at the boys' lunch period when she should be in class, making faces through the window of another teacher's classroom. So, I am strict and watchful in my class that she guts it out, sitting in the front so she does not distract the other girls.

These other girls find Jessie weird. They sense differences, and they do not know how to navigate them socially. Some of the crueler ones might have even targeted her with unkind language if they knew what to call her. But even they are at a loss for language. They do not exclude her because she is sort of scary and interesting. Jessie also knows this about herself. She has no illusions that she's unlike the other girls. She is what I call a gender anomaly. She is making many of us most uncomfortable because she is not acting like a typical seventh-grade girl.

Unlike the other girls in my class, Jessie is also making me, her teacher, incredibly uneasy. She is not falling into the acceptable gender picture that I am accustomed to. And habits die hard. We all want to think of ourselves as enlightened and aware. But her lack of boundaries makes me nervous. She is regularly noncompliant. Jessie is an all-day exception to established gender expectations and constructs. Her pushy energy feels like something that needs to be dealt with, like I need to call another meeting. We all feel like we need to huddle around this kid and solve her, fix her, and make her like everyone else. And the truth, it is we adults, including myself, who need to do the work. I need to get beyond my own fears regarding gender, my own uncomfortable biases, and get to know Jessie. We would all like to maintain our perceptions of Jessie as misguided, unaligned, and in need of finding; she needs to find herself. She is categorized as a lost object that we mistakenly believe needs to be "found."

Schools are not just places of lost opportunities when working with students as much as they are places of lost objects. Everybody loses everything all the time. Students run out of classrooms at the beginning of class because they cannot find their notebooks. They dash to lockers, then to a previous classroom, then sniff the hallways like hound dogs. Folders are misplaced in a nanosecond; pencil cases line the hallways at the end of the day. Lunch bags are picked up, put down, and forgotten, as are snacks. A student will be holding a pen and then turn around and it has magically disappeared. They look under their desks, at their feet, they will literally rip the pen or pencil out from another student's hands to check if it's theirs. It's like working in a full-time magic show. Lost and found departments at schools are like city-wide flea markets: Jackets (WITH names on them), glasses, toys, bags, school supplies, gym bags, and clothes. And books. Books all over the building. Paperbacks, textbooks, math workbooks, language handout packets. Students can be carrying the object they are looking for and ask me, "Excuse me, Mr. Ablin have you seen…" Backpacks have legs.

Teachers? Also. An email goes out almost every day. "Has anyone seen my keys. I had them in the faculty lounge. It's a green keychain…with keys on them," an adult writes. "…and they have a pendant on them that says DRINK COFFEE OR DIE."

Particularly for the students, the lost object phenomenon is not all on them. They go from the classroom, to a specialty, to lunch, to gym, back to class, circling to another classroom for science, and on it goes all day. And every day can look different. They are in constant movement and transition. It's hard enough in elementary school, with teachers moving you from place to place. Middle schoolers can be in six to eight classes a day, lunch, gym, recess, after school activities. They are also rendered helpless by normal developmental trajectories which make absentminded a way of life. Cognitive development in children means uneven blood flow to regions of the brain which help with self-regulation and the monitoring of details from moment to moment.[2] Dislocation in time and space are the norm and adults lose, quickly, the feeling and sensation and memory of that age and its challenges. When you speak to high schoolers, they often can recall what those years were like. Adults lose their patience when they lose their keys. Imagine if every object you picked up or were responsible for was cognitively up for grabs. Teachers, coaches, and parents are quick to chastise and scold, but imagine what it would be like if adults were able to remember the sensation of teething. We would all be doubled over in pain with our hands over our mouths recalling enamel ripping through flesh. We are trained to forget such periods for a reason. The frustration of even losing one object can drive us to *agita*. Imagine that sensation happening all day long.

And keys are not the only thing that teachers misplace in schools. Because students are in constant developmental flux during these years, educators tend to rely on markers, often unconscious indicators that students are heading on the correct trajectory. We euphemistically call this a process of discovery. The dilemma is when our students are discovering or "finding" themselves, we are too much in the business of defining for them what it means to be found. As my student, Jessie could be described as lost. She is not. The adults are just confused because she is not checking the boxes associated with often confining and dehumanizing definitions of gender. Educators need new levels of awareness while students are doing what they are supposed to be doing, discovering for themselves who they are.

My own journey at adjusting my teacher/educator lens began over three decades ago, and really by true happenstance.

It is the fall of 1994, and I am in my second year of full-time teaching and my role as the English department chair of a school with a unique structure and environment. The school is one single entity but separated into separate girls' and boys' campuses which are three minutes and forty seconds apart by car. The teachers taught the girls in the morning and then went over to the boys in the afternoon. When hiring new teachers, I could almost predict exactly when they would switch from thinking that the best place to be was at the girls' school rather than the boys' campus. It took about two months of teaching in both places.

Personally, I feel like I am rocking my profession. After surviving the traditional gantlet of the first year, the parents are all clamoring to have me be their child's teacher. I am the *soup du jour*, and by my own twenty-eight-year-old humble estimation, the best teacher in the school.

That bloviated confidence began its steady deflation process in October. Four postdoctoral students in cognitive psychology asked my principal if they could study my classroom for the year. And so, they visited on a number of occasions, observing me teach my tenth-grade girls in the morning and then my tenth-grade boys class in the afternoon. They made clear that they intended to study gender. I am all in, because they are going to learn so much from me about how to make these two classes equitable and fair. With my sensitivities and sense of fairness, their observations of my teaching will give future generations of teachers a clear road map for eliminating discrimination in the classroom.

After a year, we sat down together to review the data and results of their observations. These are cold statisticians, researchers with no chits in this game, and really, on some level, completely uninterested in how I assimilate their findings. For that reason, they are exactly the medicine this young teacher needs. You can run, but you can't hide.

I spent the next three hours in one of the most personally and professionally excruciating evaluations of my character, ever. Their numbers and spreadsheets ripped me apart. They had several positive things to say about me as a teacher in general: I was well prepared for class, my energy was high, I had an easygoing rapport with the students. But I could hear none of it. I was too humbled by what they had to say about how I handled gender in the classroom. To wit:

◆ I let girls off the hook. They were only called on when they raised their hands. (I called on the boys regularly, often when they did not raise their hands.)
◆ I interrupt their answering of questions. Constantly and predictably.
◆ The girls get to kick back, daydream, and be disengaged. My problem, not theirs.
◆ I am passive about their passivity.
◆ I tell them, in all sorts of ways, that risk-taking is over-rated and not for them.
◆ I limit my sense of humor and appropriate levels of sarcasm for the fear of hurting or offending, as if they are fragile objects.
◆ The girls are largely not engaged yet I think they are. I have established their obedience as a standard, a classroom value, and a sign that the class is functioning well.
◆ The girls disrupt the class, in a different way than the boys, and yet I do not firmly express disapproval.

Whereas:

♦ I am tough, often too tough, with the boys.

♦ Their leash is so short, they are scared to get out of line. Talking even quietly to a neighbor is responded to with aggressive raising of my voice.

♦ But I celebrate their risk-taking. Even when they add important insight, I let them interrupt me and other students, often in mid-sentence.

♦ My banter with the boys is looser and less confining. The boys trust me in a different way than the girls, and they benefit.

When I look back on the differences between the way I taught the boys class versus the girls, I also recognize that, to align myself and relate to the boys, I took an overly tough stance with them; it gave me instant credibility by triggering their traditional notions of masculinity. The problem is that this posture also does damage. Such interactions calcify narrow and aggressive versions of masculinity which then lead to confirmations and reproduction. I become a part of the problem in the way I teach the boys.

Finally, the four grad students communicate clearly that I do not know any of my students well enough. In other words, I am not paying attention to who they are in order to serve their educational needs.

Wow. This last point was particularly devastating because I saw myself as close to my students and truly desiring to get to know them. Teachers often confuse friendly and personable and approachable with the ability to get to know children well. What I learned that day was that the former is a personality trait which drives many into the field of education with the latter being the ability to truly understand students as learners, which is a skill that requires years of practice, refinement, and training.

How do I know that this was such a defining moment for me? Because I have thought about it every day that I walked across the threshold of school doorways and entrances. From that day on I have worked hard to discover who students are, not attempting to discover *for them* who they are. And the predominant set of stereotypes and biases that I need to combat inevitably come back to gender and their formations in students. For me, it has meant being much more patient and letting students tell me, in all sorts of ways, who they are, listening well and suspending judgment as their identity stories unfold. It is a constant battle but one I am forever grateful to wrestle with based on a seren- dipitous encounter with a group of grad students at the begin- ning of my career.

In workshops I run for teachers in their own schools and graduate education programs, I ask participants to do a simple language exercise. I give them a list of the following student de- scriptors and ask them to separate them into two lists, one for girls and one for boys. I allow them only a minute or two to do this exercise. I want to eliminate, as best I can, their prefrontal lobes from engagement. The words are:

Sweet
Energetic
Clever
Caring
Careless
Collaborative
Gifted
Hardworking
Kind
Active
Capable
Smart
Intelligent
Cooperative
Talkative
Advanced
Neat
Physical
Inattentive
Silly

Here is how the list usually divides itself:

Girls are:

> Neat
> Intelligent
> Kind
> Hardworking
> Silly
> Collaborative
> Caring
> Sweet
> Talkative
> Cooperative

Boys are:

> Clever
> Physical
> Careless
> Energetic
> Inattentive
> Advanced
> Capable
> Smart
> Gifted
> Active

The two words in these training sessions that cause the most debate are "sweet" and "silly." Sweet boy or sweet girl seem to be interchangeable, until approximately third grade, when boys stop being seen as sweet. Girls can be silly and sweet until high school. Quite a way to describe a young adult.

The two issues with these words for teachers in describing their students is only indirectly related to gender. What eventually becomes most problematic about these words is that firstly, they have nothing to do with education. They do nothing for anyone in terms of understanding what kind of learners we are discussing. The other critical piece is that they have nothing to do with showing an understanding of the students. These words represent broad categories of judgment, rather than refined understanding of actions and behaviors which either outline a successful, developing learner or the attributes which are getting in the way of that occurring.

As a school administrator, I read teacher narratives three times a year which will go home to parents as part of their report card process. I am easily reading 2,000 narratives a trimester, many of them a page long each. Sounds like an arduous, unenviable task? I love it! Whereas teachers get to know, primarily, the students only in their classrooms, I get to know everyone. I am invited to watch the ups and downs, the highs and lows of every single student in the school. I formally ban the list of words above, plus several others, when teachers write narratives. Nor are they allowed to use these words when we discuss a struggling child in sometimes highly sensitive student support meetings with parents, teachers, and counselors.

Initially, teachers pull their hair out looking for alternative language. Then, I guide them through a process of detailed note taking over the course of a trimester. Simply put, they open a doc, make headings for each student, and begin to write down observations as events occur in real time. The results? Real stories about students learning, to show, not tell, who these children are. The process of eliminating these words forces teachers, through a backwards process, to know their students in a much deeper, richer sense.

I have found that when teachers do not have specific understandings or language to articulate students, they gravitate to language which neatly slides students into a predictable gender box. This tendency is not just a question of language, but a reflection of deep biases in thinking we all have, reinforced by years of socialization and accommodation, and the never-ending cycle of being part of institutions, such as schools, which reinforce these understandings. Parents are comfortable with this language, for the most part because it is exactly that, comfortable. They like to hear that their girls are growing up to be girls and their boys to be boys, even if the ramifications are far-reaching and damaging to their education and beyond. The more that teachers utilize this default language, the greater the problems and discriminating attributes become. Studies have shown that people are more likely to group information by gender type rather than what would be considered the category type.

> ...people who were highly sex-typed were most likely to remember words in gender-related clusters (e.g., bikini, butterfly, dress) rather than in category-related clusters (bikini, trousers, nylons), supporting the idea that highly sex-typed individuals engage in more gender schematic processing than others.[3]

Also, when engaging memory systems in small children, they will remember pictures and illustrations of activities that fall into stereotypical gender consistent models. Do I think that teachers do this on purpose? Absolutely not. Teachers do not intend to cause harm in this arena. They are largely unaware of the way that they are organizing and codifying learning around gender norms and biases. But this is what I call, and will discuss later, one of several micro-confirmations that work to silo children by gender. The pull toward gender categories is so fierce, that active, consistent steps need to be taken with teachers to break these patterns of thinking and then how these thoughts are ultimately expressed in language.

This leads us back to Jessie. How would, and should, we describe her? What would we say? From the lists above, she clearly falls much more into our boys' categorizations than the girls'. She is not sweet, not hardworking. She is neither collaborative nor cooperative. She is, however, clever, careless, energetic, and advanced. And it might even be a single one of these traits that jars educators like me, making her an uncomfortable character to work with in class because she stands out. She forces us to shift our mental frameworks. What we need to imagine and be self-reflective about is that this issue has nothing to do with her as a learner. She poses an opportunity to confront our own prejudices and biases in a constructive way.

Jessie's parents give us clear clues as to why she doesn't fit into the mold. As mentioned earlier, the father is raising the kids. Unfortunately for Jessie and the rest of us, he's not very good at it. He barely gets them to school on time, he never seems to know what is going on with their schoolwork and when you talk to him, every conversation seems to make a 180-degree turn from discussing his children to talking about himself. He is the parent that you start heading in the other direction when you see him on the street or in the hallways of school because your entire day could be shot if he corners you.

The mother, in contrast, is a high-powered analyst of mergers and acquisitions for a major multinational corporation. She makes vast amounts of money as a female executive. Just like her daughter, she is an anomaly in that way. She is short with her words, clear-headed to the point of unnerving, and has no patience for wasted time or fools. Most of Jessie's teachers run for the hills when they see her coming.

Whether by nature or nurture (does it really matter?) Jessie seems to have inherited her mother's sharp analytical skills, making her by far the most talented math student in my class. Jessie is so talented in math that she catches my mistakes even before I make them. If it weren't for the high distractibility, lack of self-regulation, and general chaos, I am convinced she would be one of the top math students in the school. But the two attributes that stick out most about Jessie and make her such an exception to our preconceived gender rules are her risk-taking and self-efficacy.

It should be no surprise that girls suffer from the inability to assert themselves when they are not entirely one hundred percent sure that they will get the right answer or be correct. In a number of studies involving high-stakes multiple choice exams, girls as early as nine and ten years old were willing to default to the passivity of a non-answer (particularly when warned that points are only taken off for wrong answers). Or, when they were given the option, they fell into the "I don't know" answer mode. Boys are much more likely to go for it and, by extension, not worry and perseverate over their choices and their ramifications. Such strategies and approaches are not taught, and therefore are indicators of gendered responses.[4] Why would this be? Because girls are taught and trained to maintain outer layers as people pleasers, to keep it all together in public spaces. Therefore, the risk of getting something wrong and being exposed is much greater than trusting your inner instinct and intelligence. As we saw with Siena in Chapter 1, "I don't know" is a natural and socially acceptable answer for many girls (other than the Jessies of the world). It is less of a risk to take less of a risk. The value proposition does not make it more uncomfortable to remain passive and not speak if possibly proven wrong than to say something even far-fetched, weird-sounding, and clearly inaccurate. How do I know that this is not some genetically ordained reality for girls? Because I have seen talented and exceptional teachers create safe and, at the same time, adequately "dangerous" environments for girls to take risks, get stuff wrong without the world coming to an end, and watch them thrive. Remember me teaching that tenth-grade girls' English class where I was studied by those grad students and making it totally acceptable for the girls NOT to take risks? I had to learn how not to do that. I had to train myself how to make that happen for the girls in my class, whether in a single sex environment or a gender-mixed classroom. It takes time and work and care to get to know your students inside and out.

Jessie is not lost. Calling out wrong answers, questioning how I was solving certain problems, jumping up to the board and getting it partially right, but mostly wrong until eventually she understood it better than anyone else. She doesn't fear making mistakes. She also displays a simple, but important rule. Just start. Make mistakes over and over and sooner or later you'll stop making the mistakes and it will make sense. No self-imposed boundaries. Trial and error become a critical means to learning. She also has strong spatial recognition skills, a cognitive skill set that is often associated, in rigid research models, with boys not girls.[5] Jessie is quite comfortable with geometry and its relationships to measurements. As Kimura states, in *Sex and Cognition*, skills are not "immutable," even for boys. They can vary across seasons and even times of day.[6] Jessie might make everyone uncomfortable, but she is teaching us an important basic lesson about learning. Because she stands out, we learn more from her than she learns from us. Our job as educators is to listen, observe, and not perceive her as lost when she is anything but. She may have difficulties right now being the "perfect" student (handing in homework on time, knowing when we have a test, paying consistent attention), but in all her seeming chaos, I see the seeds of enormous success in the future.

One would think that her mother would be pushing her or blaming the school for how Jessie is doing academically. She is not. She analyzes the facts, understands that this is Jessie, and leaves us to do as best we can.

"I know who my daughter is," she says bluntly at yet another student behavior meeting. "What's the plan this week?"

Jessie is an opportunity, not a problem to be engineered or "fixed." The idea of an anomaly is an important scientific concept which is used in significant and groundbreaking research. David Gardner, the Harvard psychologist, in his seminal work, *Frames of Mind*, uses the concept of anomaly to understand potential categories for types of learners. His research primarily hinged on findings from patients who suffered from either brain damage or lesions on particular regions of the brain.[7] From understanding how these patients functioned following a physical trauma, he was able to localize certain types of thinking or functions that were critical for learning, such as fine motor skills, auditory processing, kinesthetic (physical or touch). This form of reverse hypothesis based on the exception not the rule, then creates an understanding regarding learners. It was also a necessary way of drawing conclusions because, absent of tinkering around in a live person's brain, it becomes nearly impossible to understand the functioning of the most complex and mysterious human organ. Several cases present themselves where important findings regarding brain functioning have been "discovered" through anomaly. Antonio Damasio's analysis of Phineas Gage,[8] Ramachandran's work with patients with phantom limb,[9] and Speer's work with patients already receiving brain surgery, getting their permission to keep them awake during the process, and then asking them questions as they are in surgery.[10] Speer's work led to the critical understanding of lateralization and how the two hemispheres of the brain function together and independently. But none of this would have been possible without the anomaly, situations where inquiry meets the exception to a perceived rule. Constantly sticking electrodes into the brains of mice and watching them run around a maze or searching for a single cell is critical science but, regarding a system as complex and vast as the human brain, it is the slow road to understanding human functioning.

Schools, if utilized correctly, would be extraordinary places to do research. I am not talking about looking at student surveys or test results. I mean a deep dive into schools, based on research questions which would need a full year or years inside of institutions to understand how students learn and what schools are doing to either facilitate or inhibit learning. There is no replacing the wisdom and knowledge of experience. It just does not exist in the lab or in an experiment. The classroom is a unique social, biological experience which is only captured in real time and understood completely by seasoned educators. As the prominent cognitive neuroscientist, Stanislas Dehaene, states, "The classroom should be our next laboratory."[11]

Gender seems to me a ripe and ultimately critical area in which to do this research. One of the great obstacles to this has two faces to it. The first is that researchers would have to see teachers and educators as partners or collaborators in this work. They have the capacity and the ability to explain learning outcomes and goals and the schools' particular strengths and weaknesses in meeting those goals, gather critical data, and identify students like Jessie to greatly focus the lens of researchers as they are looking for patterns in attitudes toward gender and potential bias. We need to stop seeing Jessie as the problem and look inward at schools and how they function. The flip side is that teachers would need to be able to see this role as being part of their jobs inside of schools, as doctors in teaching hospitals are often involved in research throughout their careers. Just as physicians can see themselves as scientists contributing to better understanding of how to treat their patients, educators need to see themselves as researchers capable of impacting their field in critical areas like gender.

Teachers would also need to be open. Remember the skewering I took when those four researchers came into my classroom and unpacked me like kids do to their luggage on the first day of a vacation? While it was painful and difficult and even humiliating, it changed my professional life for the better, for-ever. I was able to merge my very deeply felt beliefs about gen-der equity with real-world application and self-awareness that equipped me to serve all students more productively and pos-itively in the classroom. The structure of the school, with both a campus for girls and one for boys, with shared faculties and shared desired educational outcomes, made it a unique and ad-vantageous arena for research. It was a gift of being in the right place at the right time, for which I am eternally grateful.

Teachers need to be ready to hear some difficult realities about their own self-perception. Perhaps, when those post-graduates picked apart my gender assumptions and behaviors, it was a bit easier because I am a man. The line drawn from man to insensi-tive about gender was not a tough one to follow. But what about our female teachers in their classrooms, who self-selected into a workplace where for years they were told they were "kind," and "sweet" and "caring"? These were words that were never used to describe me in school and not really at home either.

I have also had numerous conversations, with female teach-ers working in schools, with potential hires during interviews, and with graduate students I teach in education programs that the reason that they are in education or going into education is because they "love children," or have been told that they are "good with kids." These are code words for the relationship be-tween the maternal, female social constructs, and how many fe-male educators identify. They do not seem to me to be a very compelling understanding of what constitutes a great educator for all students. I am not inferring that having these feelings about working with children negatively impact one's ability to be an excellent educator. Teachers pride themselves on self-understandings such as being fair. Given that we are all part of this system that is a genderized merry-go-round called school, where we all seem to end up largely where we began, how much clarity do we really have and how ready are we to individually change to ratchet up the entire enterprise of education?

Again, the boundary setting I established with Jessie in my classroom was enough to make sure she did not disturb other students' learning and, at the same time, I was able to identify and encourage those habits which were clear benchmarks for successful learning, such as risk taking. By pulling back where necessary and not allowing my gender assumptions to dictate my responses, I took the long view with Jessie as a human being and a student.

Kenny constitutes another perceived anomaly. Currently, he is sitting in my office strangely giddy about the fact that he is about to get suspended. He cannot help himself so I will not hold it against him.

The reason that Kenny is excited about his current predicament is because it is new to him, unfertilized ground in his long thirteen years of life. Kenny never, ever gets into trouble. He is perfect beyond recognition. He is a star student who loves poetry and photography, popular with the other boys. He is a soccer whiz, which gives him immediate cred with his peers, although he seems to pay no mind. He likes the game, but it does not consume him. He has it all in balance. He is also a math genius. I have had to place him, year after year, not in a section with some designation on it, such as pre-algebra or algebra, but in "Kenny Math." By the time he was finished with seventh grade he had completed Algebra II and was working with a retired college professor on Calculus. I never got the sense that it was more important to him than anything else he studied. Kenny loved it all.

He is self-regulated out the wazoo. I have known him since he was eight and what he has more than anything else is boundaries. He knows where he ends, and you begin. He listens until the other person stops talking and then answers a question or addresses them. He waits his turn without pushing or shoving. Even when he raises his hand in class to speak, it is only after another student has finished speaking, rarely ever blurting out *while* his hand is raised. This is unique for any child, but my experience teaches me that girls develop this sense much earlier than boys do. Girls appear more located, almost as if they have a GPS system that begins to lock in more keenly to space and time. And it's certainly generated by gender driven expectations.

"Oh, Kenny," teachers would moan at me when they heard his name. "I wish they could all be like him," meaning the other boys. When I ask teachers to go deeper, to tell me what makes

Kenny the utopian student, they have difficulty coming up with specifics. However, what does get intimated, even more overtly suggested, is the exact nature of Kenny's sexuality. Is he gay or is he straight?

The ongoing assumption is that boys who like areas of study or interests that are not traditionally aligned with their own gender and clearly aligned with the world of girls must be fitting into some other category of gender identity, one that is perceived to be outside the heteronormative paradigm. As educators, we may want more students like him, but there is also a persistent need to label his sexual identity in the process. We need to feel comfortable with Kenny. We feel the need to discover him *for* him, rather than just let his identity play itself out. Kenny is lucky in that he is popular, part of a tight-knit community, and does not experience much of the bullying from other boys who typically associate creative, artistic, uninterested in physical horseplay, verbally respectful and contained…etc. with being feminine. He is being told, mostly, that everyone accepts him; even though they recognize his anomalous nature. Instead of asking what makes him so special and what makes Kenny so able to encompass a fuller broader sense of his own interests and passions, we also peculiarly put him into a box because we can't figure him out. In other words, we celebrate him for many of the wrong reasons such as, not causing a ruckus on campus, not acting out aggressively, doing as he is told. There is that validation of obedience as an educational value sticking its ugly head up again.

Kenny also helps to make clearer what I mean by a gender anomaly, which is not that boys seem to be acting like girls and girls like boys. Teachers can default also to another form of binary language of immature/mature which tends to lead us down the biological argument rabbit hole again. But this is a not-so-easily dichotomized conversation. It is when they are bucking so hard against established often implicit social norms that students seem out of place. Eventually our presumptions and communicated labeling can make them uneasy as well.

The reason that Kenny is sitting in my office is that he has done something worthy of suspension. He has taken a picture of one of his teachers, outside of school, and posted it on one of the more popular social media sites. He has also decided to put a snarky, less than complimentary quotation underneath it: "Teachers trying to be real human beings outside of school." He does not even realize that more than three quarters of his classmates are not even able to understand his attempt at sarcasm and wit. One of the clues as to why Kenny is so comfortable with himself is that his father is here, not his mother.

"So, you decided this was how you were going to prove yourself to your friends, that you are…edgy?" the father says to Kenny. He is a very successful and extremely busy physician who flies around the world as a cancer researcher as well as seeing patients. I called his wife to ask her to come in. Dad showed up. And even though he regularly shows up at school, I called his wife. Of course, I did. Moms take care of schooling issues. Dads work. Another way in which we perpetuate gender stereotypes in schools. Schools are also partially guilty in supporting these norms.

"Your suspension will be an excellent opportunity for you and me to sit down at home and figure out how you are going to fix this, how you are going to make it right," Dad says. "I promise you; you will not be feeling the same way about this incident in twenty years." The smirk leaves Kenny's face. Kenny is thinking. He looks at me and apologizes. In a moment, he realizes why everyone thinks so highly of him. It's because his parents have raised him not to denigrate others. He had chosen to try to fit in with his peers rather than be himself.

Now, to see how we can combat these issues on a more school-wide basis, we are going to look into a school that went through a transformation to become more aware of its students' needs from a gender perspective. What practical steps did the Marlborough School in Los Angeles take to best support its students?

Some people are fans of Arianna Grande or Bono. Some worship Venus Williams or Lebron James. Me? I have Barbara Wagner.

For years in Los Angeles and then nationally, Wagner was the Lebron James of independent school education. Wagner ran the Marlborough School for twenty-five years, a well-regarded all-girls independent day school. It has long been considered a place of excellence in academics and learning. So, why do I have such admiration for Wagner? Because she took an already terrific school and made it better. She crafted it so that it better cared for the educational needs of its students and its mission.

I am not going to spend time here getting knee-deep into the arguments regarding mixed gender and single gender educational experiences. Which is better? Which serves students' needs better? Does it solve the gender issue? Firstly, the discussion has always been politically loaded which ultimately gets in the way of discussing the real matter of learning and how to truly improve our schools. Also, from a gender equity standpoint, it is a red herring, and in speaking to Wagner about her experiences at Marlborough and providing the reader with her critical insights, you will see why.

During my years as head of school at a large independent day school, I had the opportunity to speak to her about some of the minor and major issues of running these types of schools. The two characteristics that stood out more than anything else were her authenticity and clarity. She said what she meant and never dodged an answer to give some politically acceptable response. There was always such disturbing competition between the schools for reputation and status that Wagner's candor was like finding an oasis while walking in the desert. You always felt as if you were having *the* conversation, not *a* conversation.

Everyone also had such profound respect for Wagner because she was getting paid. At the time, she was one of the most well-compensated heads of schools in the United States. In this case, she was both the exception and the rule. The exception and the rule were that women heads of school are paid less, just like in other industries there is pay disparity, and she more than deserved her compensation and proved it, where men who were doing less were making close to the same.

The most damning disparities in both status and leadership opportunities regarding gender are in the field of education. While gaps in pay equity and opportunities for leadership throughout industries and professions are well documented, how is it that the field of education, so disproportionately female, also suffers so acutely from such imbalance? Approximately seventy-seven percent of the teaching profession is made up of women. Yet, in 2004, just over eighteen percent of the 13,724 public school districts in the country had women in charge.[12] Women often go through more training, receiving more advanced degrees than their male counterparts. But they still find themselves on the margins of school leadership and decision making. The assumption is the "women cook but men are chefs" syndrome, that women are teachers but should not be shaping the priorities or needs of our country's educational system, that important work should be left to men. What we are left with is an educational system with a bias toward male constructs and male priorities. And I am not so obtuse to understand that I have benefited in my career from this bias.

When she first came to Marlborough and the next year took over as head of school, Wagner inherited a school culture that she defined as "macho." She felt as if she had come to a school that was co-ed, but without the boys. There was a "raw testosterone feeling" throughout the curriculum and programming. With its zealous commitment to sports teams and curriculum that had very little female representation or role models, there was a clear confusion between the school's mission and how it functioned daily. Bias was "ringing through the school, and that bias existed in other ways" because it was an all-girls school. Educational leadership structures were largely paternalistic and hierarchical, with pay and faculty equity issues favoring men. Even at Marlborough, one of the premier girls' schools in the country, she found that ninety percent of its math and science teachers were men as was much of its leadership structure. When high school girls were asked to draw pictures of a scientist as an exercise at the beginning of the school year, they overwhelmingly drew portraits of men, with crazy hair and glasses and lab coats, but still men. The same patterns of allowing girls to remain passive, unengaged, and unassertive were practiced in classes.

"What the hell was the purpose of these small class sizes?" Wagner thought.

She regularly heard from small groups of girls the frustration that they were the only ones to raise their hand in class to answer questions. There remained a very strong culture of, "don't take risks and therefore you won't fail," even in an all-girls environment supposedly committed to empowering young women.

"Just because you are in a single-gender environment does not mean you take care of all those (gender) issues," Wagner stated years later.

There is evidence to support this claim. A large comprehensive study of private schools that consisted of twenty girls' schools, twenty boys' schools and twenty co-educational schools indicated that the same patterns of gender discrimination existed in all three environments. The report not only considered data on post-graduation results and attitudes of students, but also classroom observations which focused specifically on gender interactions.

> ...in studying the classroom interactions, Lee and her colleagues found teachers initiated similar types and frequency of sexism in all three types of schools. The sexism ranged from teacher's encouragement of sex stereotyping to teachers' use of offensive uncensored, sexist language.[13]

Wagner's goal at Marlborough became to create a balance in the faculty (because that would benefit the students most) and place a high emphasis on girls feeling confident and competent in math and science. She also sought to change the faculty culture to be more collaborative and more gender balanced. Wagner and her faculty also looked hard at the physical facilities. "How do the classrooms support different learning styles and differences regarding gender and the individual needs of students?" The theory was, as Wagner expressed to me, that "if it is good for girls, it is probably good for boys too."

The proposition of a place like Marlborough is to allow a girl to find her voice and as importantly, to focus on each student, to know them well enough that the learning needs of individual students come first. What Wagner is referring to is using gender differences as a gateway to better acculturate and train educators to be more sensitive to the individual differences of any learner, regardless of gender. As educational researchers Jeremy and Paula

Caplan put it, "…when sex differences are found they are regarded as the canary in the mine." Sex differences and their relationship to learning are more often not causal but correlative. They indicate the variables which play a direct role in diminished educational outcomes such as "stereotype threat, locus of control, anxiety, parent and teacher influences and math-related experiences."[14] The goal for the educators is not to focus on the gender difference, but to use it as a doorway to tackle the true variables that deter learning.

When I had the opportunity to speak to parents who had sent their girls to Marlborough under Wagner's leadership, they all reiterated a powerful message: Upon graduation, their daughters were ready to tackle the world. They seemed confident in ways that indicated a sustained overcoming of previous obstacles and an environment that stayed focused on them as individuals. That sentiment sounds macho to me but in an entirely different way. Whereas what Wagner saw in her early years at Marlborough maintained oppressive and confining male defined systems for its female students, now the girls were expressing a deep sense of self-confidence and willingness to take on risks and challenges because of the way their school made them feel and experience learning.

What Wagner was tackling at Marlborough is what I call the myth of male learning. We have these very cliche ways of viewing the act of learning or discovery. It typically revolves around an individual, in a lab, or reading some text or in front of some computer screen. He has discovered something, solved some long-nagging problem that everyone around him has been waiting to solve. The most important word here is "him." We rarely see a woman in this eureka moment and we imagine that brilliance is a siloed experience. The learner, in our imagination, has something deep within his own resources that leads to enlightenment and understanding. It is the false promise of the Eureka Moment mentioned previously.

The truth about learning could not be further disconnected from this mythology. We are deeply interconnected to one another in ways that we cannot even fathom. All sorts of human interactions, inputs and outputs, neural connections which extend beyond our own physical bodies are necessary and essential for learning. In fact, our brains are not only tied into constant and never-ending learning cycles, but to teaching cycles as well. We are literally designed to teach what we have learned to someone else.[15] Our survival as a species has had much more to do with our ability to pass on what we know to someone else, to instruct someone how to build, craft a tool, hunt, weave, or plough than to learn or discover it on our own. However, as this myth perpetuated itself and we saw these towering visions of male invention become the false idols of learning, our schools began to take shape inside of such constructs. Instead of teaching students to educate each other and learn from each other, we, as teachers, sat behind desks at the front of rooms, said a bunch of stuff and imagined that learning was just going to magically spring out of children like a rabbit out of a hat. Wagner struck out against that male mythology of learning, not because she was the leader of an all-girls school, but because the learning would be better, meeting the needs of her students in more productive and authentic ways. She did go out and hire female math and science teachers, passionate and skilled ones. And she also spent years focusing professional development for faculty on collaborative-based learning approaches such as project-based learning. "Mostly," Wagner told me, "people who go into education tend to be traditionalists. They live within the lines; we follow the rules." The problem is, "the lines in this country have a strong bias toward men and males in all ways."

A great example of this was on display in the year 1999 as we barreled towards the new millennium. Another myth, which turned into a puff of smoke, was building over this time: Y2K. By 1999, Y2K was on everyone's lips. The rumor was that with all our technological brilliance, we had not foreseen a potential disaster with the coming of a year with all those zeros at the end of it. The millennium bug, as it was called, was a calendar problem. Would machines and systems and software used to reading years by only the final two digits understand that the new year was 2000 not 1900 or 1200? Would our water systems start to shut down? Would planes fall out of the skies? Would cash machines start spewing out twenty-dollar bills when the clock struck midnight at the start of 2000? `

However, all this populist fear did not get into the ecosystem right away. In fact, many tech companies saw it originally as a low-level glitch, not worthy of many resources or top tier talent to solve. So, to whom did they give the task to solve?

Women, of course. According to Mark Frautschi in his analysis of Y2K leadership teams, women were given the task of leading teams to eventually solve the Y2K problem. As we moved closer to the date and these companies and the general population became more alarmed by the possibility of a real problem, they found the people leading the charge to fix a potential disaster were women.

When all the hype and noise cleared and the world did not fall apart, many men and women who were on these teams found the skills and approaches to leadership that these women had brought to their work were effective and empowering. Some of those included:

- ◆ Ability to identify relationships and dependencies.
- ◆ Ability to nurture relationships and partnerships.
- ◆ Ability to embrace the whole.
- ◆ Ability to work effectively in flat, self-organizing environments.
- ◆ Ability to manage multiple, highly detailed, co-evolving issues.
- ◆ A willingness to lead while being publicly vulnerable.
- ◆ A willingness to lead from not knowing.
- ◆ A willingness to lead from a process perspective, rather than a system perspective.
- ◆ A willingness to lead favoring flat, self-organizing webs rather than hierarchies.
- ◆ An emphasis on respect, dignity, and integrity.[16]

When the culture assumes one set of principles (male definitions of leadership) then how do you break through? By applying the same gender biases and then having them thrown in your face, of course. Y2K, particularly for the tech industry, became a wake-up call, not about the coding of years and dates, but on breaking through mythologies and cliches regarding leadership.

What existed previously as an anomaly, women occupying leadership in Tech, shifted the paradigm when we looked more closely at what was critically missing because women had been excluded.

Jessie and Kenny make us necessarily uncomfortable with assumptions regarding gender and learning. When we apply gender cliches and biases to learning, we miss entire opportunities to educate students in more student-centric ways. Students should be able to feel like they are more than just their prescribed gender profile. Barbara Wagner's restructuring of her school to better the educational experience for her students was not based on what girls needed; instead, it was based on being able to access the individual strengths and challenges of her students so that they could be their best selves. She was looking and searching for the anomaly as the rule, that we all learn differently.

(See Appendix C for two exercises designed for teachers to engage in deeper conversations about their students.)

4

The Writing on the Wall

The Gender Influence of Student-Teacher Interactions

When teachers stand in front of a classroom and begin instruction, model a process for students, cut a piece of paper along a dotted line with a group of kids at a table, recite the alphabet in a song, count up and then count back down, they trigger a powerful and necessary part of the learning process. Our students' developing brains are ripe and ready to not only assimilate information, but also activate neural pathways that take someone else's motor skills, actions, and goals and create a learning template in their brains. As the University of Southern California cognitive neuroscience and education researcher Mary Helen Immordino-Yang puts it,

> The job of mirrors is to reflect what is before them, and mirror systems in the brain, as they have been described, reflect the actions and goals of another person. In this sense mirroring suggests a direct internalization of another's actions, emotions, and goals which are automatically experienced in parallel in the onlooker.[1]

This process takes place in what the cognitive neuroscientist Antonio Damasio calls convergence zones, where sensory and

DOI: 10.4324/9781003217022-5

motor processing skills converge in the brain, leading to representations, thoughts, and then goal-directed actions based on other factors as diverse as culture and social context. These CDZs (convergence-divergence zones) can exist throughout the brain to fulfill various functions of assimilating information for use and can even be linked to one another to create even more efficiency in learning and brain function.[2]

We educators often have this fantasy that the process is simple. Many times, teachers without a background in how the brain assimilates learning imagine this process as an input-output system. It is not. Other corollary and competing values and experiences and perceptions come to translate the learning into a unique representation in the learner's mind.[3] In other words, no matter how hard we try and how much we desire learning to be streamlined, it is in fact very messy. And, ultimately, we are better off for it. I would argue, human creativity, discovery, and progress are based on our capacities and experiences to make learning our own. Learning looks more like an experimental stew than an ancient family recipe reproduced thousands of times over, tasting the same generation after generation.

Who absolutely needs to know more about this process of learning and the cognitive processes behind it? Teachers, of course. Who, in general, know very little about the neural and cognitive realities of learning? Teachers, of course.

In this section, I want to blow out the common perception of how we, as a society, see the importance of teachers. I argue that they are, in fact, at the foundation of any civilized society we hope to create. As mentioned earlier, teaching is the largest profession in the United States by a long shot and yet, I believe, its status in our country is at an all-time low. I will also be arguing that educators' inadequate status in our culture is related to the fact that it is perceived as a "women's" profession. Therefore, not only will we see the importance of teachers understanding their role in schools regarding gender discrimination and bias, but that ironically, the lack of attention to this critical area in our schools, in part, has also led to the sinking perception of the field as a whole.

In the United States, there is currently a new low regarding how Americans view educators and schools. The cliches abound!

"Those who can't do, teach," is a common one. "Teachers only work ten months a year," is another, which correlates teachers with laziness. Television shows, movies, and social media are rife with images of the incompetent teacher, the teacher sleeping at her desk, the teachers unable to control their classes, the teacher whose eyes glaze over when students are in greatest need. School leaders? Principals? We cause all the problems in schools; we are actively complicit with creating incompetence and even corruption. We promote scandal. While there is a reverential and often nostalgic tone for teachers and what they do for our society, many educators feel that the pressures and the attitudes that come from parents, school boards, outside agencies, including the federal government, are driving educators from the profession. Everything from the constant requirements for testing, the lack of support with issues in the classroom and the general politicization of education, from across the spectrum, have left educators feeling as if they are not trusted to run the schools or bring their professional skills and abilities to impact schools.

But the most significant evidence of how teaching as a profession and as a cultural value is being regarded is how we remunerate teachers and support them economically. Teachers in many parts of the United States barely earn enough income to survive. A 2019 broad-based public-school teacher poll showed that over sixty percent of teachers felt underpaid. Almost fifty percent of those teachers did not feel supported by their local communities and were considering leaving the profession.[4] With their benefits slashed, many teachers apply for social assistance programs such as food stamps just to make ends meet.[5] We value what we pay for and only a few districts in the United States have made education a feasible profession financially. In other words, money speaks much louder than all the false sounding accolades and ego stroking that we hear from political leadership and civic leaders.

Teachers are also expressing great dismay about the lack of support from the parents whose children they serve. Thirty years ago, when there was a discipline issue, the school and the parents sat on one side of the table and the child on the other. Now, it is often the school on one side of the table and the parents and child on the other. Coupled with a new low regarding how teachers perceive they are valued by their communities, these feelings are now the third highest reason teachers given for considering leaving the profession of education permanently. Student behavior is number four.[6] Parents are having a difficult time holding their children accountable for their actions and behaviors.

Other professions claim a certain kind of extended training that educators often lack. None of us went through the rigors of medical school or the grind of law school. Teachers have a much lower bar of entry into their professional lives and must do much less in order to maintain their status. Teacher training programs and MA programs are notorious cash cows for many universities. And, while most school districts and communities require a certain degree of training, experience, and background, the truth is the rigor of our certification and degree programs do not pass the muster of other key professions. There is no extremely difficult equivalent of a bar exam or medical boards to even get your foot in the door of the profession. I have never met a teacher from any state who had to spend six months studying for their state's certification exam. This might not seem a fair assessment, but this reality in our country leads to perceptions of professional attainment.

This reality does not have to do with the people who go into education. Many of them are talented, intelligent, motivated, and high energy individuals who are drawn to the psychic income they earn in the profession. The larger issue has always been a lack of nation-wide coordination and professionalization of the field. The national board certification program[7] was created to support greater professionalism and prestige for the field.[8] Many districts give significant bumps in salary if teachers go through this program. If we want to raise the level of the profession, this program should be made as rigorous as possible. Every teacher in the United States should have to enroll and pass the program by the end of their fourth year in teaching, and then teachers should receive significant pay raises to match their new status. Teachers I have met who have received national board certification tell me it was the most comprehensive and productive and challenging professional process[9] they had been through in the field of education. Only forty percent of first-time applicants receive their certification after the first attempt at passing.

Not everyone can teach. Attributes that define the great educator are as follows: High energy, focus, excellent boundaries (who is the adult and who is the child), endurance, and attention to human detail. I have had a number of second-career people come into my office wanting to make the transition into education. Lawyers, accountants, advertising people, business executives. They have a Pollyannish vision of what it means to teach a group of students in a classroom, something between "To Sir with Love" and "Stand by Me." After three months of being in a school, I have a number of these individuals either crying in my office, or quitting, or telling me that they have never worked so hard in their lives. It's not that teachers teach ten months and are then off for two; it's that they work the equivalent of twelve months in ten.

But what makes the difference between a truly great teacher, and a good or a mediocre one is their ability to find the sweet spot and walk the fine line with each one of their students. It is both a gift and a skill learned over time: How to push students to their edge of discomfort. Great teachers know what types of questions to ask which students, in what settings, under what circumstances. Who needs to be pushed harder and at what point during the day. Who needs to rely on a reward system to meet their learning goals. Who needs the threat of an email home to pull it together and get to work. For elementary school teachers, whose students can be in such a developmental flux throughout the year, the teacher must be particularly aware that what a student needs in October is not what they need in February. For middle school teachers, whose pupils change so rapidly in all aspects of life, students can be like volcanoes that need constant monitoring. For high school teachers, the success-at-all-costs game requires a much more thoughtful monitoring of students' stress levels. Many students in this country are working after school to help support their families. High school can mean four years of a relentless pressure cooker that has enormous human implications. Schools need to feel safe and protective of students' multiple developmental and emotional needs and, at the same time, edgy enough to shift the ground under students' feet to challenge them and help them grow. Great teachers know how to comfort the afflicted and afflict the comforted while maintaining that feeling of a warm, nurturing environment. This is a complicated, nuanced talent that often has little to do with how smart or intelligent you are. We will now see, through the eyes of a student, how teachers' lack of awareness regarding gender constructions in schools has a direct impact on learning for all students.

If there was anyone who could organize herself, and everyone else, out of trouble it is Donna. While I posted at the beginning of the school year what a math notebook has to look like to get an A in my class, Donna has taken it to a mind-bending level. She is dedicated to organization! Every piece of paper is in its proper place. No divider goes unmarked. Her notes look like they were typed. Sheet protectors carefully cover all her work like shields protecting ancient documents for museum display. She has kept everything handed out and submitted from the beginning of the year. Whenever Donna is out of town, she acquires every stitch of missing information and homework, not to miss a single detail. She utilizes online sources independently to support her work in the class. Her inquiries more often support her need for organization rather than clarity on the learning. Here are samples of the types of questions she peppers me with:

"It's a long weekend, are we going to have our weekly quiz on the same day, or will it be moved up a day?"

"I have a dentist appointment tomorrow. Can I come by your office to pick up the next unit's notes packet that you said you were handing out?"

Other teachers experience the same types of behavior. One colleague shared with me an Instagram screenshot where Donna presents her notebooks laid out over her desk at multiple angles. It looked like a fashion photo shoot.

Is Donna at the top of her game with study skills? Yes. Resourceful? Absolutely. Math skills? A disaster. I hand out a quiz at the beginning of class and say to myself, this is the moment! This is the moment when her obsessive behavior pays off. She is going to rip through this assessment and use that systematic and sequenced mind to crack the code. The light bulb will go off and she will get at least seventy percent. But no. That doesn't happen.

During a quiz, I watch her stumble through the first and most simple problem. She is trying to do all the calculations instead of really examining the nature of the problem. The question requires two steps. She has turned it into twenty. There is some long, convoluted digit with a decimal tailing off the end of the page she has put as her final answer. I cringe with sympathy and feel compelled to intervene. Donna is an enormous people pleaser and cares very much about what I think of her. So, I approach with a certain degree of caution.

"Donna," I whisper, putting my finger on her answer. "Do you see how this can't be correct? Look at the original problem."

"But," she answers with a look of confusion, "I was always taught to…"

I used to think that a teacher's gender had a minimal impact on students, particularly the younger ages. That statement could not be farther from the truth. In math education, the influence of female teachers and their own thoughts and personal feelings regarding math has had a multi-generational impact on women in our country. And let's get real; young boys are being equally impacted in literacy education with the lack of role models in the field of education.

In the situation above, Donna's mirror neurons are on full display. She is reproducing years and years of mimetic experiences, thoughts, and emotions that she has experienced in classrooms. Teaching is brain-on-brain combat. You insert yourself into the minds of students and they insert theirs into yours. This is a biological principle, not a philosophical one. She has already spent almost eleven years imbibing how her teachers think math works and their own personal anxieties about math education. They have been literally passing these perceptions, goals, and cognitive representations on to their students. This is also one of the reasons why Donna is so successful and strong as a student. I do not want to give the impression for one minute that her organizational and time management skills are wasted effort. They are not. They put her in a great position for future success. The child of immigrants who barely speak English, Donna has a great attitude, with older siblings who have all excelled and modeled hard work and fortitude through challenges. I have no question that there are excellent things ahead for her.

The issue is that, as with many girls in school, she thinks that following the rules has a value in and of itself. When she says to me at the beginning of the quiz, "I was always taught to…" she is deflecting her lack of understanding by mimicking a process rather than thinking through the problem.

And this leads us to Hans the Horse.

The French Neuroscientist Stanislas Dehaene, in his extraordinary work, *The Number Sense*, retells the story of Hans and his trainer, Wilhelm von Osten, at the beginning of the Twentieth Century. von Osten claimed that he taught his horse to do remarkable feats in mathematics and reading, using his hoof to stomp out solutions to arithmetical problems and spell out words. The horse was not only able to respond to its master's verbal questions, but also to written instructions on a blackboard and to others who asked him questions as well. While other experts validated the claims, it did not satisfy a young psychology student by the name of Oskar Pfungst.

In a series of highly controlled and carefully designed experiments, Pfungst both uncovered the mystery of Hans and provided us with a profound understanding of teaching and learning. The horse was extremely talented, but not in the way in which von Osten imagined regarding the cognitive skills of math and reading. Hans was, instead, able to read very fine and barely detectable changes in facial expressions, a twitch of the lips or a movement of the eyebrow, that indicated the right answer to the question. If von Osten, or anyone else, was aware of the right answer, Hans followed their non-verbal cues to indicate it with his own non-verbal stomping gesture. The outcome wasn't based on calculation, but on an extraordinary feat of attention.[10] Hans demonstrates the power of the teacher to influence the student through every single movement of her body, triggering responses that are embedded into a student's biological system. It can be as simple as recognizing a teacher's smallest gestures.

Mimesis is an incredibly important part of the educational process for all genders. Good teachers teach a subject, great teachers know they must begin with modeling. Given the material you want to teach, the modeling that the teacher provides, allows those mirror neurons to begin to connect between the students' motor skills and the complex tapestry of their students' brains and therefore minds. Students take this process and then make it their own and hopefully begin to translate those representations into independent thought. Donna's strengths as a student are also her weaknesses. She is great at the mimesis; it is the conversion into independent thought that gets in her way. There are two reasons for this, I believe, that have to do with gender.

School, for Donna, has become a series of hoops to jump through based on the fact that she is rewarded for being a good girl. Her behavior, as we discussed earlier, is her calling card. Teachers have nice and confirming words about her politeness, her deference, her big smile. While receiving all this praise, she appears to be a role model for other students. She is not only seen as not causing issues, but she is an ally in the never-ending fight to get students to follow directions and stay organized. Her impeccable notebooks are an outer veneer of success in school. However, they tell another story when you take a closer look at the work.

The other reason why Donna is mimicking rather than learning the math has to do with the teachers and how they perceive the learning of math. As we will see later, learning math is a messy art form. It is more like a Jackson Pollock painting or a Picasso than a lifelike Renaissance portrait. The math itself can be exquisitely beautiful once you see and understand it, but the road to get there is bumpy and dark. Most math teachers at the elementary school level did not opt into education because they perceived themselves as accomplished at math or even competent. They bring their lack of self-efficacy, anxiety, and their experiences of stereotype threat into the classroom all day long. This has real ramifications when students are expected to perform on high stakes standardized tests.[11] Young men are much more likely to take independent routes toward problem solving, applying creative methods to answering math questions which include risk-taking, analyzing the best possible solutions to a given problem and applying those solutions back into question sets to come to conclusions. They, in other words, gamify tests and worry less about the ramifications of a wrong answer. Young women are more likely to stay inside the confines of practice and execution and take fewer risks, even if eliminating a couple of obvious wrong answers and taking an educated guess is worth the risk.[12] If teachers view math as a narrow set of neatly out-lined steps that lead to some narrow conclusion, female students are more likely to mirror and mimic this approach.

Where do I see teacher attitudes toward math on display the most? At Back-to-School Night.

Parents pour into their child's teacher's classroom and sit at their kid's desk. Maybe the student has written their parents a note which sits waiting for their parent before the presentation begins or the teacher asks the parent to write a note wishing them luck as the new school year really kicks off. The teachers then launch into their ten-minute presentation running through more information than anyone wanted to hear. Most of it has to do with classroom routines, materials, where they are kept in the classroom, what parents need to bring and when. (Remember Donna's extreme levels of organization). Then the curriculum. When I first arrived to work at the school, I timed each elementary school teacher's presentation to see how many minutes were committed to discuss the math curriculum which, by the way, was a huge selling point for the school. Four percent. Long explanations were given to describe the literacy program, or the cool butterfly experiments they were doing, or learning the States. Math? Four percent.

Often, as they explain their math curricula, teachers hand out sheets that explain the scope and sequence of what is being taught for the year. Several teachers show the cover of the workbook and then put it immediately away. Others indicated their own discomfort with the subject matter being quite blunt about their feelings.

"Hey, we all know how much the kids hate math, so we are just going to make sure we get it done."

"If you have any questions about the math homework, you can look it up on Khan Academy. Asking me is a waste of time. Math is just not my thing."

I was horrified.

Now imagine the dissonance that Donna has been experiencing. She is moving through her math curriculum as a series of steps that need to be accomplished. If your paper is neat and you have followed the steps, then you've won. Worksheets are flung at you; teachers are nervously moving through the material hoping that students will not challenge the actual thinking behind the math, and girls are imbibing large doses and generations of anxiety from their role models. Think of Hans the Horse. Are the girl students in these classrooms paying attention to the math and thinking through the problems, following a confident and passionate math teacher or are they responding to the 1,000 micro signals and confirmations that tell them that the subject causes stress, anxiety, or worse, indicates a sense of insignificance or unimportance? There is no beauty, no creativity, no magic. This is a battle you need to endure and get through.

Examining teacher practices, as we did in the previous chapter with how teachers talk about students will help us see the work we need to do in schools to create more gender fairness and equity. In this regard, everything a teacher does matters. The physical space of classrooms and schools is another fruitful area to focus our attention.

***

When I began working as a principal for the first time in a school with an elementary division, I quickly realized that setting up and decorating these classrooms and learning spaces was a *big deal* for the staff.

First week before school starts:

Will we have time to set up our classrooms?
Will they be cleaned in time?
Do you know where they put the classroom rugs?
What's our budget for materials and decorations?
My throw pillows are worn out. Can I buy some more?

I would find teachers staying two or three days in a row until ten at night taping up charts, cutting crepe paper, organizing shelves with pens, scratch paper, crayons. It was impressive what sweat and pride they put into these rooms, to make the rooms stimulating (perhaps over stimulating) and engaging for the students.

As I began touring the rooms after school started, I started taking photos of the classrooms. In fact, every inch of every class. Over 500 photos. I then culled this down to twenty-five for our next faculty meeting. I then posted the photos around the room and I asked the teachers to take a gallery walk to gather information and record it with the central question being:

"According to the walls of our school, what do we teach at this school?"

I should mention that all the teachers in the elementary school are women. Twenty-two faculty members and eleven assistants and not a man in sight, except for the principal, of course, who happens to be a man. As the teachers toured the room, they began smiling. One teacher put her head in her hand, realizing what she was witnessing. After we all sat down together, this is what the data gathering revealed. According to the wall photos, the school teaches ninety percent literacy and the arts, four percent history, four percent science, and two percent math. Our classrooms reflected a very powerful message to our students, not about what we were teaching, but what we thought about what we were teaching.

If you asked any of the teachers what should be and what was the actual balance of instruction, math, science, and history would take a much more prominent percentage. However, the teachers' attitudes about teaching math were literally on full display. And the fact that all our teachers were women made this reality neither shocking nor surprising. By their own admission, they were reinforcing their own challenging experiences as math students. Many had brought their anxiety, fears, and feelings of failure with the subject into the classroom where they are the greatest role models for girls. It is a generational dilemma of inherited bias. The walls are telling the girls exactly what they should think is fun, interesting, and exciting to learn and it sure isn't math.

And the boys? Well, guess what they learn? That to identify with literacy is going to threaten their sense of maleness, so stay away! Rather take in all the other gender triggers, that men do math and science, they are inherently and innately good at it, and that literacy is for girls, like my teachers, as clearly noted on all the walls of the classroom they designed. Boys and young males need to construct what educational scholars Rob and Pam Gilbert call a, "school self – how to perform as a schoolchild – and this learning is not disassociated from gender."[13] In their extensive interviews with primary school boys, literacy was regularly associated with the boys who are neat, wear their clothing properly, like the girls, who go home to do their homework instead of being interested in the physical activities that boys do and being a good boy for mommy.[14] These binary feminized and masculinized defaulted manifestations of school identity get baked into the road to academic failure. And, the proof, again, is in the data.

While some progress has been made around girls and math education, both in terms of access and perception, many women still report, even those who are accomplished at the highest levels of mathematics, that they feel inferior to men in this arena. An Organization for Economic Cooperation and Development's 2015 report that looks at test results and surveys for fifteen-year-olds, shows a persistent lack of confidence with females regarding their math education and science, despite being successful in these classes in school. "What emerges from these analyses is particularly worrying," the report asserts. "Even many high-achieving girls have low levels of confidence in their ability to solve science and mathematics problems and express high levels of anxiety towards mathematics."[15]

The more damning problem, one which we have largely ignored, is how males are suffering under this gender paradigm. While men still post at the highest level of math testing and assessment, they also occupy the lowest end of the bell curve. Internationally, males represent the bottom twenty-six percent of math learners in developed countries. And the literacy picture is much graver, with a significant number of men graduating high school marginally to functionally illiterate. The PISA (Program for International Student Assessment) results regularly indicate that women, while on average hold a slight disadvantage to men in mathematics, they maintain a whopping thirty-two percent advantage to men in literacy.[16] These numbers are no longer ig-norable, and the issues need to be addressed through the lens of gender. If we can make inroads with girls and math, we can do the same with men and literacy.

The teacher influence issue extends itself well beyond at-mosphere and space consideration and straight into practice and pedagogy. The implicit bias is found simply in the time by which teachers give students to answer a question or as researchers call "the bombing rate." And an aptly named measurement at that. Teachers are giving students, on average, approximately less than a second to answer a question, no matter how complex or sophisticated the thinking necessary to answer the inquiry.[17] In an attempt to move through the curriculum and not waste time, students can become flustered and anxious, even embarrassed if they do not come up with a response quickly enough. The irony is that, for many of us, these moments are the actual education. What students remember or learn exactly in the moment is less important than a student's self-confidence, their ability to get something wrong and feel okay about it, and the ability to think through something carefully and hone their critical thinking skills. And to listen to others and themselves, to think.

All students would benefit from extended time to respond to a teacher's question. But in this instance, again, young girls are getting even less opportunity, by a magnitude of three to one, than boys to respond. Teachers are less likely to interrupt boys when they talk than girls, leading to retreat, a lack of willingness to assert themselves, and in the case of Donna, needing to prove herself more by being a "good student" than by developing her thinking and analytical skills.

So, what can we do in schools to make the atmosphere of the school more gender balanced and fair?

The first thing we can do is start to acknowledge that the atmosphere really matters, much more than we think it does. Teachers running around at the beginning of the school year with tape measures and scissors and crepe paper may have a concept. They may even have a theme for the year, or they may even be putting up the same materials they have from the first year that they taught. Maybe it seemed as if it worked, and it helped the class function better. Just design the classroom the same way again, particularly, if it is not broken.

If we start by giving these classrooms the intentionality necessary, then we need more than a theme or an idea. We need to answer a vital question: How is my room going to be the second (or third) teacher? How am I going to utilize the space to foster the best kinds of learning in my classroom that supports *all parts* of the curriculum and is not just a reflection of what I am most excited about, insecure about, in terms of learning as a teacher? Classrooms can serve as another full-time instructor if designed well and transformed throughout the year. Donna was not just interacting for years with a teacher and other students in a blank, colorless silo of space. She was surrounded, all day long, with signifiers and signs which told her exactly what to believe about herself as a learner and about the purpose of school for a young girl.

Here is where school leaders and instructional leaders can help. Don't tell teachers what their classrooms should look like. Instead, ask teachers specific questions that they can use as a form of self-reflection before they put all that work into their learning spaces. When administrators meet with their teachers beforehand and start to think through these questions and then use them to observe the first six weeks of school, the results can be mind-bending. You will discover everything from a piece of furniture that is blocking student movement and needs to be rearranged to language on walls which speaks to boys, but maybe not to girls.

Here is a sample of thought-provoking questions that teachers can ask:

1. What is the process for keeping the room orderly and organized?
2. Is the room safe? Do students have enough room for movement?
3. Are supplies, bookshelves, materials clearly marked? Would a stranger know where everything is?
4. What do the walls reflect in terms of student learning and why? From their physical vantage point (height), what do they see?

5. Are the walls organic and flexible? Will the students see in April what they saw in September?
6. Are the walls under-stimulating?
7. Are they over-stimulating?
8. Does your space facilitate critical thinking? Is the room filled with inquiry and questions, not just information?
9. Does the room make clear our fundamental core programs, in equal measure? (Math, literacy skills, science, history.)
10. And finally, how does the room suggest that all students have equal access to learning?

As you can see, these questions move from the mundane to higher order, a bit like Benjamin Bloom's famous taxonomy for learning. Even though I believe that explicit questions regarding gender representation need to be asked, magically, you will see rooms transformed into spaces which represent a greater inclusiveness of student needs. It will raise awareness, not just before school begins; teacher thinking will also be altered throughout the year because of this process. (**See Appendix D for a complete space observational tool**).

On Saturdays, Daphne Orenshein walks. She does not do it alone. She has a group of friends who put on their running shoes and do their power walk together. They do it not only for the exercise, but also to talk, laugh, and enjoy the gift of year-round glorious weather in Los Angeles. But Daphne has a secret. On these walks she is not only communing with her buddies or sweating her way to health. She is also registering each of the house numbers she sees, to figure out if it is a prime number or not. Then she tries to calculate its prime root.

"My head, my mind is just always swirling with numbers, with math," Daphne explains.

She is a master teacher. A teacher's teacher. Her classroom has a rhythm. It has a calm. It has an excitement. All in the same breath. She does not merely teach a given curriculum. She tears it apart until it is embodied and then translated into a completely organic manner. She is always in motion when you walk into her classroom and so are her students, and, at the same time, so much gets done.

Daphne is also her own kind of anomaly, just like Jessie and Kenny were as students. She has taught early childhood and elementary school and her real passion is teaching mathematics. It is not that the teaching of math comes easily to Daphne: It's that math is the lens by which she sees the world. What is the greatest indication to me that she is so brilliant at what she does? When I visit her classroom, it takes me several seconds to even realize that a math lesson is occurring. There are no boring worksheets, no teacher talk from a smartboard in the front of the room. There are games and weird songs and representations that transform into math learning. Rather than some old chart hanging on a nondescript part of the room, domino tiles are placed on tables, where students need to physically manipulate them to find the right answers. Most elementary school teachers are not talking about math outside of class or even school. But Daphne does.

The reason that Daphne is an anomaly is that women with her skills, passion, and love of math typically do not make their way into education. The truth is often the exact opposite. When teachers choose elementary school education, it is because they have endured years experiencing and listening to schools tell them that math was, "not for them," that it was "for boys" and even that their genetics did not program them for careers or the talent for the world of math and science. College students in elementary school education programs report the highest level of math anxiety of any major. What we are left with is a cyclical and repeated pattern of math having a secondary status in our schools and young girls experiencing, through no fault of their own, a generational dilemma of something called stereotype threat.[18]

Researchers in the field of gender, who make assertions about how schools and children function, do not help matters. In fact, in attempt to forge arguments regarding the biology of gender, researchers misinterpret what is going on in schools and therefore reinforce patterns of gender bias and discrimination in the classroom.

Developmental psychologist Sir Simon Baron-Cohen (Yes, this is Borat's cousin!) makes an odd claim in his work on male-versus-female brains, *The Essential Difference*. In the book he quotes research by Kimura, which asserts that, "sex differences in math have been documented in children as young as seven years old." He adds:

> ...the *same* teacher teaches both the calculation (in which girls excel) and mathematical problem solving (in which boys excel), so it is hard to see how the teacher's *general* expectations or teaching style could produce a different pattern of scores in the two sexes.[19]

This understanding of how teachers and more importantly the classroom work is on the verge of bizarre for those of us who have worked and observed classrooms. Cohen's logic is the reverse for what we know to be true, and therefore educators are so needed in partnership with researchers. Educators know the *opposite* to be the case: It is exactly because of who stands in front of a classroom that we are getting different results with boys and girls in mathematics. Teachers, in general, bring their own biases and unintended micro confirmations of sex into the classroom leading to different results. Daphne Orenshein's anomalous nature as a teacher of math at the elementary school level lets us know this.

Kimura in, her work *Sex and Cognition*, makes another corollary point that belies the researcher's lack of knowledge regarding the classroom. She states,

> Some have argued that the males' better performance on math aptitude tests largely due to socialization factors, such as different expectations teachers and parents supposedly have of the sexes, beginning early in life. This argument assumes that such attitudes determine the acquisition of math skills in children (rather than the skills determine the attitudes). The fact that girls, if anything, get better marks in math courses than boys do, does not seem consistent with this explanation.[20]

Again, the assumption exposes Kimura's misunderstanding of the gulf, as mentioned earlier, between an aptitude test and what students experience over the course of an entire year in a math class. In a class, students have many ways to demonstrate knowledge of the subject and the ability to be an excellent learner. Strong teachers are looking for both and are rewarding students with both. Again, classrooms and teaching are not output in, input out. They are organic experiences where students get to grow in multiple ways and demonstrate a variety of learning, emotional, and human skills, which can then lead to excellence in a subject matter. The relational nature of school is a big reason we are drawn to the model in the first place, not only to learn the math.

Donna is the perfect example of this reality of school. Do I know that Donna is going to begin to excel at math at some later date? I have no idea. But I do know that her chances are much greater because she understands what it means to work hard, what it means to show up every day ready to try and push through difficult dips in understanding and what it means to organize a mean damn notebook. These are numerous important skills that have nothing to do with math. The hope is that she will then grow to translate those skills into how you write down a math problem, how to work through a math problem, how not to make mistakes, how to check your work, how to navigate multiple steps and concepts simultaneously. All these steps can be missing pieces that reinforce the gender gap.

Problem solving versus calculation ability and the gender divide that exists with these two skills also has more insidious origins as well. With girls being rewarded for following rules (compliance) and the assumption being that boys are rule breakers (troublemakers on the one hand, but out-of-the-box thinkers on the other), stereotype reinforcement demonstrates itself in the classroom as teachers are much more likely to ask boys analytical questions or to rethink incorrect answers to their inquiries and girls receive many more yes or no answers. "Research in student-teacher interactions revealed that due to gender-stereotyped expectations…teachers may unintentionally encourage boys and girls to employ different problem solving techniques in mathematics."[21] In Dr. Elizabeth Fennema's groundbreaking research on differences between gender in math problem solving, one conclusion reached is that the more the teacher focuses on the individual needs of a student, the more likely they are to apply (unconsciously) gender perceptions to students. The promise, ironically, of focusing on the needs of the individual learner leads to broad gender stereotyping on the part of the educator.[22]

It does not surprise me that girls tend to do better at calculation and men at problem solving. I have watched countless lessons where elementary school teachers think that calculation *is* the math. For someone who struggles with their own math confidence, the easiest way to frame math is as if it is about following some preset pattern of rules that should lead you to some objective result. For those who know, love, and live for numbers, you know that math is a complex problem, a puzzle, an interesting question where the calculation is a means to an end. If girls are consistently associating and cognitively connecting with gender role models who believe that calculation is the end game, then that is what they are going to excel at more often than not. The beauty of math gets lost in anxiety and fear.

Where Baron-Cohen and Kimura miss the mark most heavily is the question of who is that teacher. And this speaks to the convergence which I alluded to earlier concerning the history of gender equality in schools and the history of education in America. The "who" of teaching is so critical to this entire endeavor and the parallels between how we think about teachers and questions of gender equity are too obvious to ignore.

***

As I mentioned in the introduction, one of the great innovations in American life which took place in the Twentieth Century had two components to it: The first was the then radical idea that everyone, regardless of gender, economics, racial and social backgrounds should get an education. The road to that becoming a reality was not overnight and it took exertion and will by those who were determined to make it happen. For sure, what that education looked like – its accessibility, its quality – differed greatly across regional, racial, and neighborhood lines. And gendered ones as well. The second issue that paralleled this development was the understanding regarding what purpose this education served, not only for whom it was for. This battle took place in my opinion, to our detriment as a nation.

In 1893, the National Educational Association (NEA) convened a commission to make recommendations regarding what would be the content, context, and rationale of high school education given the realities of the day. Chaired by the president of Harvard, William Charles Elliot, it was comprised of himself and three other college and university presidents, two headmasters of prestigious private schools, and one high school principal. Note that no teachers sat on the committee.

According to educational historian Thomas McCambridge, "What they would produce reflected an attitude based in an Enlightenment conception of education." This concept, McCambridge says, had two parts. First was the basic ideal "that all were educable" – or rather, perhaps not people of color. And second, "that the development of 'personal culture' and of a clarity of thinking would lead to a successful life defined by the individual and consequently to a successful society made up of enlightened, clear-thinking people devoted to the ideals of democracy..."[23]

The committee's recommendations were aimed not solely at preparing students for college. Instead, they believed an education dedicated to the fullest development of the human mind was also excellent preparation to lead a meaningful, purpose-filled life. The standards they set forth were sky-high. The results, whether a student was college-bound or not, were meant to be in the best interests of students' development, which then would be of great benefit to American society.

But by 1911, less than two decades later, this entire vision was under attack. A new committee formed by the NEA, largely populated by professionals in the field of K-12 education, had completely redefined the purpose and goals of secondary education while simultaneously admonishing the views of the earlier committee as naive and utopian. The new committee's work became the template for the 1918 *Cardinal Principles of Secondary Education*. It designated schools as primarily a place of *training*, a caste system that drew on and reinforced gendered, racial, and class divisions.

The new committee argued that the Enlightenment-influenced vision of the 1893 Committee of Ten was

> responsible for leading tens of thousands of boys and girls away from the pursuits which they are adapted and which they are needed, to other pursuits for which they are not adapted and in which they are not needed. By means of exclusively bookish curricula's false ideals of culture are developed.[24]

The president of Stanford University, Ellwood Cubberley, was even more explicit. He wrote in 1916 that,

> Our schools are, in a sense, factories, in which the raw products (children) are to be shaped and fashioned into products to meet the various demands of life. The specifications for manufacturing come from the demands of twentieth-century civilization, and it is the business of the school to build its pupils according to the specifications laid down.[25]

I would argue that despite our pretensions, it's the 1911 vision, not the 1893 one, that became the ideological blueprint for our educational system today.

In it, students who do not fit into this narrow system are not useful. Their duty is to be assigned a role. To fit into the model, like an assembly line. Gender can be an industrial category as well, depending on the utilitarian needs of the nation.

The educational system is subservient to the economic plans of a young industrial society. It purposefully and consciously under educates segments of the population to provide the fuel for the needs of the economic machine of America. The 1911 report dismisses academic standards as "bookish,"[26] with a nefarious impact on our culture.

As mentioned earlier, who is driving the classrooms? Women. Who has been and is mostly driving leadership in our educational institutions? Men. Education becomes nothing more than a form of training for an economic marketplace and machine. If

Hollywood were to make a movie about this moment in United States history, the word "conspiratorial" would be all over the reviews. And the results have filtered down into a sharp divide between how teachers and schools see the purpose of education versus the communities which they serve.

By the 1960s, we see the educational assumptions of the 1918 cardinal principles being questioned and openly attacked. The atmosphere in education was full of desire for reform and rethinking the purpose of education. This debate was largely framed as a question of social justice and equity, coming from minority groups, the poor, and, yes, women.

The women's movement had made significant strides at this point, both inside and outside of schools, but more was not enough, and equality is equality. It is an objective reality measured in access to jobs, pay equality, and human safety and security. It is not the subjective understanding of those in power over those who do not have as much power, namely men over women.

The backlash against women and schools and the profession of teaching has parallel tracks by the 1980s. Ronald Reagan came into office and sectors of the population retreated into previously held social constructs. I cannot give any greater justice to this issue for women than does Susan Faludi in her brilliant and comprehensive *Backlash: The Undeclared War Against American Women*. Education snapped back ideologically and has not really recovered. The reputation of educators seemed to reach new lows at this period as well. Ironically, as more women entered the non-educational workforce and did not need to fill the classrooms of our schools in order to earn a living, the field of education felt the brain drain. The perception of educators also started to take a tremendous hit. Shows on television, such as "Saved by the Bell," portrayed teachers as dithering schoolmarms, who had no clue what was going on with their students. Male educators were portrayed as prudish, geeky, figures whose sexual orientation was ambiguous or open for question. Because what real man goes into teaching? Representations of school leadership, in the form of principals, were worse. With nothing better to do with ourselves, teachers were roaming the hallways, bothering students, or getting their incompetent selves into problematic or even corrupt situations. In a seminal "classic" movie from the period, "Ferris Bueller's Day Off," the conniving, dimwitted principal, Edward R. Rooney, spends his time stalking Ferris through his day because he obviously has nothing else to do with his vindictive small-minded self.

Our changing attitudes and cultural assumptions concerning education had to do with several factors. Economic circumstances in this country began to change rapidly as we moved from an industrialized nation to the hybrid consumer/service/technological model that we have today, and which will continue to progress in that direction. As the Harvard economists Claudia Goldin and Lawrence Katz point out, the forward progress of technology relies on workers to acquire more and more sophisticated skills, not just technical but in the traditional liberal arts areas of problem solving, creative thinking, and communications.[27] Ironically, the Cardinal Principles of 1918 designed an educational system exactly contrary to the needs of a technocratic culture.

What also arose in this transition to a consumer economy is the need for people to consume. And consume. And consume. Growing up in the United States during this period, I can personally attest that, by the 1980s, America seemed obsessed with the marketplace. Business, Wall Street, financial services and its macho, testosterone fueled value system were at the center of the American consciousness. The idea that you proved yourself as a man by the size of your bonus or paycheck seemed to take on new mythical proportions. As Faludi points out, this reassertion of the macho status of the male money earner was also part of the backlash against women who were heading into the workforce in record numbers. As men were being portrayed as "economic victims" of the feminist movement, "the start of the '80s provided not only a political but an economic hair trigger to the backlash."[28] Any kind of notion that education was to serve a larger purpose, to provide people with a sense of meaning, inherent worth, a sense of freedom and even for the health of a democracy seemed completely diminished and dismissed. In the Phi Delta Kappan 2019 poll of parents and teachers regarding schools, seventy-one percent of parents perceive that schools primarily roll as academic/work preparation with only twenty-eight percent seeing school role as to become good citizens. Less than half of teachers saw school as the primary place for preparing students for citizenship.[29]

So, what does this have to do with gender? Schools, as places of learning, had also become genderized or even feminized. In 1880 in the United States, men represented over forty percent of the teaching population. By 1920, it had dropped to below twenty percent. While the number has gone up and down over the years, it currently holds at around twenty-five percent for males.[30] In other words, girls were certainly finding schools to be places of success, but which ultimately reinforced certain gender notions as well. Faludi also argues that the forces of a turn to the right in this country also fostered a sense that the gains of equality, found through the schooling system and the vision of equal education for all, were under full assault. She points to the relentless attack on the Women's Educational Equity Act (WEEA) program, a publicly funded program which was doing important work to provide equal access to women in several areas. The program provided small grants which funded such projects as "a guide to help teenaged, handicapped girls; a program to enforce equal education laws in rural school districts; a math counseling service for older minority women returning to community college." A "tiny, underfunded" program became the target of right-wing think tanks and religious organizations that distrusted it as some sort of feminist enclave. Much of its work was just to help enforce Title IX legislation. So why all the hubbub? Why all the focus on this almost non-existent office? Because the far right in this country knew that education could be at the forefront of bringing about eventual radical change to the male hegemony of American society. Therefore, any efforts to further this agenda had to be eviscerated. Women's ascension to equality was predicated on equal access to this central human institution of learning. The emerging empowerment of women around them was coming from an ever-expanding access and success of women inside of the educational system. The attack on the WEEA was not just an attack on feminist values but also on values of equality in general. It was an assault on the very vision of education, its values and principles, as a greater equalizer, equally deserved by all. What the feminist movement was championing for itself had much larger ramifications than just for women. Thus, education itself had to be reduced in status and concern. And efforts by the religious right aimed to do exactly that as they attempted to eliminate federal legislation that demanded equal access and rights for women in schools and re-established separate but equal *zeitgeist* back into the school, to the point of denying federal funding for schools that portrayed women in nontraditional roles outside of homemaker and mother.[31]

And for boys, schooling has become, for most, a means to an end, a way into the economic marketplace. There also lies the difficulty that our boys face when they come into schools. They are rewarded if they do well, joining an ever-narrowing group of elite learners who can find their piece of the one percent, or school becomes a place of unrealized potential and often a threat to masculinity because of our notions about what constitutes a man. In the area of math, boys and young men can dismiss their teachers' own insecurities about math because they do not react to this stereotype threat. Young boys often take great pride in coming home and telling their parents about how they "corrected" the teacher regarding some math problem. And, in relation to literacy skills and attainment, they can be equally dismissive, this time of the content and learning, no matter how enthusiastic the teacher, because she is, nine out of ten times, likely to be a woman. Reading and writing is not for them. "Where is it going to get me?" they may ask. "I'm not going to be a teacher, that's for women."

And the studies on employment have borne this exact point out. Women have surged in increasing numbers both into educational opportunities in traditionally aligned male fields and therefore into these occupations. But the same has not been true for men going into traditionally female aligned fields, such as education.[32] In fact, the number of women going into education compared to men has only *increased* over the past forty years, from being sixty-six percent of the teaching pool in

1981 to seventy-seven percent by 2018.[33] The reasons this has been the case for women are varied. But for men, it remains a question of gender perceptions which keep men from seeing a wider range of career opportunities. Employment traditionally viewed as women's work is also traditionally undervalued and undercompensated. This phenomenon reflects a huge part of the problem regarding how we see gender and begs the question: are we really liberated from gender constructions in schools because women are doing better in school and have greater access to the workplace? Men still cannot break the psychological bonds of their perceived individual value in society beyond pay and perception, and the gender–education nexus has real consequences for how Americans view education in general. A 2018 global index ranking positive perceptions of education places the field of education at below forty percent in the United States.[34]

How have I experienced this reality? My great "research-based" litmus test is when I fly. On both domestic and international flights, I can gauge American impressions of educators by the person I sit next to on the plane. If that person is American, they pause and say, "a teacher?" when I tell them what I do for a living. They adopt a tone of strangeness and curiosity as if something must be wrong. I then tell them that I was previously a teacher and now I'm a principal. That statement usually makes them less uncomfortable, but the conversation typically stops dead in its tracks; it's as if they have met someone whose English is not good, and it is hard to conduct a real conversation. The talk usually ends with, "That's really nice," or "That's a hard job."

When I am sitting next to a foreigner or a recent immigrant to the United States, party on. They give me the impression that they have just sat down next to George Clooney or Bill Gates. I am an absolute rock star. A teacher? Amazing! A principal? Drinks all around! They cannot stop asking questions, they cannot stop talking about their old school days, their teachers that changed their lives. I am a towering cultural figure and a thought leader all wrapped up in one. If this were not so tragic it would be a hilarious contrast of cultures.

Another important benchmark of experience, which I also believe is a recent phenomenon – all of us in education have these war stories – is the lecturing we teachers and school administrators get from unqualified people, mainly parents, about how to do our jobs. No one goes into a lawyer's office and says, "Let me tell you how to conduct my case." No one, when wheeled into surgery, gives the surgeon advice on where to make the incision. Only in education do people come to our classrooms or offices and say, the following preamble clause, "You know I've visited two schools" or "I taught for a couple years" or "I sat on the board of a school" or "when I was in school…" They come from the highest offices of political power. They are radio talk show hosts or parents. They all think they know what schools need, what teachers should be doing every day, and how schools should be run. No other professions in the United States need contend with everyone having an opinion about what we do. To appropriately borrow terminology from the feminist movement, no other group of professionals gets mansplained like educators. The impression of incompetence is high. The idea is off the table that the profession itself has a certain set of learned skills and competencies and required nuances to be successful. In a twisted sense of reality, this is what makes anyone who goes into education today extraordinary. Those who last for the long haul must constantly be standing in contrast and contradiction to the value proposition of current American culture.

As a person who has spent over twenty-five years hiring, training, supervising, and sometimes firing teachers, at this point, I would much rather hire a woman than a man. Sounds sexist? Perhaps I am making a statement that applies more to the field of education than any other workplace, and I would hate it if someone used this logic to prejudice women or some other group from fair opportunity. However, my experience is that women know what they are getting into when they get into the field of education. They do it from a place of positive choice and strength, needing to dispel all the negative noise and stereotypes about people who go into education. They feel like they are spending a significant amount of their day making the world a better place. Men? I wish they would make such choices, and I have met those who feel they have found the profession that suits their professional goals and aspirations. But often it feels like they are settling. They often give off the air that there is something better waiting for them outside of education. They also feel the gender pull to be the money earners in their homes, which either drags them out of poor-paying teaching jobs or propels them up into the ranks of administration to "lead." How many times have I heard men in the field ask me career advice about becoming administrators when they had no business even considering it. How many men have told me about a "side hustle" they are doing that is their real passion. My experience with women is that when they are in it, they are in it. Again, I do not believe this is really about the nature of men but how we have taught them that education, as a profession, is really for women and for those who are perceived as not being able to do anything else. Do we notice who gets to be connected in that one sentence and therefore thought?

The answer to this self-perpetuating dilemma is not necessarily to encourage more women who love math and science to go into education or to push more men into education in general. This seems counterintuitive and too high a fence to climb. The more direct and immediate solution is to train, guide, and encourage those passionate and exceptional human beings who go into education, particularly elementary school, so that they become awesome like Daphne Orenshein. Teachers need to confront and encounter their own inhibitions and challenges to allow math, and any subject really, to be celebrated and nurtured regardless of gender.

Teacher practices, in general, also need to change. Gender awareness, active engagement and patience need to be more broadly pushed in teacher education programs.

Teachers need to guarantee that:

1. Girls get called on, whether their hands are up or not.
2. Boys must demonstrate that they are listening to others.
3. Everyone is called upon every day.
4. Be relentless. Do not let kids off the hook. Get past their fears and anxiety about speaking up and struggles with

subject matter. Have them answer questions about their opinions, classroom norms...etc. Whatever makes them comfortable with having a voice.

5. Conversely, don't interrupt students, particularly girls, when they are speaking or asking a question. Be patient, even when you know what they are about to say or ask. Allow full articulation.

6. Do not let school become a litmus test for girls to figure out how to please us. Obedience is not a learning goal or value.

7. Boys should never feel that parts of school are not for them or that they get a free pass in areas such as reading or writing. If they do a poor job, make them do it over. They are what they do, and they need to put their best effort into doing it all.

8. Teachers should start to self-reflect on their own anxieties and fears regarding learning. What are we bringing into the classroom that can impact our students' sense of self-confidence?

9. And finally, look around you and inside you. What are the micro-confirmations and implicit thoughts you are generating that could play a major role in gender bias and discrimination?

It can be as simple as reading the writing on the classroom wall.

(See Appendix E for a two-step observational tool addressing Student Engagement and Bombing Rate.)

5

Learning Liberation and Integration
It's Not about the Math!

"Let's settle in," I say, waving sheets in my left hand over my head like a ground crew guiding a jumbo jet into its gate. "Backpacks away, let's cut out the chit chat. And you need a pen, NOT a pencil."

"Wait, what are we doing?" Toby asks, looking surprised.

"It's Wednesday, we have our weekly quiz," I answer.

"But we just had one last Wednesday, why are we having one today?"

"Because it's been a week, thus the idea of a weekly quiz." It's January. We've been doing this for four months.

"Thus…" Siena repeats my phrasing and tone to herself. She thinks it's funny.

"I am totally unprepared. I don't know anything. I studied for four hours last night."

"You did not," Abigail says. "You were on Snapchat for like sixty hours last night." Hyperbole is a blood sport for middle school girls.

"I'm waiting. It's your time."

"This is beyond stressful. Why do we have to do this?" Jessie puts the back of her hand on her forehead in a gesture of deep, exaggerated persecution and arches backwards, looking like a

DOI: 10.4324/9781003217022-6

1920s distressed Hollywood star from the silent film era. I try to calm everyone's panic, a bit.

> It's on 4.6, 4.7 and 4.9. I skipped 4.8 because there was mass confusion yesterday. LCM and GCF. Tara and Sage, please get real pens, the pink and baby blue markers are not going to fly. I mentioned this before. This is not the magical mystery tour.

They both smirk knowingly.

"Sergeant Pepper's…" Sage whispers into Tara's ears. Tara nods her head. They reach into their backpacks and pull out two pens, one orange, the other lime green.

"Wait a minute," Kendra's head shoots up on her shoulders like a jack in the box. "LCM what! I thought the quiz was on Least Common Multiple and Greatest Common Factor!"

"It is," Caytlyn calls out and rolls her eyes in disgust. "That's what LCM and GCF stand for. Even I knew that."

"Oh, got it. Thank God. I studied all last night. For like twenty hours!" I start distributing the quizzes, perhaps too soon.

"Wait," Donna interrupts before I am about to hand out the papers. "But you wrote on the school site to study section 4.10 also. I studied that as well. Is that on the quiz?"

"I'm sure I didn't write that, and does it matter? So, you studied that too."

"You did write 4.10. I'll show you on my iPad."

"She's right," Candice chimes in. "I just checked."

"And how many people studied 4.10?" Only Donna's hand goes up, which the class realizes collectively is a problem.

"Well then, problem solved. Let's take the quiz. Donna is now ahead."

Sophie raises her hand, not waiting to speak. "Oooh. Mr. Ablin, can I go to the bathroom?"

"You know the answer to that, Sophie. Let's get on with it shall we?"

"Shall we…" Siena repeats, laughing to herself again.

"But I just got so nervous. Now I really need to go."

"You can wait for fifteen minutes. Let's get started."

"That's really mean," Jessie says. "She sounds like she really needs to go."

Cassandra and her hair are ruffling in her backpack for something, and Rachel has one finger on her watch indicating time's a wastin'. "Let's go!!" is screaming from her expression. I agree.

I take two steps back, put the quizzes behind my back and silently wait. The girls straighten themselves out and I place a quiz on each desk face down, walking around the room, eyeballing each of them and measuring their temperature.

"Don't turn it over until I give the signal," I say as I see some of the students turning it over without thinking. Do they look prepared? Are they calm? Anxious? Already defeated? Confident? As I move to the front of the classroom, five hands have already shot up. Now I know who is struggling with the very act of just starting.

"You people know the rule. How long until I answer questions during a quiz?"

"Twelve minutes forty-three seconds," Rachel answers while already hard at work, with her head so close to the quiz, she might molecularly merge with the desk.

The hands go down except for one. Donna's is still up. I go over to her with my "what could be so important right now?" look on my face. She looks me straight in the eyes and asks, "Are we going to have a quiz next Wednesday?"

I stare at her for a full moment, straighten myself out and, unknowingly to my students, walk part defeated, part amazed back to the front of the room. Within eleven minutes twenty-two seconds, multiple hands will rise.

Creating excellent assessments, tests, quizzes, writing assignments, essay topics, and lab experiments is an art form. Done well, they reveal student ability and knowledge in a whole range of ways. They can inspire, demonstrate, and activate student growth. They are sometimes better than teaching. Great ones *are* teaching. You know that you have executed a moment of true learning through assessment when students look both drained and immensely satisfied right afterwards. They feel accomplished, excited, smarter, and more grown up.

"Mr. Ablin, when are you going to grade them?" a student will ask. "I want you to read what I wrote." Pride and true self-worth trump grades every time.

Assessments also bring to light the types of thoughts and impressions students have about themselves. Do they feel like they know how to study? Do they know how to work hard? Can they focus? Can they do all these things, but anxiety will take over and dominate their thinking? As I mentioned previously, the differences between the experiences of students taking high stakes standardized tests and what they do in school to demonstrate growth and learning are like night and day. The emotional and biological interplay of school and assessment can be a great tool to support students, or it can be used as a weapon to try and knock them down.

Testing and assessment also, depending on the subject and the group of students, reveal much about how students respond to learning based on gender. At least part of the hyperbolic and frenetic behavior that morning in class, even for my brighter students, has to do with persistent feelings of inadequacy when it comes to learning a subject like math or literacy which is so stereotypically gender aligned.

For three years, Chris, a very thoughtful and committed science teacher, and I conducted an informal experiment during one of the most stressful moments in a teen's life, the AP exam in Chemistry. Well known as one of the most difficult exams in the Advanced Placement arsenal, students flocked to Chris's class every year. Was he a terrific science teacher? Absolutely. Was the class considered incredibly challenging and all consuming? Absolutely. Your final grade could wreak havoc on your overall GPA if you were not in the game. Well planned, creative, organized, and supportive, Chris did everything possible to help students achieve. He insisted on no gates or roadblocks into admission to the class. There were no science prerequisites required, no entrance tests, no previous level of math acquisition or competency. Did students try the class and drop out? For sure. But Chris wanted the students to find this out for themselves. He wanted them to try and discover and come to conclusions about where they wanted to spend their time and energies. The door to his classroom was always wide open. Students just needed to walk in ready to put forward their best effort.

Chris's classes were also an oddity, in that we always had more girls take the class than boys. AP Chemistry, with its heavy emphasis on math skills, and with the science/premed sensibility always tips toward heavier male enrollment. But not Chris's class. Young women felt welcome and supported throughout the process. He was passionate and excited in class about the study of science; however, he also exuded a one-on-one calm that engendered confidence and a sense that the class would get through this together. Chris was also 6 foot 8 inches tall.

Constantly bumping his head on hanging lamps and barely clearing door frames, his reed-like frame saunters through the hallways, smiling with abandon. His thick English accent booming, "Hallo, how'yre doing?" as he went from classes to meetings to the faculty lounge. The boys believed that he must be good at basketball because he was so tall. Nope. Hated it. He played a little soccer, but most of the time he and his long legs awkwardly slipped in and out of the Chemistry room to prepare for the next lab or experiment.

After the AP exams every year, Chris would come to me in despair because, as with any semi-decent science geek, Chris broke down the results of the twenty to thirty students who had taken the test. He worked so hard with the girls, but every year they were always a tick below the boys and it bothered him. Consistent with national statistics, his female students were doing as well or better than his male students in class, but the standardized testing environment, and its pressures and triggers, knocked his female students off their game. No matter how many practice tests he gave them or after school cram sessions, the results were basically the same.

"I'm too nice to them," he would say. "They're just too used to the support and it's holding them back. I'm not tough enough." I looked up at his upset face, looked back at his classroom, and tried to imagine what it must be like to be one of his students. There was always such joy and laughter. Students couldn't wait to come to his class every day, because of him. So, with that information, we decided to change the chemical balance.

As with all standardized tests, there are rules. Who can take them, when they need to be administered, how students can take them, what they can have with them when they take them, what they can be doing before, during, and after the exam, and most importantly who is allowed to proctor the exam. As opposed to the SATs or ACTs, individual schools are responsible for administering their own AP tests with the one clear understanding that the teachers who teach the curriculum and course are not allowed to proctor their own exams. AP teachers pace anxiously outside their students' testing environment, wanting to know what is on the exam, how the students are feeling and if they are taking it seriously. Many AP teachers see it as much a test of their own abilities as what the students can achieve. Such caring about student accomplishment is appropriate, yet some of it can verge on narcissistic or self-important. Students are not natural extensions of us. They are their own emerging people. Most of the time, we are not in control of their learning the way we would like to believe. They are not input/output machines. But the influence, as we discussed earlier, of a well-trained and passionate teacher can make all the difference.

Chris and I descended the steps of the school with anticipation that morning before the students arrived. We carried a big piece of cardboard, him on one end and me on the other. It felt like we were pulling off some crazy high school prank. We walked into the massive space, two classrooms combined, that would be where the students took the AP Chemistry test that morning. In front of the classroom, we placed an enormous cut out of Chris, all 6 foot 8 inches of him, smiling with his big grin, and with one hand raised with a thumbs up. Chris quickly left the room, and I waited for the students to pour into the class.

They did not notice the cut out at first, but then a few began to smile, laughing and cracking jokes about the cardboard likeness of their teacher eagerly cheering them on. The test began, and I observed students picking their heads up at certain moments and glancing at Chris's one-dimensional face staring back at them. They would stare for a few moments and then get back to work. The students finished the exam and some of them came up to me and mentioned the cut out, but most were absorbed with talking about what was on the test and if they had answered the questions correctly. And many did!

All the students, on average, did better on the exam, with the largest gains coming from females. We would love to believe that learning is rather one dimensional, like that cutout of Chris at the front of the room. But Chris is not one dimensional and neither are his students. The social and emotional triggers that occur, both positive and negative, during the learning process are real. They embed themselves into our psychological and biological selves in profound ways. What Chris and I discovered was that he and the subject matter were deeply associated in the minds of the kids, and particularly the female ones. The positive learning environment that Chris had forged with his students mitigated many of the biases and negative feelings that they felt walking into that rather cold and disassociated learning environment of standardized testing. Chris's face served as a reminder that he had their backs. They had worked hard, they had learned the material, and ultimately could accomplish much on this test.

How students identify internally with their academic abilities is not only complex but has to do with how educators construct and make apparent to students how learning takes place. Similarly, binary gender constructs play into how teachers and schools divide and compartmentalize learning as students age through our educational systems. We will now see how the ramifications of such approaches continue to aid and abet both students' perceptions of success and school perpetuated gender bias.

As mentioned earlier, if there is one area where men seem to achieve at a higher level than women regularly and predictably in their math studies, it is spatial skills. Defined simply, spatial skills "involve the ability to think and reason using mental pictures rather than words."[1] Perhaps this skill is also tied intimately to another idea we discussed earlier, that of mirror neurons and how we interact with physical space. Nonetheless, constructing mathematical problems into representations seems to be a critical aspect of learning and mastering mathematics as a subject. And, when researchers drill down, they also discover that not all spatial skills represent the great divide between genders. Some skills, such as mental rotational ability and mechanical reasoning are more prevalent regarding gender differences.[2]

Spatial skills, in all their various parts, are not the only ones necessary to solve math equations or problems, but they are significant enough. So much so that in the process of problem solving, "the primary determinant of whether an examinee successfully represents a problem in whether the examinee is successful in retrieving a memory analogy that bears a structural relationship to the problem at hand."[3] Another way of putting it is that you can know your times tables and math facts inside and out and you can memorize complicated formulas and even know where and when to apply them. But without the ability to select relevant information and organize that information into a coherent mental representation, we have a limited and ultimately flawed framework for mathematical mastery.

Imagine walking into that anxiety-producing testing environment, where you are presented with information in all sorts of forms, word problems, graphing of fractions, algorithmic patterns. Not only are you asked to organize and sort through and then determine the hierarchical relevance of the information presented, but you are going to have to do it at lightning speed, perhaps even a minute per question. The winner in this little race is not the student who takes out their pencil, blows off the dust from the sharpened tip, and starts attempting multiple calculations and possibilities. The actual winner is the one who can "see" the problem, who can cognitively represent the problem in a coherent whole and *then* apply the necessary calculations. What we often mistake as math, carrying the two and multiplying by the square root, is the obvious end game for someone who can construct a spatial reality for a problem. It's not that the answer automatically appears for these students, but the representation of the problem presents itself as a coherent whole. This is at the core of why school, to apply the famous metaphor of Isaiah Berlin, celebrates the hedgehog and testing favors the fox.

Why is there this imbalance in essential math skills and are there ways of overcoming them through thoughtful approaches to schooling?

Rational and thoughtful evolutionary theories explain these slight differences in math ability. Our hunter and gatherer ancestors – invariably males – spent days, perhaps weeks, moving through changing and complex terrain to find food sources. Even if they found them, they had to figure out how to get back home! As the psychologist Simon Baron-Cohen puts it "…there are no man-made signposts and no maps. Good systematizing allows you to build up a mental map of the area rapidly."[4] Hunters needed to hold on to enormous amounts of memory regarding their covered terrain, which required efficient memory systems, potentially more tied to visual representation systems than language. Also, guess what happened to those hunters who did *not* make it home or got lost. Can't remember whether it was a left or right turn at the watering hole? Their weaker navigation and mental map skills were selected out of the gene pool. Also, because of the unreliable, shifting landscape over time as they hunted, hunters need to rely on "geometric and directional cues" in relationship to the sun, weather patterns, the stars, to guide or steer home, and ultimately leading to the greater likelihood of surviving and thriving as well.[5] Women generally did not hunt but were major players in hunter/forager communities in terms of survival. They were responsible for as much as sixty percent of the group's food supply and its critical storage techniques during hard times and understood the pre-agricultural food available, what to eat, and what not to.[6]

All of this is important to understand the greater picture of gender issues and differences. But it still falls very short of understanding learning and school and why these differences persist. To put it plainly, I cannot recall when I needed to be out navigating the Serengeti for my next meal. I try as much as possible to stay away from red meat and the local supermarket is a two-minute drive, and if I get lost on a route I have mastered some 8,000 times, I can turn on my GPS App and take the three turns necessary to get home. The "troubles on the Savannah" argument takes us only so far. Are evolutionary forces important to understand? Yes, but they do not even begin to explain the complex developmental picture of what happens in schools.

And instead of consciously ameliorating gender biases and actively working to level these differences, we reinforce them. Early childhood classrooms are a perfect example. Recently, I visited five early childhood programs in schools with anywhere from five to seven constructed classroom spaces. Two of these schools labeled themselves as "progressive" in their approaches to early childhood education. In a total of thirty-eight classrooms, all but one had block sets and all but two had play kitchens. You can imagine what I saw over time observing students in these spaces. Not only was there a clear gender split, but if the girls wanted to play with the blocks with the boys, there was active discouragement, even to the point of boys telling girls to "go to the kitchen." Three and four-year-old boys had already manipulated and controlled the spaces so that there was a clear designation between public and private, ostensibly controlling both realms and making it clear where everyone belonged along gendered lines. And the kitchen areas were not much better. The girls were somewhat more inclusive, but the boys found themselves in a very familiar role. The boys were seated, asked what they wanted, and the girls would cook for them.

In this straightforward example, students are already being asked to fit into gender specific boxes which reinforce a cultural bias and value structure, and which also directly impacts the cognitive tools necessary for a critical component of their math education. The blocks? Spatial, design, geometric, problem solving. The kitchen? Collaboration, communication, language, and sociability. Beyond the obvious gender sorting and narrow construction that was going on in these classrooms (these are two- to four-year-olds!), the educational impact can be far greater than just self-perception and societal role association and the results were consistent with research gathered over forty years ago. Not much has changed. Boys aggressively dominate the rules and activities allowed in the more open, public spaces of the classroom, without much push back from instructors. Female students and male students less interested in the aggressive play of the public space found themselves confined to private worlds of kitchen and dress up.[7] At three years old, students were already setting up traditional patriarchal structures within the classrooms.

And that issue of bombing rate mentioned in the previous chapter? Teacher interruption of students? Of the 138 times a female student spoke to the teacher directly, the student was interrupted a whopping 106 times. The boys? In eighty-nine interactions, the male students interrupted their female teachers' speech patterns sixty-two times with no push back from the teacher.

We earlier saw the clear differentiation between the time given to boys versus girls in classrooms, how girls are interrupted more regularly when they begin to articulate an answer to a thought, and how boys are given greater attention in general regarding their academic needs. The question is: What do we consider to be the real learning impact of this differentiation? This leads us to ask: What are the optimal conditions under which students learn?

The work on teacher effectiveness by the educational psychologist James Byrnes outlines conditions for effective instruction through a 3C model which stands for Three Conditions Model. Students need to find themselves with *"genuine* opportunities to enhance their skills...*willing* to take advantage (sic risks) of these opportunities...and they are *able* to take advantage of these opportunities."[8] The groundwork for *"genuine"* relies heavily on the teacher's capacities. They need to be able to create learning environments which are non-preferential to certain students and challenging and logical/sequential to learners. They need to hold high expectations for everyone, manage a classroom behaviorally, and where teachers understand purpose and are able, communicate in a developmentally appropriate way that gives a sense of purpose to the students. All of this requires sophisticated training, ongoing, reflective practice, and school leadership who can keep their focus on what really matters in schools. It requires an honest assessment, not of students but of teachers' actual abilities, strengths, previous experiences, and most importantly, an awareness of their own implicit cultural biases and expectations.

I suppose I am blessed in that I have never worked with or had to supervise anyone who was an overt racist or misogynist. That is not the point. Implicit thinking is prevalent in all of us and is particularly problematic in a field whose main goal is to educate everyone equally. While those who chose to go into education do so out of a sort of rebellion against our current cultural views toward the profession, it can also create a certain sense of *chosenness* as well. When I have foreign students or recent immigrants join schools from different places with surnames that are culturally unfamiliar, even well-meaning teachers can stumble over the pronunciation. Often, I will hear, "Oh they all sound the same to me" or "I'll just call her out by her first initial." These are perfectly well-meaning and culturally open teachers who are unaware of how they are creating a learning environment which is marginalizing and creating preferential identities for its students. Under these circumstances, it's not about math, or science, or the English…etc. The classroom has been turned into a place where students are either finding themselves inside the narrative or somewhere on the periphery. The teacher is creating challenges to his own effectiveness. Gender, I argue, is the big elephant in the room regarding this issue. It is the global issue surrounding implicit thinking.

Because of this thinking, despite the small discrepancy in gender spatial skills, many girls simply believe they can't do math, especially if they are voracious and advanced readers and math, science, STEM are not nurtured in the home environment. Another student example is that of Tara and Sage. Teacher Chris would have been proud.

Tara and Sage are not the first twins I have taught. I have taught twins, (over forty pairs), triplets (four sets), and quadruplets (one). What I have come to realize is that teachers (and perhaps parents) want them to be different but expect them to be the same.

Sage and Tara early on rejected any kind of notion that they could be competent in math. Open and candid about their perceived ineptness in the subject, this view was reinforced by the fact that they came from a highly literate environment and were years ahead of their peers in terms of writing and reading. Their parents celebrated reading at home. Their mother, an editor at a magazine and their father, an engineer, kept reading for themselves and the girls at the forefront of home life. Both girls produced glorious prose, with rich vocabulary, and they read from an extensive home library. The family listened to many genres of music and early on made regular trips to museums, the theater, and dance that many other students wouldn't consider, if at all. Both unpretentious and nerdy, they were also my favorites. (Yes, as a teacher, I have favorites. We all do!) Why did I like them so much? Because they were so familiar to me. Just like me, they did not grow up with a television in their house. They did not have cell phones. They also got all my stupid jokes. Why? Because they have the nuances of language and reference. When one of my cultural references came flying across the room at some random moment (Sergeant Pepper), many of the girls responded with a confused, "What?" In contrast, Tara-Sage would laugh knowingly.

Here is another dirty secret: They were both competent to brilliant in math but never knew it, and no one noticed enough to let them know.

I was convinced for many years that math and literacy were separate competencies. For years, I would just nod my head in department meetings when math teachers told me that math could only be taught "this way" or "that way." They would integrate project-based learning as a matter of public relations or because they felt they had to help weaker students pump up their grades because they could not handle the "real" math. The discussion about math education is often a very narrow one, partly because of elementary school teachers who struggle with the subject themselves or math teachers who just got it when they were learning math. Only later in my career did I meet teachers who were doing extraordinary things with math, and I began to believe it could look differently. Math teachers are slow to change and skeptical about the results.

There are several reasons that math educators hold on to this narrow notion of math methodology and expertise. Many of them are men and many of them experienced the same type of failings in literacy throughout schooling that women faced in terms of learning math. They found their true strengths and the positive reinforcement in school through leveling up every year in ever more complex and ever more challenging math classes into and beyond the university system. Not only did they feel competent and receive the rewards of feeling part of a special club, but they fell in love with it! So much that they became math educators.

Another reason is what I call the tax code phenomenon. Accountants who do your taxes want most people to imagine, as much as possible, that they are the only people capable of navigating the tax system (and math) to do your taxes. Accountants rely on this mentality to keep themselves in business and it is often people's math phobias that keep this myth alive. The same is true with people who come and fix your computer. However, their clients are really avoiding a learning curve that can be steep, but that's all it really is, a learning curve. Not only fear, but an investment of time, keeps people from learning things they are being told is best done by an expert. Math educators fall into this kind of language about what they do all the time – that there is some specialized set of skills and either you have them or you do not.

Nonsense. I never hear this kind of language from English or history or even science teachers. This is a particular kind of spell that we fall under because of how we perceive school and its mythologies.

How do I know that Tara and Sage can perform well in math? How did they stop fooling me with their protestations and poor scores on math assignments and quizzes? It came down to trees and the final question on all my tests.

When you learn about factoring, either Greatest Common Factor (GCF) or Least Common Multiple (LCM), I often resort to graphs and charts to explain it to students. They needed a visual representation to isolate the numbers, like a game. Learning LCM and GCF are critical concepts for working with parts of numbers, particularly fractions and then equations which have fractions as part of their notation. Some students are fine with graphs and flow charts to isolate their final solutions. Some need trees, with birds on the branches and clouds in the sky. And then a select few need trees with poems next to them.

In speaking with Sage after another failed quiz experience, I asked her to write out her understanding of the math verbally, as if she was telling a story. Sage would create elaborate tree structures and then insert numbers into simple poetry that sat next to the trees. Not only were her answers correct but the poems *explained* the concept. She needed the tree and its visual representations, and language was critical for formulating her full understanding. She then began studying this way and then inserting the numbers that I had put into the quizzes into her poetry to help figure out her solution. In other words, she started with the language piece, her strength, and then tackled the mathematics.

Tara was a more complicated case to crack. She would present me with the most miserable set of mistakes, errors, and miscues on her quizzes. She would start a problem in the right direction and then veer off track because of a string of miscarried places with subtraction or multiplication and division errors. This stemmed from a lack of confidence with the simple and sequential nature of working through a math problem. I used to stand near her during quizzes and watch her pen shake back and forth with indecision.

But then there came the last problem on my tests and quizzes. Often, I would put a word problem with some useless piece of information that they needed to discard to get the correct answer. Or I would insert a problem that turned some principle we had learned upside down to see how they would handle it. I wanted them to think, not just mathematically, but to think. Tara would get to these problems, stare at them for less than a minute and write down the solution, usually in an intense shade of fuchsia.

"How did you do that?" I would ask.

"Do what?" she answered.

"The last problem…how do you just write the solution without doing the work?"

"I don't know," she would say sheepishly, worried that she had done something wrong.

"It's okay," I reassured her. "You simply slapped the answer on the page. It looks like there was no struggle for you, no fight with the numbers."

"I know. I just read the problem and I saw it. It made sense."

Tara's struggles with the material were not that the math was too hard. It wasn't hard enough! When she finally started to see math problems represented in language that were much more difficult, her mind went to a different place. It was like one light was turned off and another was turned on. The last problem on my tests no longer allowed her to fall into the trap of how she had been taught to do math previously; therefore, it allowed her to use other tools, her sharp language resources which had been previously untapped to solve the math. She was invited into new mental frameworks. What, I believe, she was freed most from was something called compartmentalization.

In his seminal work, *The Number Sense*, the cognitive neuroscientist Stanislas Dehaene argues that there is nothing innate about learning math. He states that humans are wired to understand numbers, but the process of learning math is counter intuitive to how the brain works. It is, by definition, as opposed to many language skills, something we must practice to master. "To influence the learning of number words, this protonumerical module must be in place before the exuberant language growth that some psychologists call the 'lexical explosion'..."[9] Children develop a sense of numbers and value at six months old, perhaps even earlier. The danger is imagining that this is all smooth sailing, that this is all some clear linear line of human development that can be counted on as a benchmark for learning in schools. The truth is that transitioning from this innate sense of numbers to studying math takes a lot of work. Language and memory systems interplay to support and become an obstacle at times as well. The sophisticated processes in the brain connected to associative memory become a primary example. We use associative memory systems for all sorts of complex retrieval of information to create analogies and relational connections in thought. When one idea becomes related to another, it provides the basis for insight, creativity, and problem solving. With something like the multiplication table, it becomes a hindrance.

"When faced with a tiger, we must quickly activate our related memories of lions," Dehaene wrote. "But when trying to retrieve 7×6, we court disaster by activating our knowledge of $7 + 6$ or of 7×5."[10] Just because we have memorized our multiplication tables, as all of us have slogged through in third grade, does not guarantee that our minds are cooperating when we do more complicated math. In other words, the more our brains understand how math works, the less likely we are to trigger misconceived pieces of information that do not help in the process. When a teacher describes or practices math as a series of hoops to jump through or calculations to make, over and over again, educators are actually playing into these contrary often conflicting systems. And as female students relate to math in this way more than their male counterparts because of the gender associations with female teachers, as mentioned in the previous chapter, we are literally gender-hardwiring student brains towards error, rather than understanding.

What Dehaene argues is that while some learning activation around math is localized to particular parts of the brain, namely the prefrontal region, several different areas, such as additional language centers, are necessary in order to learn mathematics. "Neither an isolated neuron, nor cortical column, nor even a cerebral area can 'think'. Only by combining the capacities of several million neurons, spread out in distributed cortical and subcortical networks does the brain attain an impressive computational power."[11] The false idea that the brain works in isolation or compartmentalization also mirrors, to a large extent, the constructed gender biases we have in instruction in general. As students get older and lessons become more divided by subject matter, by the time of day (an agenda list on the whiteboard which lists what will happen in segments and parts) or by the materials and exercises that the students are exposed to, this approach does not support how their brains work. Students are trained to see subjects as either for them or not for them and this often aligns itself with gender expectations. And, back to our boys, the struggle for them is not just with their connection to reading and writing and communication skills.

The crisis for boys is that they are almost twice as likely to suffer from learning or attentional issues, often language-based ones, such as reading disorders like dyslexia. It is still unclear which is the cart and which is the horse, but a preponderance of students diagnosed with ADHD also have a learning issue.

Several studies indicate that there is a comorbidity between read-ing disorders and diagnosed ADHD based on shared genetic propensities that inhibit information processing.[12] And they are more likely to be boys. Data indicates that boys are at least twice as likely to be diagnosed with learning disabilities and with speech impediments.[13] So, when doing math, we have students who are much more likely to reject language and literacy instruc-tion and then potentially the entire enterprise of school, driving that decision and feeling through masculine constructions and stereotypes and fears rather than true proclivities and interests. It would also help if we did more than just wait for our students to be identified late in the game as having learning issues when they are already at some point of crisis and hating school. The educational testing which is currently used is sophisticated and robust. Why don't we just universally profile all students in first grade? This would help us learn more about individual learners, take the stigma away from the process, and identify the students up front who need the support.

This discussion of how children feel about school goes well beyond the lament, "I don't want to...." that teachers often hear or that parents experience in the fights and crying that occur as they are trying to get their children to school in the morning. When students experience failure in the form of relentless con-fusion or stereotype threat, they develop this fatalist emotional reaction to learning. This psychological disengagement can stem from a period of poor performance or even in anticipation of one. The next level of this defeatist state is identified by schol-ars Paul Davis and Stephen Spencer as, "a permanent strategy of domain disidentification." This identification is defined as a "defensive strategy of eliminating a domain as a long-term basis of self-evaluation."[14] The amount of work it takes to pull even young students from these defeatist states is nothing less than herculean even at young ages. Gender biases lay at the heart of this reality and are reinforced in our culture and in our schools on a minute-by-minute basis. Tara and Sage, when I met them, were in full on disengagement and it took me a year to remove the obstacles. As I spoke to Tara, whom I booted up to the upper-level math class the next year with stronger students, she was still fighting these internal feelings. However, our work together helped us to realize that it was not about the math. While it was certainly not their fault, Tara and Sage needed both a cheerleader and someone who would not tolerate the internal mythologies that had been constructed for them about what they could and could not do regarding academics.

Much of the research into the state of this long-term disengagement revolves around females and math. However, there is no reason to believe that it also does not have to do with boys and literacy, and school in general. Boys are, I believe, placed into domain disidentification not only with literacy but with the entire enterprise of school, leaving them economically, socially, and emotionally vulnerable with no avenue of recourse. The trade school conversation seems to be a narrow-minded and condescending answer to this dilemma.

This trend also leads to strange interpretations of research that does not rely on the experience of girls and boys inside of classrooms and instead focuses on outcomes. Researchers need to focus less on assessments and test scores to discover what is happening in classrooms. They need to focus more on process and a recycling of old patterns that eventually lead to easily predictable outcomes. Teachers are constantly using language to teach math and they are using math principles to guide literacy instruction. The two realms are in interplay all the time and it is the job of the educator and school mission to construct learning experiences which integrate the two so students can see this reality. The gender fallacy is that they are separate.

Understanding which regions of the brain deal with the concept of numbers just proves that what is necessary is not necessarily sufficient. If the brain is an integrated whole that relies on robust neural connections across the various systems of the brain, it also means a needed re-evaluation of how we think of math education and its very purposes. Dehaene recommends doing away with the route learning of computation and even calculation, particularly given the extraordinary machines we have around us that can easily handle the workload of these mathematical tasks.

We cannot hope to alter the architecture of our brain, but we can perhaps adapt our teaching methods to the constraints of our biology. Since arithmetic tables and calculation algorithms are, in a way, counternatural, I believe that we should seriously ponder the necessity of inculcating them in our children.[15]

He advocates games, both physical and on computers, to engage students and expanding on this notion, I would include literacy education as well.

The most complex and integrated learning environments are often found in the early childhood departments of schools where learning of all sorts is almost entirely integrated. Apples aren't just apples. They are lined up, word labeled and then counted, becoming sums, and are differentiated from the oranges lined up next to them. As students move away from this integrated approach, not only does the learning become more compartmentalized, but students lose the concept of the *system* or context that the learning sits in the middle of. This pertains to such concepts as relevance, problem solving, inquiry, viscerality or the physical application of learning. Sage and Tara were not only convinced that the math was not for them, but that all those other extraordinary skills and abilities that they had were somehow not applicable or relevant or to be usefully accessed. Boys would also benefit greatly from such approaches because it would allow them to feel liberated inside of these systems of learning, less stigmatized from the necessary and critical literacy piece.

Constructed and developed thought should look far less binary and far more holistic. Integrate curriculum, particularly literacy skills, into everything. Compartmentalization inherently feeds binary gender constructions of knowledge and learning. We learn better when we learn *from* the world around us rather than just *about* it. Our lives, everything from language systems to spatial awareness to number sense are integrated systems. Schools should look the same. Instead of getting students to "do" math, we should be developing programs that help them understand and conceptualize what they are learning. Their entire brains need to be engaged, regardless of gender.

6

It *Is* about the Math

Gendered Mediators and Executive Functioning Skills

Schools are successful when they can create just a tolerable and fair amount of disturbance and affliction throughout the course of a school year. This is when real growth happens. Discomfort is a key ingredient of any successful education. Students need to be at least slightly uncomfortable with a question asked in class which is currently beyond their reach academically. They need to experience a reasonable amount of stress over an assessment coming up, even when they have prepared well. A recess yard that feels like kumbaya all day is a failed learning environment. Conflicts occur. Neither children nor adults, show up to school every day with their best selves on. It is when and how we must contend with this reasonable level of disorder, conflict, and anxiety throughout the day that true learning takes place. There is also a complicated world outside of our schools that our students need to be exposed to, even when the news is challenging and difficult, because they need to see that they have a role and responsibility to play in making that outside world a better place. They will not incorporate that message into their overall development if we create completely siloed and overly protected environments for them in schools. If schools tried to pretend that nothing had taken

DOI: 10.4324/9781003217022-7

place the day before September 12, 2001, they were engaged in educational malpractice.

In American education we also constantly talk to our students about their futures. And we often discuss more what they will be doing professionally rather than what type of people they will become. Will they become doctors or lawyers? Accountants, firemen, writers, bankers, police officers, nurses, judges, or elected officials? New media experts and technologists? We parade these professional examples through our classrooms or set up career days. To me, it often feels like a process of indoctrination rather than an introduction.

Implicit is that education's purpose is to get you to one of these places. The message is that the schooling process will play a role in impacting one's future career and that is its primary purpose: A means to an end. As mentioned earlier in Chapter 4, it is possible that schools began seeing their mission as training for participation in the country's economic machine, whether through choices regarding vocational education or advanced and increasingly sophisticated technical careers.

I find it ironic that many of the teachers I work with are acutely aware of this need for gender parity when portraying women's roles in the outside world, but spend little time discussing what their classrooms, practices, and schools look like regarding gender bias. It's as if what happens *out there,* outside of school, is more important or impactful.

This level of gender awareness and sensitivity was also not always the case. The work of career counseling offices in many high schools and colleges relied upon what were called interest inventories. The insidious nature of these questionnaires and measurements was that they only seemed to be gauging interest, as if they were neutral bystanders at a car accident. The presumption was that they were merely a reflection, not an influencer. In fact, the scales strongly promoted gender restrictiveness, "based on the pervasive and strong influence in our society of gender role socialization and the continuing existence of occupational sex segregation."[1]

One of the more frequently used instruments in the 1960s, the Strong Vocational Interest Bank, had a clear gender agenda, with separate scales for men and women. The scales pointed men in the direction of such fields as business management and engineering. Women were suggested in such fields as "Executive Housekeeper." These scales used language that reflected presumptions concerning learning. For instance, the men's profile contained a basic interest scale for mathematics while the analogous scale on the women's form was for *numbers*. "In other words, it was assumed that men do mathematics and women count."[2] The interest banks were part of a much larger feedback system, reinforcing the stereotypes that both genders experienced in educational systems. The scales were not meant to expand horizons or to create American dreams; they were meant to make sure that slots were filled, and the system maintained its integrity, largely based on prejudicial thinking. Again, this is just another example where school became the confining funnel rather than the vehicle of freedom for our children.

Eventually, the Bank and many others were revised as attitudes and expectations changed. But the insidious nature of these messages did not evaporate so easily. If we are serious about continuing these types of conversations with our students in schools, if we are going to have this conversation about the reality of the world with seven-year-olds and with young people in high school and college, we should also be honest about what women will experience "out there." Females will be paid less than men, much less in professions typically aligned with male stereotyping, and even in professions like teaching and nursing. Women will find themselves with better credentials and more accomplished than men and still not be viewed as equal candidates to men when seeking work. Women will be discouraged from seeking employment and training opportunities in many blue-collar fields. Women who show interest in these areas are discouraged because they are told that they lack the physical prowess or that they are stealing jobs from men. And we should be clear about what women can expect in terms of sexual harassment and attitudinal obstacles they will face.

The COVID-19 pandemic has been nothing less than a pulling back of a veil regarding gender inequities that women face at home and the workplace. According to journalist Tracy Brower in Forbes, unemployment for women has increased by 2.9 percent more than for men, with women being also three times more likely to leave the workforce to take care of the tsunami of household and family needs created by the pandemic.[3] About 1.5 million had left the workforce by March 2021.[4] Women have less options when it comes to work. Less of everything: Furlough time, flexibility to work at home, less paid leave, and less access to childcare.[5] Scholar Rachel Renaldo, in her blog *Gender & Society*, reports that the persistence of the pay gap has left women with, as usual, the inevitable falling back into gendered roles. Thus, their work is deprioritized, by what is perceived as necessity, rather than by the sheer injustice of persistent pay discrepancies in the first place.[6]

These realities are now re-calcifying what young children see in their homes, in a much more pronounced way, in terms of what gender inequality looks like, particularly in heterosexual homes. Children are experiencing learning loss in terms of hard-fought gains by women in the workplace and the expected new roles that men *should* be playing in the fair balancing of household responsibilities.

Indeed, parenting reporter, Jessica Grose, reports in the *New York Times* that the psychological state of women versus men during the pandemic was a master class for children in terms of hegemonic gender norms. Women are not just left with increased physical burdens but the mental focus, worry, and anxiety associated with running the home as well.

> Women's antennae seemed to be constantly up and looking for these things. Whereas men were often very happy to help once their partner had alerted them to the issue and they might've gotten to it eventually on their own, but women were consistently getting there first and either doing it themselves or saying: 'Hey, this is the thing you need to handle. Are you thinking about it?'[7]

The word "help" here is a telling one. Why do women expect help and men think they are helping in what should be perceived as shared responsibilities and expectations? Why are women the ones needing to negotiate their relationship to work to ensure the education of their children, and everything else? Are men making clear to their superiors and workplaces that they need flexibility to assist their children with online schooling during the day? What was the unfortunate lesson that came from watching their parents during the pandemic do this all too familiar dance around gender equity? It was that not much had changed.

If we think that schools are really about training kids for the real world, all students will benefit from learning the reality of gender bias and discrimination that continues to persist.

Rachel's parents have been using the C word, in this case it stands for college. "We just want to cultivate her interests and her mind," they explain, as they list five professions that they think might be acceptable for her. I wonder what would happen if I just interjected words such as artist or plumber or magician into the mix into these conversations. I wonder what their reaction would be.

Remember way back in the introduction when I had that uncomfortable conversation with my parents at Back-to-School Night? About mothers doing math with their daughters and men reading to their sons? Well, it was not the *most* uncomfortable conversation I have had with parents on such a night. That happened several years later, when I asked parents, about 600 of them, how many of them would be encouraging if their child came home and said they wanted to be a teacher. I am going to be generous when I say that approximately ten hands went up in the crowd. One would imagine that out of sheer embarrassment more hands would have flown up to dismiss any misconception regarding what they as parents thought of teachers. My homework for the parents that night was to go home and start a conversation with their child about what vocations or careers or jobs they were contemplating. Did they ever think about becoming an educator? I will share the results I got back from the school's parents at the end of this chapter.

One family responded robustly in my meetings with them – Marty and Sandra, parents of Rachel. They constantly brought up the C word – college – and even graduate school. They were concerned about how she was doing in math, fearing that it might impact her path to medical or law school. I might add here that Rachel had never mentioned to me a desire to practice either. She's just interested in getting through middle school algebra.

Rachel is doing fine in my class, not great, but fine. She gravitates between putting in a lot of effort and then falling down a rabbit hole and disappearing for weeks on end, ascending again in a burst of energy and enthusiasm. She cares and then she doesn't care. She is into it one week and then disengaged the next. She is also a great example of where the emotional life of a thirteen-year-old and their academic progress are so intimately tied together. When she pulls on one end, the knot in the middle just gets tighter and more difficult to untangle.

Her parents feel differently. "We're disappointed with her math education," they say in my office for visit number fourteen about this issue. Now, I happen to like Marty and Sandra as people. They have a good sense of humor and when I can explain how children learn, they listen and take it in. There is a reason Rachel gets so wound up: Her parents' anxiety about her professional success many years down the line. "Fine" in seventh grade algebra is not good enough.

"We're thinking of getting her a tutor," Sandra shares.

"What does Rachel think?" I ask. They pause for a moment.

"She told us if it will get us off her back, she's all for it," Marty says.

"You know that all the other students in the class and mostly in the grade look up to Rachel, right? They really admire her." Sandra and Marty start staring at me in a different way. They are drunk on my words. It's as if they just needed to hear something positive about their daughter, something to cut through the tension at home.

"Other students can tell when one of their peers has a real backbone. Rachel stands up for herself and speaks up. She has something to say and speaks with a kind of thoughtfulness that can be unusual for her age. It happens all the time at town hall meetings. She is a born leader. She's most comfortable when speaking in front of a crowd. It's impressive. All the other students stop talking and listen when she speaks."

"She never tells us anything. She is silent and morose from the moment she steps into the car. I know she is thirteen, but she used to tell me everything and now she wants nothing to do with us. Marty is the only one who can even get a laugh out of her."

"She'll start to like you again," I smile. "Right around eleventh grade, she might even want to spend some time with both of you."

I try to reassure them. "Math…might not be her best subject now but once she gets into high school, she's going to do great. She may not be a super genius math student, but she will put in the effort to succeed."

That didn't work. They continued to press the point about tutoring so that she can be best prepared to apply for high school ten months from now. According to her parents, Rachel needs excellent grades so that she can get into a super selective high school so she can get into an Ivy League university.

Their need for constant updates on her progress and their obsession with Rachel's math makes her feel defeated, even with her spurts of hard work and desire to do well. Rachel does believe in herself. She has ambitions. When I ask the students to do a math journal entry on why math would be important to their future, Rachel began her answer, "*When* I take over my father's business…" This kid has a plan and confidence to express it. But her parents are killing her spirit. Not only do they want her to go to one of the top private prep schools in the country for high school, but they think math is the most important subject to getting her in. Parents and our society have reached a level of lunacy regarding this issue. If education is all about economics, about outcomes, and about becoming an uber bread winner, then math, then science are the most important subjects. What seems to be the utilitarian nature of these subjects also drives their import in a largely utilitarian and increasingly nihilistic society.

I bring up this point to show how parents can have a pernicious impact on their children's success or failure with math education. As more and more of the burden of, not only the educational but also the emotional and social outcomes, are placed on schools, parents are becoming less and less aware of the role they play in reinforcing gender stereotypes or ignoring and counteracting them. Teachers are certainly responsible for what happens with students in classrooms. But they have little control regarding what the kids bring from home in their heads and hearts.

Parental attitudes toward math and gender are considered better predictors of future math success than even their prior performances. Research conducted in the United States and Thailand with thirteen-year-olds indicates that parental beliefs influence future performance.[8] These attitudes are not only about conversations or expressions of traditional gender differences, which clearly play a role. Parents also tend to provide different learning opportunities for their children whether they are boys or girls, sports versus arts classes, summer science or computer programs versus more socially oriented activities. There is even evidence to suggest that parents are more likely to intervene to push and prod school administrators to advocate and elevate their sons into advanced math and science classes than for their girls. In studies of parental influence, the gender split in families also shows a clear divide with fathers expressing greater confidence with their sons' abilities in math than their daughters. The divide becomes worse as students get older and the need for support and encouragement is much more pronounced. This leads to a sliding down effect whereas the challenges and the need for strong self-perception go up, the gender identification and perception piece becomes more challenging and starker.

As the education and gender scholars David and Myra Sadker write,

It is within the family that a girl first develops a sense of who she is and who she wants to become. Committed parents can create a climate of possibilities – or of limitations. Girls poised on the edge of adolescence struggle to retain their authenticity and vitality, for pitfalls are everywhere: physical vulnerability, the emphasis on thin, pretty, and popular; the ascendancy of social success over academic achievements...Girls who succumb to these messages are at emotional and academic risk, in danger of losing their confidence, their achievement, and the very essence of themselves.[9]

To be fair, evidence exists to suggest that parental influence can be marginal in reinforcing gender stereotypes. But that the amelioration or minimizing of gender bias gaps in math education relies heavily on parental influence. Girls who have positive affirmation and support from their parents in this realm tend to have higher standardized test results.[10]

Marty and Sandra seem to be a perfect litmus test for this type of conundrum. On the one hand, they have high expectations of Rachel in math. They are not settling for established, traditional associations of where she should succeed or even find interest. They are dead set on her accelerating in math. On the other hand, speaking with Rachel is another matter. She spends two hours a night, four nights a week in a dance class. She has been doing it since she was five years old. She is really into it and really good. Her parents have encouraged her passion for dance and simultaneously do very little to promote an interest outside of school in areas that might support and nurture her abilities in math and science. They also simply lack confidence in her ability to do well in math. You can hear it in their voices. Unlike boys who are pushed and prodded into accelerated programs whether they can do it or not, Marty and Sandra are communicating their lack of confidence in Rachel every time they have this conversation with her. Getting a tutor for a student who is performing well enough is a vote of lack of confidence. They are caught in a very common modern gender puzzle. Therefore, the school becomes the focal point of all their anxieties and frustrations. They want to have their gender cake and eat it too. Rachel is supposed to be awesome at a lot of things and she is also supposed to fall neatly into gender choices and paradigms that make everyone feel normal, comfortable, not threatened.

Our current national obsession with math and the sciences, computers and coding, STEM and STEAM and Innovation also appear to be another example of how entrenched gendered thinking in in education. We have become fixated on these areas of study. While reading the research from the past fifty years, what is striking is how the emphasis on math education also seems to be a type of reinforcement of the very bias it is trying to alleviate. By placing these traditionally male-dominated fields at the center, don't we also suggest that the male perception of reality, the way the world should orient itself, becomes squarely placed at the center of our collective consciousness? We have taken up the banner of the male hegemony as a way to create equity. This seems odd to me. Particularly regarding schools, complex human ecosystems, by overemphasizing these technical fields of study, we avoid a significant and growing issue which is male illiteracy. The goal to provide gender equal opportunities for women in math related fields is necessary and critical, while we also elevate the notion that women are simply more successful and capable in school because they are well-trained readers and writers and thinkers. We need to push our schools to make literacy a necessary part of the entire equation for males; otherwise, the societal gender picture will continue to get addressed on the fringes, not in its totality.

But the question remains. Should we be so focused on the math/STEM education of girls and the boys who are finding themselves on the bottom end of the bell curve or for any student for that matter? The answer is a resounding yes, and for very different reasons than the other narratives would suggest.

I didn't really understand how important math education was until I taught it. For many years, I struggled with the insane emphasis in math education at the expense of other concerns. And my eventual ability to better understand my investment portfolio or to calculate the tip in a restaurant or even understand the data and statistics of cognitive neuroscience research did not convince me. Part of this was clearly based on my own biases growing up. My house was awash with literature and politics, philosophy, and big ideas. My mother was the best read person I have ever met. So, when the discussions arose concerning math this, and math that, it just did not click with me as an educator. I needed more of a reason than it was going to help someone get a good job or even pass their pre-requisites for medical school. However, being in a classroom, day in and day out, with a group of thirteen-year-olds slugging it out with everything from rudimentary computation to more sophisticated principles in math, I began to witness other skills and other habits of mind develop which were unique to the type of thinking we were doing in class. And, because the learning of math needs to be taught and does not happen naturally, we see a number of critical skills, particularly in the areas of executive functioning (EF), which develop because of math education. These mental and cognitive habits are not just used to crack a difficult concept or to solve a puzzle. They are essential ways of being that make us better citizens, spouses, parents, human beings. Our goal must be to reach the highest levels of math education, regardless of gender, in order that people can master the executive functioning so critical to adult life.

Executive functioning is a large category with multiple cognitive systems working together, alongside each other and sometimes in contradiction with one another, to create different types of thoughts, understandings, and abilities. These skills allow us to plan into an uncharted future, although we are simultaneously processing new, often competing pieces of information with which we are confronted. Specifically, three sub working areas necessary are working memory (short term), inhibition control, and attention shifting. To break these down simply, holding on to information to do something, deciding A not B, and realizing A equals B but A also equals C.[11] Sounds simple? Well, it's not. And for children learning multiple rules, exceptions to rules, processing multiple layers of information from academic to emotional to social, it is a miracle that anyone gets out of school alive every day, particularly our children. It is a testimony to how hard wired humans are to learn, how natural it can be, and under the right circumstances, the miraculous potential of the brain is in context to human reality. Many of the learning disorders that I have seen in children have to do with one of these systems being even slightly less than up to the task. Imagine how intricate and sophisticated learning systems are and yet so fragile at the same time.

Math education has some perfect representations of this system at play. Teaching students how to do something as simple sounding as subtracting can involve all three of these sub areas at once. Issues arise when we ask students to learn to subtract one larger number from a smaller one, such as fifty-two minus forty-one, and then we ask them to subtract fifty-one minus forty-two. And then when we ask students to subtract 502 minus 416. Notice the different permutations of information that must be engaged to just subtract. There are rules and then exceptions to the rules and then other rules that need to be applied while maintaining the earlier set of assumptions about the idea of subtraction.[12] Then most math teachers ask us to do things like to "take away," "borrow," and "carry." We evoke such language as ways of triggering students' memory systems and rule applications. They are in fact tricks that have very little to do with the math concept that we are trying to teach the children. Place value, the numerical value that a digit has by virtue of its position in a number, is the much more relevant piece of information that students need to understand, process, and then synthesize all of these varying applications.

Math teachers, particularly elementary school teachers, who relied on these shortcuts and tricks in learning math, are now passing on these systems, as methods for understanding and doing the math. Dehaene writes, "We are now condemned to live with inappropriate arithmetical associations that our memory recalls automatically with little regard for our efforts to suppress them."[13] Not only are we by-passing the real math understanding when we teach this way, but we are also compromising the much more important development of strong executive functioning with our students. If we even put to the side if any of this type of education is necessary due to the machines and digital systems that we have available to do this type of math for us, real math education is so critical because it necessitates the use of so many systems that make us better thinkers, predictors, and problem solvers. What we want is the type of activities and math learning that require students to synthesize information and then eventually create "novel combinations," coherent expressions of thought based on numerous sources that can align but that can also contradict one other.[14]

This type of ongoing novel learning leads to new neural connections and avoids routine setting in, which shuts down the prefrontal regions of the brain responsible for advanced thinking and the development of executive functioning.

So, what does all of this have to do with gender?

Previously, I explained how stereotype threat and self-efficacy are impediments for girls (and, I believe, boys) and how therefore gender bias plays such a critical role throughout our school systems. Now it is the time to pull some of these pieces together to demonstrate a much greater impact on learning and the success of our children throughout their lives and in any subject of learning.

When looking at the reasons for differing performance between boys and girls in academic settings, we need to take much greater care in terms of making causal claims about sex differences and their relationship to educational outcomes when they are really indicators of correlative distinctions. The danger of making assumptions about "discovering" sex differences that are connected to school performance is that they often end up being interpreted as definitive genetic differences between the sexes as the explanation. There is a long-complicated leap between hormone secretion in early development and doing poorly on your latest geometry exam or essay on Kafka.

Simon Baron-Cohen considers such understandings or distinctions between that which is "common cause" and actually causation as a "nicety that in practice the brain ignores."[15] For Baron-Cohen, inside the world of the lab, this might be the case; however, in schools our main leverage is the biological interplay between one human being and another, and the learning becomes the third leg of the stool. He is making an essentialist argument regarding gender and learning which does not accurately represent what happens in classrooms. Certain information in these settings for establishing effective interventions is just more vital than others. Assigning some inherent gender distinction is virtually useless; whereas, looking at what we call, mediators, provides us with much richer information which focuses on the individual students, not on assigning potentially further damaging biases.

Mediators such as self-confidence, stereotype threat, self-efficacy, or past experiences with learning are not only likely to be more causally related but also more easily treated and addressed to support students and create meaningful corrective interventions.

One of the more fascinating aspects of stereotype threat is that the more a student excels in a subject, the more susceptible she will become to the anxiety of performance and gender roles. Math study is this perfect storm where the perception of the "maleness" of the discipline creates the circumstances for student perception. Areas such as science and computer science are not far behind. This issue becomes acutely pronounced in test taking environments where "struggling with the test becomes doubly threatening as you begin to worry not only about failing the test, but also about fulfilling a negative stereotype targeted at your gender."[16] Several studies have revealed that the differences in scores between men and women virtually disappeared when women were convinced that the test had been washed clean of gender bias and that men and women performed equally well in the past.

In one of the more interesting experiments, researchers Michael Inzlicht and Talia Ben-Zeev did not work from the angle of perception of the material but through the makeup and configuration of the testing environment. Beginning with an all-women's testing cohort, they continued to add men into the group. As more men joined, the test scores of the women dropped proportionately. Just the presence of males reinforced a negative message regarding women's own capacities and who should be equipped and able in math.[17]

The power of stereotype threat extends far beyond gender as might be expected, into race and ethnicity as well. While this book is not necessarily the place for an extended discussion on its larger effects and what they tell us, we should be awed by the impact of social and environmental constructs through simple suggestions and implications. Take one study of white males who were high achievers in math-related areas in college and graduate school programs with a heavy investment in math achievement. The students were told, prior to taking tests, that Asian students were highly successful on these exams. There was no indication of diminished capacity of the white students' ability to do well, only the projection of a standard stereotype/racial profiling regarding Asians that they can "do" math better than any other group. The white males who heard this slight consistently underperformed on the test. "The study made it clear that this reaction was not coming from a self-believing, self-fulfilling negative stereotype, but rather from an intense situational pressure that happens to individuals who are invested in doing well in the domain."[18]

When we look at the results of students in schools, we see that stereotype threat is also a phenomenon that plays itself out more in testing environments than in classrooms. When girls have the opportunity to build confidence and relationships with teachers who show their support, students can truly perform at their best. Again, testing environments are weird to the point of useless. Several studies have shown the psychological impact on performance. Why do we even put a time limit on tests if we are serious about wanting to know what students know and can do? How is this somehow a reflection of what future adults will be expected to do in their lives?

Another critical area of concern previously mentioned is self-efficacy as a mediator between sex related differences and competencies/successes in schools. Self-efficacy is a simple concept with much clout when it comes to student success; it is merely and substantially the belief in one's own abilities. Not only do men have a higher self-efficacy than women, but it also comes to predict their success in math and generally male related fields of study, where they even tend to overestimate their abilities.[19]

Now, let's complicate matters and give a more complex understanding and definition to self-efficacy which will link several of these pieces together and give us a more fruitful understanding of what girls and boys are experiencing in schools, particularly in subjects where gender biases are at play. If we go beyond self-efficacy as a form of self-confidence or self-belief and expand it to mean "one's beliefs and capabilities to organize and execute the courses of actions required to *manage* (italics added) prospective situations,"[20] we enter an entirely different realm of challenge. If self-efficacy is merely a sense of confidence or self-perception, then the intervention is rather straightforward. Greater support, belief, and encouragement from all adult parties surrounding the child, including teachers, administrators, and parents, would at least ameliorate this issue. It would also punch a hole into the socially generated assumption that boys and girls are inherently able to do and achieve in some areas but not others. Because of gender stereotypes, it becomes more difficult to strengthen weakened beliefs than to further damage already poorly constructed self-concepts.[21] This also establishes the clear imperative to eliminate the disparaging gender messages that boys and girls receive at such a young age and throughout their learning.

The obvious measurement are those students, like Rachel, who are exhibiting and expressing feelings of anxiety, significantly high levels of stress, and generally negative thoughts regarding a measurement or expression of their ability to perform in a given academic area. In other words, the emotions are the signs of an already preexisting weakened state of self-efficacy. This can snowball to, "trigger additional stress and agitation that help ensure the inadequate performance they fear."[22] But how? What exactly is happening that allows for such a state of low self-efficacy to impact what students can demonstrate in terms of knowledge? Why should this be the causal relationship? Perhaps what we need to imagine is that the mediator needs a mediator to properly dispel the effect.

Earlier, we saw the complex set of tools that a student needs to develop to carefully work through and construct understanding, learning, and therefore execution of simple to ever increasingly difficult math problems. These tools have largely and critically to do with executive functioning skills that are so in demand, and which seem like a flaming sun when given complex problem-solving tasks, particularly in young children and adolescents as their brains are developing. They are not only developing understanding of a subject matter but constructing abilities that allow them to think as human beings and function in the world at the highest and most meaningful levels. These skills work best under certain conditions and are compromised under others. What is the best state for humans to be in to allow their executive functioning skills to be at their best? Let's call it a "calm stress." As mentioned in the very beginning of this chapter, schools need to be uncomfortable enough.

This oxymoron allows us to see the type of careful equilibrium where students function at their most competent. The oven (the brain) needs to be lit and it needs to be steady, but it also needs to be regulated, not overheated, not over exposed to forces that will make it explode. The keeper of the fire is a child's sense of self-efficacy. "Specifically, self-regulated learners plan, self-monitor, and self-evaluate at various stages of the learning process (metacognitive component), and are also competent and self-efficacious, expend effort and have less anxiety."[23] The confidence and sense of ability in an area allow a child to adopt a state of mind whereby the various tasks and mental models, such as working memory (short term), inhibitory control, and attention shifting, can work efficiently to get the student where they need to go. They then show greater motivation when encountering next level learning which fuels the fire of those prefrontal cortices related to further development of ever evolving executive functioning skills. When girls show signs of weakened self-efficacy, what is occurring emotionally is that, as defined earlier, the "capabilities to organize and execute the courses of actions required to *manage* prospective situations," are also seriously compromised. The act of subtracting a number, where a student needs to borrow from the left because the minuend, the top number, is smaller than the bottom number, becomes one where certain gender biases and therefore certain emotional states literally trip up the effective functioning of those essential executive functioning skills. What I came to learn is that the study of math is a critical arena where we can decide to strengthen a future adult's sense of their ability to be a coherent, engaged problem solver or further dismantle those beliefs and therefore their executive functioning skills for future tasks, in any field of study.

A student such as Rachel, when they exit an exam and start talking about knowing versus doing, are describing a very specific state of mind called an abulic dissociation, which "results from difficulty in one or more of the component processes of

EF."[24] She has a distinct sense of knowing that she knows something and is flummoxed, disheartened and confused by her ability to demonstrate her knowledge, leading her to question if she really knew it in the first place. There is no reason to believe that Rachel is somehow inherently weak in one of these areas or experiences a learning impairment. (That would be the case with some children who suffer from learning disorders where EF skills are highly impacted.) As mentioned earlier, she is a star public speaker who can organize her thoughts and communicate her ideas in a sequential and logical manner. Rachel is one of those students who, when she walks into a math classroom, feels the stress and weight of her gender, imposed upon her by years of messages about what she cannot do, her parents' subtle messages regarding their confidence in her abilities, and what she may perceive as not really for her. As mentioned earlier, Rachel is stuck in a contemporary gender storm. Her parents want her to have equal opportunity but are implicitly sending her strikingly gender laden messages about their confidence in her math abilities.

Males experience a different type of conundrum regarding this issue. When looking at how boys respond to issues such as stereotype threat and self-efficacy, particularly in subjects such as math where they expect and predict to do well, the tendency is to *overestimate* their abilities and capacities to succeed. Our previous story of Adam is a perfect example. This is true; even though, they may not have had a previous history to support such self-perceptions. In other words, the fact that they received a sixty percent on their previous math test does not seem to dismiss prior self-concepts nor future confidence. While girls tend to be more accurate regarding their understanding and abilities, this almost utopian perception that boys have may be to their advantage. The very notion that they should somehow be destined by gender to do well in math also seems to provide a certain level of motivation and perseverance which girls do not possess. What this demonstrates more than anything else is the power of attitude and self-perception regarding learning. Certainly, underconfident would be easily categorized as an issue, but even being realistic has its drawbacks.[25] This suggests that teachers and schools would do best to try and consistently maintain an aspirational messaging to students regardless of gender.

As a teacher, have I really created an environment where issues such as stereotype threat and mediators have been mitigated or even ameliorated? Have I truly thought through what it means for my female students to have a male teacher standing at the front of the class and what that means for their ability to grow and feel self-confident about math? I went into that classroom with the goal of understanding what it meant to face these gender challenges as a teacher every single day. That is quite different from grinding away at approaches that could support my students' self-confidence.

Teachers who were given false testing information regarding certain students meant to identify the possibility of those learners poised to excel begin to engage with those students in a significantly altered way. Their communication with these supposedly highly gifted students was more positive and more encouraging. They were given more praise and more attention when necessary. Eight months later, even though those students had been in fact randomly picked, they showed significant academic gains. As mentioned before, the attitude, approach, and sense of expectation from teachers is proven again to be imperative to the success of students.[26]

The difficulty for a teacher is trying to look back and imagine if you did enough. Did I bring my best self to class every day, being sensitive to how girls can walk into a test ready to do poorly merely because they have been taught that math is not the way for girls to define themselves? Did I truly support them to become more tolerant and create a challenging enough learning environment as well? Remember Chris and our experiment from his AP Chemistry exam? Just a cardboard cutout of his presence helped students remember that they were more than capable of achieving.

"I tried my best." Rachel would say. "I really thought I knew it; I just couldn't do it on the test." She would speak these words as if she was not only speaking to me, but to her parents and to some future self who was locked into an eternal struggle, like

Sisyphus pushing the rock up the hill only to see it roll back down to the bottom.

An important area of research would be to see how we would define students who feel that they fall into nothing that looks like a positive stereotype category. What does a boy experience who walks into a math classroom, where his peers are benefiting from, even built mostly from perception, the idea that they by the nature of their sex can feel competent and accomplished, but he does not? So, not only is he doing poorly in school, but our narrow and debilitating social constructs of masculinity have failed him. The goal seems obvious: Realign the social construct. Redefine what it means to feel good about himself or herself, along any point of the gender spectrum, in all sorts of ways. Perhaps then our students will be relieved from the stress to eventually figure out, at least, how to simplify a polynomial equation.

How do we know that these mediators, as opposed to innate biological differences, are the culprit? As mentioned earlier, female students have significantly closed the gap in performance on standardized tests and even more significantly regarding classroom success. If Baron-Cohen's genetic sex differences were the culprit, we would have seen very little to no change, even with thoughtful interventions and changes in teacher practices. The other outstanding piece of information as research becomes more globalized across cultures is that if there were inherent biological differences, we would see similar results in other countries in terms of gaps in learning. In fact, we see the opposite. In other cultures, where the expectations regarding academic achievement across academic realms is considerably more gender neutral, women are performing as well as men in areas such as math and science.

Steps teachers and schools can take to tackle mediators created by bias.

1. Balance the equation by emphasizing, starting in early childhood classrooms, spatial skills learning as a component of larger problem-solving strategies. The correlation between successful and engaged pre-school block performance and play, a standard first introduction to

engaging students with spatial awareness and understandings, reaps its rewards years later in middle and
high school test results. This approach would benefit all
students in that it would move them away from the route
computational approaches that occupy most of the time
elementary school classrooms spend on math education.
It would also refocus the emphasis of math education
more closely toward developing those critical executive
functioning skills as a primary objective for all children.
2. Pre-game assessments. Give students pep talks which
help eliminate the idea that certain kinds of learning are
for males rather than females.
3. Gather classroom attitude data during assessments. No
matter the subject, watch who gives up where and who
persists throughout.
4. Post assess assessments. Have students describe not only
what problems were challenging but also what questions
they gave up on early. This will give you information if
certain students are suffering from stereotype threat or
self-efficacy challenges. Then, you will be better equipped
to address their anxieties and unfounded self-bias.
5. Script the parents. Give parents the language and
knowledge to address their children about learning.
Parents are often unaware of the way they support
micro-confirmations of gender bias. Lobbying a male
child into an advanced math class merely because of gender assumptions, not because of interest or demonstrated
capacity, is a perfect example.

Now, back to my very uncomfortable conversation with 600 parents. The lack of excitement or enthusiasm for their students going into education as a field is, I believe, based on two ideas. One
is a protective impulse. As only a few of these parents raised their
hands in affirmation when I asked them if they would encourage
their children into education, parents intuitively know how challenging this occupation truly is. They also know that the respect
and compensation for educators are equally matched, at least in
the United States, where education has not seen significant or

even adequate increases in pay over the past fifty years. There is very little to incentivize parents to extol the virtues of their children growing up to develop young minds day in and day out.

The other reason is a failure of imagination.

There is an attitude of "well, you can now do anything. Why would you want to *limit* yourself?" Again, this is where the nexus between how we contend with gender issues and how our schools are viewed and supported dovetail. If professions which are feminized are also by extension downgraded, the talent pool will no longer be there to support our national and democratic aspirations. The societal and civic implications are vast and deep, leaving us decrying struggles we are facing and where the solutions are right underneath our noses, at our family dinner tables, and subsequently in our classrooms.

7

Rage On! Gender/Sex, Emotional, and Physical Expression in Schools

Sasha is raging at me. Even before she starts to cry, she yells and screams at a volume that draws other students to peer into the window of my office. They can't see through the shade but linger about, hoping to get a glimpse of the person who has the audacity to unleash like that in the principal's office…at the principal. I hear them whispering Sasha's name and then running off, too scared to be part of what they conceive will be the consequences for what she is doing right now. They assume she will not be back in school until the next day. Suspended and sent home.

Sasha's mouth contorts, as she cries with indignation and fury. She looks like a twenty-first-century dragon spewing fire and outrage. "This is…not…right," she screams. "Why do *you* get to make this decision!?" She leans forward and slams her palms on the conference table. It rattles. My coffee cup threatens to tip over. "You should have told me before that this was going to happen. Someone should have warned me!!" In fact, her coaches warned her. All her teachers in the four classes which she is failing signed a sheet indicating to her that she was flunking and warned her. I warned her. I sit and listen. I make direct eye contact. I even let silences occur, waiting for the next wave of hostility to stream forth. I maintain a poker face throughout. My

DOI: 10.4324/9781003217022-8

beloved uncle, Marek, once told me that when people get ramped up, you should ramp down. You must balance the conversation. But with thirteen-year-old kids, there really is no balance. The rage shows no sign of subsiding; she is exploding and imploding like a supernova all at the same time. Hollering at me, at her life, at the universe.

Why? Why is Sasha having this global meltdown in the principal's office? What was she warned about? This: I have just told her that her grades make her ineligible for the one passion in her life, basketball. She is suspended from the team until she gets her grades up to C's. While we regularly see this type of explosive behavior in boys (and often accept it as an "appropriate" way for them to communicate their feelings) I have only experienced this from a girl once before in my twenty-eight years in education. Sasha's explosion is in the top ten right now regardless of gender. She gets up, opens the office door, turns back to me and says, "You are a horrible man. You're destroying me!" I am shocked, embarrassed, and on another level, thrilled and excited. How awesome.

I am used to boys losing their temper. It starts to happen at a *very* young age with boys. They also cry and get upset, but often, they rage. They scream and yell, their nostrils flare with faces turning red like a character from a cartoon. And it is perfectly accepted. We treat it as everything from funny to cute to "boys being boys." Even when they use their bodies, hitting another kid, punching another boy (and occasionally a girl) we suspend them, sometimes even kick them out of school. But the behavior itself is somehow expected and allowable even when we do not condone it.

Sasha is flat-out failing my math class and three other classes. She is even failing art! She does no work, has a poor attitude, and makes no excuses for herself. Her parents are consistently unavailable and do not communicate with the school. There is no crisis big enough to bring Sasha's parents into school or to answer the phone. They either do not care or do not know how to care. Since I am not only her math teacher but also her principal, according to the rules of the school (which I bend or break at different times given the situation), it is my job to suspend her from the basketball team due to her academic performance. This moment is always awful and ninety percent of the time I am talking to boys. Ninety percent of the time it is for the best. Ten percent of the time it is meaningless; it does not turn these kids around. They are not incentivized to put effort into school, and they can fall even deeper into a hole. For the ninety percent that the policy does work does not seem worth the ten percent where it is a failed decision. And, when I do get the rare female I need to suspend from a team due to grades, they invariably listen, say "okay," walk out of my office, and burst into tears. What Sasha is doing right now is…special.

Sasha, refreshingly, is not like the other girls in many positive ways. She does not get mixed up in their destructive forms of interactions such as gossiping or social media conflict. She dismisses these conversations, the offhand slights, the exclusionary behavior, the relational violence. She is friends with everyone. She does not discriminate or insult or reject. She has close friends and even closer friends. Everyone basically seems acceptable to her and worthy. She also stands up for people. She has a strong sense of social logic and communicates directly. No one seems to frighten her, neither girls nor boys. She loves basketball, a LebBron James acolyte.

Why are boys "allowed" to lose it, while girls have to keep themselves anger-free, sublimating feelings of rage? Why do girls scare us more when they get angry? I used to believe that this was an issue of maturity, that according to how we see girls and young women, they mature faster, are therefore more capable of self-regulation, and can take bad news with a certain degree of understanding. Sasha is also different from our friend Jessie whom we met earlier. Sasha had a moment that reminded me, us, as educators to not make assumptions about student reactions. The truth lies in what we consider reasonable for both boys and girls in public spaces. Obsequiousness, deference, and obedience for girls versus openness, risk-taking, and anger as a form of emotional expression for boys. Girls push down their upset to be the good little girls they are supposed to be. Boys learn to rage as a poor excuse for communicating their emotional hurt and needs, their vulnerabilities. Girls tend to say, "I am not sad, everything is okay." Boys, in contrast, insist they are not sad but really angry. Both answers lack truth and are inadequate. Both should not be tolerated as responses. Both answers establish binaries for behavior that perpetuate gender myth. How do these developed, even curated gender standards hurt our girls and our boys? We will now look at some of the experts in gender scholarship and psychology to understand the expectation and what we can do to change it.

Students like Sasha need us to be aware of the biases we hold within us to allow them to react the way they do without judgment or assumptions. While Sasha may not be responding to my news about her basketball future appropriately, my adult response to her cannot make her feel that her inappropriateness is based on the fact that she is a girl and not a boy.

Educator and author Rachel Simmons, in her thorough analysis, *Odd Girls Out*, depicts girls and their various forms of expressing rage and aggression as occurring across socio-economic and racial lines. She outlines both indirect aggression, "covert behavior" in which the aggressor makes it seems as though there has been no intent to hurt at all, and alternative or social aggression which is "intended to damage self-esteem or social status within a group."[1] While she identifies the middle school years as the hotbed for these types of passive-aggressive expressions, girls are getting primed for this type of approach to emotional expression at a younger and younger age. Imagine an elementary school environment where boys are receiving a disproportionate amount of teacher attention and teachers are often, "letting girls be girls," merely because they are not physically destroying something or hitting someone. The elementary school classroom, recess yard, and lunchroom become laboratories and testing grounds for expressing aggression in cruel and demeaning ways, defined as relational violence[2] mostly toward weaker girls and girls who threaten social orders. Relational violence or aggression is when the actual relationship between two people is leveraged to cause pain and suffering to the victim. It can include behaviors such as ostracizing someone from a group, damaging reputations, or forcing some to engage in involuntary behaviors under social threat.

Much of this behind-the-scenes, "who me?" behavior is based on maintaining constructs of outer perfection. Girls are made to feel that they need to present perfect versions of themselves: People-pleaser, well-behaved student, well-groomed and put together, dutiful, kind, and sweet. In the meantime, behind the scenes, starting by the middle of fifth grade and mostly de-accelerating by the beginning of ninth, they are treating each other like garbage, bullying, excluding, disinviting, shaming, and triggering each other.

Most parents will tell me that home presents a very different story. In that private familial space, girls feel comfortable to act out. They unleash their inner rageful, angry monsters. Siblings and parents receive the brunt of it. For girls, the gender dilemma is one of public personas versus private, and only when parents think that issues have reached a crisis state do schools begin to hear about it. Over the past fifteen years, I have been flooded with parents sending me the latest screenshot of a meme, a group chat thread, or a posted picture that has been photoshopped to either mock or malign someone else. Ironically, I find it is often boys on social media who tell other kids to cut it out. Whereas we tag girls with having the more heightened emotional and psychological sensitivities, boys are often the ones who recognize when a line has been crossed. This would be an excellent avenue for research. When parents come to me to complain, expecting a fierce response from the school, they often do not realize that they are coming to me about an ongoing narrative, not a one-off or the beginning of a problem. Girls have been in practice and training for these moments for a very long time and we have all allowed these gender manifestations to simmer and fester to the exploding point.

As Simmons also points out, this need by young girls to maintain these outer layers of perfection reach their peak when they are at their most developmentally vulnerable, insecure, moody and where the fear of isolation and loneliness become acute.[3] It goes from the elementary school version of, "no one wants to play with me" to "no one wants to *be* with me." Their lack of permission to communicate these acutely painful feelings directly leads to indirect expressions of rage that do not do physical damage but do damage regardless. It maintains the individual and group's gender constructs while allowing girls their own, almost condoned, form of aggressive expression. There are also other ramifications when girls, like Sasha, express themselves as typically associated with males. Adults, when girls act out and express themselves like boys, are likely to view them as having "a character defect" as opposed to boys who are just asserting themselves.[4]

I also know that girls are watching boys. They see them often physically out of control, being reprimanded and chastised for breaking and throwing stuff, and hurting each other through pushing, wrestling, punching, and kicking. For the most part, this is not a tenable avenue for girls. It is already so overtly displeasing to the adults around them, that it might shatter their ability to construct the well-behaved girl persona. It is what boys do and what is expected of boys. It is for boys, not for girls. And it is scary. The adult response can also be so swift and condemning that this too is quite frightening. If a kid smacks another kid, he can expect immediate suspension or even expulsion. This kind of male aggression has nothing in it for girls. They do not benefit in any way from a gender standpoint. You want to be disinvited from a party or excluded from a trip to the mall? If a girl in middle school hits other girls, the entire community may isolate you.

While girls are viewed as conniving and scheming, boys get away with their physical aggression, not only because it is viewed as "boys being boys" but because it is seen as a more direct form of communication. There is at least partial praise inside of adult circles because a punch to the gut is somehow seen as a form of honesty.[5] Boys, unless it's truly chronic, join the club. You're just being a boy.

Parents come to me earnestly distressed about how their daughter is being treated or how their daughter is treating others. When parents identify their daughter as being the aggressor, they often want solutions and feel responsible for what is going on. My first response is to calm their nerves. Their students will go off to high school and find themselves in a very different social paradigm with very different, if equally challenging, social issues. I also then direct them to important resources and readings which can give them practical tools to support their children. But I am partly lying to these parents. While high school kids know that they need to pivot socially when they get to high school, that no one really tolerates what is considered "childish" forms of meanness, these gender stereotypes start to become more subtly embedded into young people. For girls this often takes on the new face of extreme performance insecurity and anxiety in school. Their sexual lives and identities come more into play as well and they find themselves needing to navigate scary and uncomfortable circumstances with the personas of pleasers, not necessarily as the defenders of their personal dignity as well. They have not practiced asserting themselves directly and there is no time to text or send out some secondary flare for help when encountering a male with no boundaries, with his own male stereotypes fostering physical violence and male status through sexual assault. I am in no way suggesting that this is a woman's issue. Males are responsible for sexual assault and rape and, therefore, it is their problem to fix. but I also want women who are well-equipped and completely comfortable speaking loudly and directly and assertively toward men who would hurt them, or anyone else. Even the girls who led the pack at younger ages, the queen bees, are expected by their peers to begin acting more benign in high school. Otherwise, they run the risk of being labeled a "bitch." Or worse.

But this passive repose by young females may be changing. In 2018, when the #metoo movement was gaining significant public attention and momentum, I received three phone calls from principals (two high schools and one middle school). Through professional circles they knew of my work with gender and schools and wanted to discuss what was happening on their campuses. From other educators I follow on social media, I knew what was coming. These principals were reporting that their campuses felt like war zones. Young females were exploding on campus. Physically aggressive behaviors directed mainly at young males. What was the issue? They were tired of being touched without permission.

Everything from squeezes to the midsection, both hands on shoulders as approached from behind, bras being snapped, bottoms being touched, and hands on head and hair. Responses and reactions ranged from screaming in hallways, throwing of textbooks, shoving away bodies and slapping hands. Other girls, perhaps for the first time, were collectively responding when an incident occurred, surrounding their aggrieved friend in collective pods of response. One boy, who tried to sit in a girl's lap uninvited, was pushed off, fell, and slammed into a set of lockers opening a cut on his forehead. These principals communicated that they were untangling altercations all day for weeks. One of the principals, who was a woman, told me, "I get it, but come on, what's with all this physical…fighting!"

My initial thought, which I kept to myself, was "good!!" Finally young females were standing up to aggressive male entitlement, meant to put these young women into positions of psychological and social subordination through unwanted physical contact. All three principals indicated that the problem was somehow with the physical and violent reactions of the young women. "If they could just calm down," one administrator said to me. They were made uncomfortable by these girls crossing some artificial border from relational/social aggression (expected and approved) to the physical aggression associated with males (also expected and approved). My first response was why should they calm down? For years these young women have been dealing with a type of physical assault or controlling aggression toward their bodies. Now, is it their fault for literally pushing back? I am not advocating for physical violence in any form. In fact, I propose we train all our students in effective ways of reducing violence and learning how students can respond before violence even occurs. My next response to these principals was, "So what do you think you need to do with these boys?"

We have long acknowledged the social and emotional toll that the denigrating behavior of relational violence can have on girls, both individually and collectively. Not given the tools to emotionally express their greatest fears and concerns, they can either turn inward, too frightened about the ramifications of wrecking people's impressions of their perfect gender constructs or lash out at others to try and expel feelings of rage. The worst position that we can take is suggesting that this is somehow some "natural" process that all young girls go through, and we should just let it happen. That it is an easy way to ignore the emotional damage caused to others, failing as adults to accept responsibility for the social dynamics around us. While often these behaviors simmer at a low heat, when they do boil over, I have found that creating concentric circles of conversations with groups of girls involved can set a better course and give girls who want this behavior to end a more significant voice. Having responsible faculty and administrators break down students into individual scripted conversations, then small groups, then entire grades, if necessary, gives everyone a chance to be heard. The power alignments shift when students feel there are adults ready to listen without judgment. The process empowers those who feel marginalized and reduces the impact of those girls who feel they need to control others and the social narrative.

The other issue with allowing these behaviors to persist is that it condones a value system in schools which helps create the problem in the first place.

Remember when I mentioned in Chapter 1 that girls rock school? This has a good news/bad news dynamic to it. In many ways, schools are really designed for female success. There is a much greater probability that the way in which we construct the school experience is centered around how girls are socialized and the expectations placed upon them at the earliest of ages. Everything from the way we expect girls to play with one another to how they are introduced to language as a primary skill of engagement. The landscape of school has a much more open-ended definition than what boys experience.[6]

Boys are much more locked into a narrower set of definitions regarding the physicality of play and their bodies as a tool for self-expression. Their role models for heteronormativity – athletes, professional wrestlers, even gamers I would argue – are primarily body talkers. Words and language are not a primary or secondary tool for expressions of maleness. And schools are about language. They are about learning to follow multi-step directions, reading instructions on an exam, following along with a set of arguments in a history class. To do many of these tasks, one needs to develop listening, patience, and self-regulation.

Females, because of their gender socialization, are much more likely to be on the road to developing these skills and habits of mind early, therefore garnering success, feeling positive about school as a place where they can be their best selves, at least academically.

Even when boys use language, there is often a type of violence that is associated with it. Everything from the competitive landscape of male talk to comparing physical strength to actual threats of physical harm suggest that boys and young males are given few tools for working out their grievances or conflict or simply being able to socially problem solve. As Barrie Thorne, UC Berkeley Professor, in her sociological study, *Gender Play*, points out, "…boys' social relations tend to be overtly hierarchical and competitive. They repeatedly negotiate and mark through insults, direct commands, challenges and threats."[7]

The darker side of this equation is that with this sense of success comes another value system that does not serve girls well. Obedience, to the point of obsequiousness, becomes an educational value and goal in our schools. Schools unduly congratulate and praise children who are not asserting themselves and are quiet and passive. We have a "don't ask, don't tell" social contract in our schools which girls are more than willing to adhere to. In other words, if you go along with the program, whether you are struggling or not, whether you are even learning or not, then you are awarded with the approval associated with success. With the chaos that can sometimes occur in school, teachers spend much more time dealing with boys and their behavioral issues. When the teacher does get around to girls, they are much more likely to be addressing academic concerns. In other words, in this system, girls only appear as if they are winning.

I am obviously not condoning the behavior of boys. They also suffer in this gendered system, terribly. When formal schooling ends, they are probably worse off for it. The issue is that girls suffer in the moment. They are not required to assert themselves, to speak up and have a voice. Rebecca Solnit, in her essay, "Men Explain Things to Me" calls it "an invitation to silence."[8] Not only should obedience not be a school value, but it should also be an educational anathema. We need to teach girls to show up and be part of what is going on around them, to, can I even say it, misbehave, talk back, disagree, refuse to cooperate. The rebellious side of them needs to be nurtured and most importantly in public spaces where the gender stakes are the highest. They need to be uncomfortable with obedience. And parents can play a role in this as well. They need to allow disobedience to flourish in positive ways, full-on debates at the dinner table, encouraging them to speak up and not retreat into being shy wallflowers. Smiles are great, but not when they become masks for insecurity and fear. Again, the significant way to get our girls to feel more comfortable expressing themselves in more direct ways is by making sure teachers do not value obedience.

One effective technique is when teachers apply a "no hands" rule in class. It means that when a teacher is calling on students for answers during a lesson, then this is precisely what is happening, whether a student's hand is raised or not. More students are encouraged to participate, again, without judgment, and girls cannot be assumed to be paying attention because they are sitting quietly. Some teachers will use popsicle sticks pulled from a cup or can so that everyone knows they will eventually be called on by the end of class. Getting along to go along should not be tolerated just as much as a student calling out in the middle of class or disrupting learning by throwing an eraser across the room or…punching another kid in the face.

It is me, then David, and then Brandon sitting on the recess bench, but there is not the usual chaos of the recess yard. There is dead silence except for David hollering in grief. He is crying so hard that he is unable to catch his breath. His back heaves up and down as his body convulses with his emotional outburst. His head is also bobbing side to side as if he is fishing and is in a battle to pull in a catch, except there is no fishing rod, there is no fish. He is in contention with his own body. He will slow down for a few seconds and then it will start all over again. His shirt is drenched in tears. His hands stay on his knees almost to stabilize himself, as if he raised them, he would just keel over from his emotional catharsis. This has been going on for the past seven minutes, a long time for a crying episode. Brandon sits next to him, stone silent and staring forward with a stunned look on his face, mouth slightly open. His nose twitches as if it is its own autonomous appendage. He is in his own world, almost in a trance. His hair is matted from sweat to his freckled forehead and he is having no reaction whatsoever to David's distress. We are waiting. We are waiting together. We are waiting for David to calm down. We are waiting for David's parents to arrive, and we are waiting for just the right time.

David has just punched Brandon in the face. It was not an errant elbow during a football game, or even an open-handed push that lost its mark. It was a fully closed five fingers, arm cocked back into a tight rubber band effect that went hurling sharp, fast, and quick into Brandon's nose.

The physical pain is the least of it, although there is an important reason why getting punched in the face has such high currency and happens so rarely, especially when you are ten and nine like David and Brandon. A seasoned educator knows when students are roughhousing and when there is true aggressive tension hovering over a gathering of kids. But sometimes you are thirty seconds late to the main event. When it ended in a punch to the face, the victim lay on the ground, crumpled up. The results can be severe.

One of the first subjects you learn about in cognitive neuroscience is human's relationship to the senses. For any species, our senses are a critical way that we interpret and react to the world around us. We take in information and need to sort it out, taking the bits and pieces that we need and discarding or ignoring the rest. Taking in every sight and smell and noise would incapacitate us or overwhelm us. Our brains need to find a coherent system to sort through the millions of data points to make decisions and function coherently and safely.[9] For humans, the eyes are a critical piece of sensory equipment. When early neuroscientists gave us a physical representation of the human senses and their relevance to human functionality, it often depicted a human head with huge, exaggerated eyes bulging out. Of the five senses, sight represents most of our needed functionality to survive.[10] That is why getting punched in the face is so frightening and creates such terror of vulnerability. We need to protect our precious senses at all costs, and when they are exposed to physical assault, we are jeopardy. A shiner or black eye is no Hollywood punch line, it is no joke.

The fight took place because Brandon irritates his peers. It is not his fault that he was punched in the face, but he skipped a grade in kindergarten and his social skills did not skip with him. He is constantly trying to make friends, constantly picking the wrong friends, and constantly imagining that someday the way that he tries to interact with other boys is going to work. Sitting on the bench that day is one of the first times I have seen Brandon with his mouth shut. He follows other boys around all day long, talking and talking right next to them, giving them no physical space, and right into their ears. He rambles. I can be next to him at any given point during the day and he is pontificating on something like a radio talk show host. He does this in class (when I visit his classroom, there is always the low-level hum of Brandon that everyone has learned to ignore). He does this at lunch, lineup, and dismissal, and he does it at recess.

Recess for boys is the sanctum sanctorum; it is holy ground and is to be respected as such. For most boys, it is physical lunacy. They wait for it all morning. Some talk about it at home the night before. Some even dream about it. And all that male physical expression in games and sports and competitiveness is a big fat mask for wanting to connect: A male sanctioned way of building relationships.

We give them few words if any, we let them grow up being admired and praised from afar and all they really want is a good friend, or a good group of friends. And, for many of them, this is just too much to express, too many words, so they get out there and feast on kickball, shoot hoops until exhaustion, or plan elaborate football leagues and games to relate and feel connected. Recess can also be a place where the less athletically obsessed find time for their other interests, including trading cards, pretend games, Minecraft, and even stillness. The yard can be a precarious place for these boys as they both struggle to fit in and remain fearful of being ostracized for not fitting in or for not playing an acceptable part in the drama of masculine development. Masculinities scholar R.W. Connell calls these experiences for males, "gender regimes" or the overall creation of "gender orders."[11]

The rigid, narrowly defined standards for gender performance rely on broad performative masculinity and can be in sharp contrast to more difficult and challenging skills developed in early literacy, such holding a pen correctly or unpacking written symbols on a page.[12] Thoughtful schools will roll out carts with crafts and games on them to legitimize other activities on the yard and create a more balanced acceptable set of activities to define success on the yard.

Study after study suggests that physicality is just the way boys are. They tussle and wrestle, unlike their female counterparts. What is also clear from looking at these studies is this behavior and reaction is a *tendency*.[13] It is not a preordained reality to which all of us, parents, and schools, need to surrender. The chemical agent testosterone gets thrown a lot when we have these conversations. However, as Stanford neuroendocrinologist Robert Sapolsky points out, rising and higher levels of testosterone measured in males are a *result* of already triggered aggressive behaviors, thoughts, and feelings, not the other way around. The psychological state actualizes the biological/chemical response in the body.[14] These popular, yet false declarations of biological and essentialist tendencies often read like some elaborate excuse why we can't seem to teach and encourage boys to express a whole range of emotions that pull and tangle them up inside until they explode. Professor of philosophy, Myriam Miedzian, in her comprehensive work on the sources of male aggression and violence, *Boys Will Be Boys*, puts it best,

> It is the universal fact of human existence that what we know best, that which forms part of our everyday landscape, is that which we most take for granted, and question the least. And, to some of our strongest jolts to our awareness, the deepest reorientations in our thought, often come from being confronted with the obvious.[15]

Acting out in class, not seeming to have the tools of self-regulation (some of it is just pure entitlement), not being skilled at following directions, and ultimately the physical expression of rage would certainly be addressed by having more conversations with our boys. They need to learn how to talk and verbally express their feelings, especially negative ones. We need to assure them that their thoughts and feelings and emotions matter. Which they do. Because, otherwise, they could end up punching someone in the face.

Brandon would not get out of David's ear. David told him to go away, but he would not. David was playing handball and Brandon kept positioning himself an inch away from his head until finally David had enough. One boy could not stop talking. The other one could not talk.

What I learned when David's mom came to pick him up is that his parents have been fighting and fighting for the past six months. David has been listening and listening and listening with no avenue to express his feelings and no one expressing concern about whatever he is feeling. He has kept a good poker face. His explosion on the bench after he punched Brandon was because hurting someone is scary; he thinks he is in terrible trouble. When I ask, quietly, if anything is wrong, he shakes his head in defiance as if to say, "You're not getting a single word out of me."

Male rage and aggression are both more simple and more complicated than what we tackle with female counterparts. While girls use their language to express their feelings and emotions, the outcomes are often skewed by what they imagine people want to see from them. The damage they cause is generated through language. Therefore, a more direct avenue to course correction is potentially obtainable. Eventually, we hope to support girls in using this critical human tool in an appropriate manner. The damage that they can cause is very real, but its potential solution is found inside the very system that supports it.

The issue with many boys, who then become men, is that they lack this emotional toolbox. We have not helped them develop a method to express their rage. We know what the issue is. It's so very clear. But the work can be a real slog if not addressed early. And the ramifications are catastrophic. Just under ninety percent of the violent crime in the United States is perpetuated by men, much of it against other men who become their victims. A woman is beaten every nine seconds in this country – mostly by men. More women are injured by physical assault – again, by males – than by any other source.[16] A reported rape takes place in this country nearly every six seconds. That does not include all the incidents that go unreported. Rape and sexual assault are crimes of violence. It is about physically brutalizing someone else, controlling them, and ultimately denigrating them in the worst possible way. It is rage at its most exposed. It is entitled male aggression which, until very recently and still in parts of the world, was and is culturally sanctioned.

This patterning happens early and gets established as part of the schooling process. We spend an inordinate, almost criminal, amount of time contending with boys' behavioral issues at schools. Boys receive significantly more attention than girls in schools and much of it is based on adults correcting what is perceived as disruptive or negative behaviors.[17] The entire gamut of what teachers deal with throughout the school year and in their classrooms is a form of missed opportunity at real communication played out in everything from clowning around to bothering other students to getting into fights. The amount of time that these students lose that they could be using to learn and thrive inside of classrooms is unnerving and frustrating. No wonder that, as mentioned previously, boys are forever finding themselves on the tail end of the bell curve of literacy and communication skills. We are not doing the work of fostering these skills as relevant and important for them to have, even on the critical and basic playground of human interactions. We may want to teach our boys and young men how to read, write, and speak so they can find success in life, but what better reason to teach them these skills so they can express their deepest joys, frustrations, sorrows and yes anger, instead of physically hurting someone else.

I do get to report that Sasha, after some effort and hard work to get her grade point average above a C, was reinstated on the basketball team. She did not magically come back to me and tell me that getting suspended from the team was the best thing that ever happened to her. But she did return the next day, after cooling off, to apologize for exploding in my office. I felt comfortable validating for her that people get upset and angry sometimes and that there is also a respectful way of expressing those feelings. The last thing I wanted her to feel was that her outburst was not normal or that, even worse, this is not what girls do.

The end results with David and Brandon were more complicated. By suspending David, I could tell that he felt terrible about what he had done, but he was not going to take claim to it so easily. He leveraged his incident on the yard to keep Brandon from bothering him, using his body on several occasions to imply that he was willing to get suspended again if Brandon did not keep his distance. For David, this was a very male way of solving a problem. Threats of violence are easier than learning how to peacefully negotiate a difficult situation. Brandon had no interest in getting punched in his face again and, even after being told that he needed to give other students their space, he was unable to connect why talking incessantly at other kids was causing him painful social isolation.

In the summer of 2018, I was fortunate enough to work with a talented group of educators from around the globe to design a program of self-defense for boys. While this sounds like placing one problem on top of another (teaching boys how to be violent) one of the central goals of the Empowerment Self-Defense for Boys (ESDb) program is teaching young boys psychological and physical techniques for violence reduction. By bonding young males in experiences that build confidence, allyship, and gender boundaries, we also disrupt traditional destructive forms of ever narrowing masculine development. And yes, I am also an enthusiastic advocate for young females learning these critical life and confidence building skills as well. These programs, for both boys and girls, should be well integrated into the physical education programming for middle school children.

(See Appendix G for a specific program to support students as they navigate school and beyond, giving them tools to ultimately reduce violence and become first responders.)

8

The Crippling Impact of Mental Health Issues and Trauma

Gender Informed Responses

Schools are built on social contracts between the school, parents, and the communities which they serve. Schools make the promise that your child will come out more enriched, more educated, and a bit smoother around the edges (socially engaged). We make the claim that the school has a direct role to play in that progress and growth. The parent's role (in the eyes of the school) is to stay out of the way, to create a home environment that is conducive to this growth, and, if possible, to be an active player in the overall well-being and health of the school environment, perhaps as a volunteer.

People of means in this country have more choice when it comes to where this social contract is forged and how it will take place, either through paying for private school education, or by having the economic means to live in neighborhoods with higher performing and resourced schools. Living in these high-priced neighborhoods also means the potential for significant fund-raising events that fill the school budget gaps, paying for extra-curricular programs and resources which create even wider gaps in equitable access with poorer neighborhoods. One of the main

DOI: 10.4324/9781003217022-9

reasons families move into a particular neighborhood is based on access to a well-functioning educational system.

> In a 2013 survey by Realtor.com of almost one thousand prospective buyers, three out of five homebuyers said school boundaries would affect their purchasing decision; nearly twenty-one percent said they would pay six to ten percent above budget to live within certain school boundaries and about nine percent would pay eleven to twenty percent above budget. Homes in desirable school districts — those rated a nine or ten on national education nonprofit GreatSchools' ten-point scale — are on average forty-nine percent more expensive than the national median, and they're seventy percent more expensive than homes within the boundaries of lower-ranked school districts...[1]

The consistent increase in property values based on school performance is another indication of how Americans are willing to pay more for access to higher performing schools and how inequity in American education continues to expand and becomes normalized by the marketplace.[2]

Another less obvious social contract is socialization. Parents believe that their children are better off around other kids all day and therefore benefit from learning how to interact and contend with other children and adults. Plus, the idea of spending sixteen to seventeen waking hours a day with their children can be so anxiety-producing that parents are willing to drop off their offspring with little or no complaint. Many parents – I include myself in this portrayal – are drooling for school doors to open after a long weekend, a winter vacation, or the long summer days in anticipation of someone else contending with their little darlings.

What schools promise in return is a sense of safety.

The idea of safety is a complex clause in this particular social contract. There is the obvious understanding that, "I drop my child off in one piece and expect not to pick her up in pieces." Physically: Is the school in good enough shape where the building will not cause harm? Does everyone know what to do during a natural or human-generated emergency? Are the adults safe for my child to be around? Do they know how to conduct themselves around children? Are there drills for active shooter situations? The horror of tragedies such as Sandy Hook and Stoneman Douglas create the perception of schools as vulnerable to extreme and unpredictable gun violence. I did not have active shooter drills growing up and neither did most Americans above the age of twenty-five. They are now standard practice and training.

Then there is the psychological/emotional sense of safety. How does the school tolerate or even implicitly sanction bullying? Are students and adults respectful to one another? Is the school paying attention to the mental health of my child and communicating home when things seem awry?

Teachers make all the difference in schools with how it feels daily for our students. A teacher who spends as much time getting to know his students as is expected of a student to know their multiplication tables will create a sense of care. Students want to know that there is an adult who is thinking about them, even when they are not around.

Educators also do not control the entire narrative. Students come to our classrooms having had fights with siblings, being screamed at or even physically assaulted by parents, all by 8 a.m. in the morning. There may be a terminally ill member of the family, economic strife and anxiety, sexual or substance abuse or just simply bad parenting and negligence.[3] Teachers are lucky if students arrive for the day in a good mood or are even capable of regulating themselves. Again, schools are constantly shifting organisms and teachers and educational leaders are meant to hold the center, to be sometimes the one steadying influence in the six to eight hours of a child's day.

As schools have become centrally identified as providers of mental health and social/emotional support for students, this chapter looks to understand how gender awareness, in both emotional challenges as well as our response, plays a central role in supporting the long-term well-being of our student populations. Trauma informed schools and education are essential components of this work, but they are certainly not enough. Programs and seminars and training can in fact create dissonance between what is known and what is done. Real change often means discarding deeply ingrained old models of response and reaction to these situations. Not only can our policies and norms miss the mark, but they can also ultimately be the *cause* of trauma and thereby Post Traumatic Stress Disorder (PTSD) that members of our school community experience.

The Centers for Disease Control and Prevention, in partnership with Kaiser Permanente, ran a three-year study from 1995 to 1997, measuring the impact of an Adverse Childhood Experience (ACE) on adults between the ages of nineteen and sixty-plus. Over 17,000 adults formed part of this broad-reaching and critical study. These experiences were examined specifically to measure the relationship between the number of indicators of trauma a person reports and impact on mental and physical health. Someone who reports having experienced six or more such incidents in their childhood can expect close to a twenty-year reduction in life expectancy stemming from behavioral factors, drug use, obesity, suicide to related illnesses such as heart disease, cancer, and stroke.[4]

Not everything a child either witnesses or experiences is an ACE. Hearing your parents argue occasionally is most likely not an ACE. Getting into fights, even on a regular basis, with siblings is not an ACE. Having a learning disability, such as dyslexia, is not an ACE. These cause drama, not trauma. The distinctive categories range from abuse (physical, sexual, and emotional) to persistent household challenges (a mother treated violently, divorce, substance abuse) to neglect (emotional and physical). Sixty-four percent of adults surveyed reported at least one ACE with twenty-two percent reporting three or more. Sixty-six percent of women versus thirty-five percent of men comprised the gender breakdown of individuals reporting four or more ACEs.[5]

In general, the impact on learning for children can be significant. The types of observations and diagnoses we see with students who have experienced traumatic events look and appear like attentional issues such as ADHD. The overlapping signs make it difficult to differentiate. Overall IQ can be lower, there are deficits in working memory and language development, and poorer self-regulation and response inhibition. And these are merely the manifestations in learning which are also accompanied by various social and emotional effects which arise over time given certain developmental stages. We will look at the neuroscience of trauma but suffice it to say that a number of the areas that children need to function effectively in school get derailed. In school-aged children, a shortlist includes massive mood swings and tantrums, inability to form trusting relationships with adults, reversion to younger ages, revictimization, reckless and self-destructive behavior and difficulty forming healthy relationships with peers and friends. These children demonstrate limited and fractured mental and psychological resources to cope with school.[6] This means that, whether we bought into this reality or not, teachers and educators and schools, become first responders to these realities for their students.

The issue is that much of this groundbreaking information and research is relatively new. Were these challenges present in families and schools previously? The assumption is yes, with a certain caveat. Due to economic stressors and social circumstances, I would argue that families are less resourced and less tied into communities that can help them through these struggles with their children. Schools are becoming the primary centers for contending with these children who suffer. Clinics now exist on campuses to provide psychological services for students. Teachers are not yet well trained enough in these areas, schools are largely underfunded in order to address these teachers' needs in their classrooms and there is, to begin with, a significant shortage of trained school psychologists and interventionists in the United States upwards of 15,000.[7] And, let's face it, one can be lucky and blessed enough to go to a school where the culture and expectations regarding taking care of the whole child are built into the system or the opposite can be the case. Schools can be places that trigger previously experienced trauma and make matters worse. One of the significant limitations of the ACEs study is that its questions only inquired about events that took place in the home, negating what might have occurred in school settings, summer camps, or after school and community-based programs.

I am all for schools taking on the responsibility of students and their mental health. Then, we need to acknowledge this as a society and fund and resource schools with everything they need to make this happen. I will argue that how children exhibit mental health issues, how they respond to trauma, and how successful we are in supporting them as they go through their schooling is contingent upon our understanding of gender and how we socialize and construct toward gender.

Sam appears regularly to be in a good mood. She often surges into class joyfully, and I am sure the sight of me or the math warm-ups on the board are not responsible for her glee. A utopian part of her wants to believe that a new day is a clean slate, a *tabula rasa*. She seems high on her own youth, her soaring development, as many kids do. We tend to focus on students' moodiness or their snarky, sometimes difficult, and rude behavior, but if you pay attention, young kids are mostly exuberant, optimistic, and hopeful. It is almost impossible to remember the full feeling of being a thirteen-year-old. I try to summon up that long-ago sensibility to better relate to my students. Not the thought, or the analytical sense, but the real feeling of experience. I see a lot of joy in kids. They love life in such a way that is tough to replicate as one gets older. I go along with Sam's enthusiasm; although, I am weary. Within five to ten minutes, I will experience another side to her that comes crashing like waves on a beach.

The problem is that her parents have been in a wickedly contentious divorce…for nine years. Even though she has a younger brother, Sam has really been at the center of this maelstrom. During parent-teacher conferences, where we have discussed issues regarding Sam and her academic abilities, the father is a voice of constant disagreement – on the phone. He's on the phone because Sam's mother refuses to be in the same room with him. She has gotten the court to ban any interaction between him and her and their daughter. I can only guess why the mother needed to do this or how this makes Sam feel.

The impact of the trauma of divorce on Sam's education is clear. She cannot concentrate. She starts off raring to go, engines roaring as she comes into class. Within ten minutes I have lost her; she sinks into a morass of pained thoughts and distractions. Her eyes go dark. Her smile vanishes, her chin slumps down and it is as if all of us have faded away. If another student tries to bring her back into the light, she gives a slight grin of recognition and then quickly recedes back into the darkness. Sometimes my jokes work with her, sometimes they fall to the ground, quickly deflected by her increasingly disconnected demeanor. Whether she is aware of how she presents herself at these moments is unclear. But there is something oddly comforting about this external honesty because I am aware of her pain. Girls tend to manifest depression more openly than boys and will more readily, over time, seek support. I'm relieved when I know what's troubling a girl, so that we can talk about it and we can get her help. It's the boys I worry about more, the boys who keep everything bottled up because they fear showing weakness or they explode about some other issue, and we are all left to guess what is occurring. David punching Brandon on the recess yard springs to mind.

The dangers go beyond students just being in a bad mood or even feeling depressed. Suicide is the number two killer of children in the United States and the ways in which sex/gender play a role in this phenomenon has not been articulated well enough with our teachers. As boys get older (late middle school and high school), their suicide rates climb. Girls tend to attempt but not follow through as much as boys. And these attempts tend to steadily decrease. In other words, girls ideate; boys actuate. These two crossing bell curves may have to do with learned behaviors based on gender constructions. Girls learn to "fend and befriend," seeking less direct help when they are in psychological trouble. They tend to seek support, less from parents and more from friends and non-parent adults like professionals. Men both seek less help from everyone – parents, family, and other sources. They go into more traditional modes of fight and flight based on evolutionary models when adrenaline kicks in.[8] Masculine norms and cultural definitions of personal autonomy and independence may isolate and alienate boys, and make them less likely to seek professional help, because it fits more into the masculinized paradigms of self-management, suggesting they can "take care of it" themselves.[9]

The physical and neurological manifestations of psychological trauma are becoming much more known to us. Bessel van der Kolk, in his brilliant personal and professional history of working with traumatized patients, *The Body Keeps the Score: Mind, Brain, and Body in the Transformation of Trauma*, outlines the experiences of conditions such as trauma as being whole body manifestations. From children to Vietnam veterans, these horrific experiences become somatized, interrupting cognitive pathways that would lead to more normative responses to events occurring. For someone who has experienced trauma, stressful events turn into five alarm fires. If everything that we encounter has the capacity to trigger a flight or fight response, then we no longer have the capacity to calmly interpret real danger. Our bodies are just too hardwired to prioritize survival first. The entire cognitive system needs to be functioning properly as a feedback loop of the myriad of stimuli and information and responses that define human existence during every living moment. Instead, those impacted find themselves trapped by memories of experiences that lead them to misread cues that the decision-making part of our brains would typically suss out. The result is a triggering of terror, racing heart rate, loss of language centers, such as Broca's region of our brain, leaving victims without the capacity to articulate what they are experiencing to comprehend and eventually cope by themselves. Kolk describes this process as one of "depersonalization."[10] Individuals can vacate themselves of feelings and disappear behind blank emotional responses, entering a fugue state. Dissociation and absence are what Sam look like in my classroom.

She also catastrophizes, another common symptom. A challenging math test is not a mere stressful moment from which she can rebound. Instead, it triggers a somatized state which she cannot free herself from – she is locked from within. She cannot possibly imagine this experience ending up anywhere but as a disaster. And imagination is exactly what she needs. A critical human skill is the ability to think about how one can overcome past challenges and distressing events and move beyond them, creating flexibility and confidence in reevaluating our present circumstances with a clear mind. If our minds and our bodies are stuck with versions of memories that do not change, we lose the ability to reimagine the past, short circuiting our capacity to shift perspectives and solve dilemmas.[11]

Kolk also recognizes that the danger for children can lie, not with the children who are manifesting their trauma in certain behaviors, but those who disappear behind a veil of passivity and numbness. "The acting-out kids tend to get the attention; the blanked-out ones don't bother anybody and are left to lose their future bit by bit."[12] I cannot stress more highly how my experiences in schools have demonstrated this reality time and time again, and largely, on a gendered basis. Girls want us to all believe that everything is fine, that we do not need to worry about them; they can fade into the woodwork of their past experiences and need no help. As I mentioned earlier, Sam is more likely to seek help as she grows older, but right now she feels she needs to please, not appearing like a burden. There is also that tendency, which we discussed earlier, of constructed female stereotypes' need to project a sense of perfectionism. Many boys, on the other hand, tend to burst forward in aggressive and unprovoked behaviors disconnected from what is going on around them. The nuance between how girls avoid help and boys signal but push away support is complex.

Both responses are problematic. For females, self-destructive behaviors and acts, such as eating disorders, cutting and suicide attempts, dominate their landscape. In their need to meld into the background, females turn inwardly destructive, trusting no one and blaming themselves for whatever is distressing them. Males, with their erratic and outwardly destructive selves, see danger everywhere. They also seem to simultaneously externalize blame for everything that is happening in the moment, but internally express confusion and a chaotic, frightened inner life.[13]

Sam falls behind on her work and misses assignments in multiple classes. While she has periods of enthusiasm and the energy to catch up and move forward, these efforts are consistently short lived. She quickly sinks into a pessimism and defeatism that leaves her without energy to complete her work or study for exams. She cycles through negative feelings about herself that become reinforced through failure at school and poor resilience and coping skills to overcome challenges and obstacles. Then, the panic sets in. The breakdown leads to a period of absenteeism, where showing up to school leads to such panic and anxiety, that she can't mobilize in the morning. We then need to all coax her back into the building by shifting her program, extending deadlines, making phone calls of concern. The school and Sam's teachers are not fixing her responses to trauma by moving deadlines or excusing homework assignments. These kids cannot just shut off their responses. They often remain in hypervigilant states well beyond the triggering event.[14] When she returns, the outward facing appearance of got-it-togetherness is there, but there is a frazzled, exhausted child who looks like an exhausted older person.

She is also quite heavy. Her weight, her appearance in the middle school years is becoming a social issue. Girls are starting to notice but do not discuss it because this is also a highly sensitive topic with the level of insecurities that all the girls feel about their bodies. We adults notice she never eats at school. In the lunchroom, she picks at her food. We believe, therefore, that she is bingeing in response to her emotional pain. This could also be the beginning of a cycle where food, purging, anorexia could become her drug of choice and lifetime disease if not addressed immediately. This possible response to her weight issues is another place where a broader topic in adolescents gets misinterpreted and therefore the possible solutions are not effective. When we discuss the larger issues of drug abuse, many of us think of hard drugs escalating into possible addiction, particularly if they are being used by students to self-medicate due to emotional pain and suffering. For young girls, drug abuse can very often mean diet and weight management aides. Thin body type, reinforced relentlessly through social media, can erroneously appear to be the road to acceptance and inclusion in school social circles. These over-the-counter remedies become gateway drugs for more serious abuse later and girls are therefore more likely to turn to stimulants rather than alcohol which boys more readily learn to abuse. Why is this gender information and distinction so critical? Because the ability to intervene early and apply solutions are also found within programs which take these gendered considerations into account. Under these circumstances, effective interventions for girls include programs that support female students' sense of self-esteem, effective communication, self-efficacy (there is that term raising its head again), and belonging. Mother-daughter sessions have also proven to be highly effective in mitigating these issues.[15]

Sam's mother has inquired several times if she has a learning disability. ADHD has filtered through our conversations about Sam for years. The school psychologist keeps insisting this is not the case. Sam's mom will then shrink into an eerily familiar look of darkness that finally emerges into an outburst of tears. These moments are not tough; they are nearly emotionally impossible.

Sam's responses to those who reach out and seek to support her are not surprising for a kid who desperately wants to please. She wants everyone to stop worrying about her and just leave her alone. Persistent attention makes her agitated and annoyed. Eye contact is avoided, particularly when it has the gaze of caring. She wants nothing to do with people who think there is something wrong with her.

Our responses to these circumstances may do more harm than good. The issue with categorizing responses and attitudes towards reaching out for support is that it becomes something of a self-fulfilling prophecy. Because of these two very different approaches, we also tend to give boys more privacy than girls and we also tend to have expectational relationships with them in times of distress. What do I mean? We then bug girls to communicate with us and leave boys alone much too much. Teens' wishes for privacy can be scary, and as psychologist Lisa Damour in her work *Untangled*, puts it,

> Some parents wrongly suspect that if their daughter is closing her door, she must be up to something, but most teenage girls close their doors to do the exact same things they used to do with the door wide open.

Believing that only boys have the right to be sullen, moody, and withdrawn as a rite of passage, but girls do not, seems to me a big mistake.[16]

We are not talking about normative situations where teens are simply struggling with identity issues or figuring out their place in the world. We are talking about students like Sam,

whose experiences have clearly left her feeling isolated, potentially not trusting of the adult world, and who disappears into
depressive states. I experience this most acutely with her during exams, when she gets stuck and feels unable to go on. She
freezes and then her entire system seems to shut down. There
is no crying, no tantrum or externalizing of her struggles. ("You
didn't teach us this stuff!!") I lean over her desk without coming
too close, giving her space. You can sense when someone might
jump out of their skin if you even tapped them on the shoulder.
But I need to get close enough where she will lift her head and
make eye contact. I encourage her to move on, go to the next
problem, do as much as she can and then we will go over it later.

"It's just one test," I tell her. I pull out the most useless teacher
cliche ever. It's the equivalent of telling someone who is agitated
to relax or calm down. Sam looks up for a second, nods her head
with a half beaten-down smile. I move away and she sinks back.
She disappears again from those around her and from herself.

I use two words with faculty to describe what should be our
relationship or way of operating around students. Presence and
attentiveness. This does not mean bugging students relentlessly
when we notice something is off or wrong. It does not mean pulling the fire alarm because a student is upset or crying. What it
means is that we have developed enough of a relationship with
students during the average times so that they know that we
are watching and are available to them. Even when boys tend
to push back, not wanting to talk or engage when they are hurting so badly, the long-term payoff is that they know there are
people in schools who care about them and are looking out for
them. This very well may not be the case outside the walls of the
building. They need to know that when they are ready, there are
people around them that care enough to be responsive. And the
same with girls like Sam.

The more dangerous and typical challenge that schools face is
that the rules and disciplinary responses to students who suffer
from mental health issues can be the trigger for school-induced
trauma and PTSD. If Sam disappears for several days, unable to
get out of bed, and upon her return we are only concerned about
"catching her up" or we are in frenetic apoplexy about what she

missed and how horrible it is that she is academically falling behind, then are we supporting her or triggering further levels of anxiety and somatic responses to her psychological suffering? Are we pushing her to spiral and ultimately to a trauma-based reaction to what is occurring? While schools are about learning, Sam can't do that right now. She's too paralyzed. Males experience this school triggering response most acutely through extreme forms of continued punitive reactions to their acting out or disruptive behavior. Often, what we know about children and their struggles do not take the central stage that they need to. We tend to apply old normative school responses to students who need an entirely different approach.

Teachers and educators are not trained psychotherapists or doctors. We need to know the boundaries of the help we can provide. Teachers need to ask themselves more readily: What is my role here? How can I best serve this student within the emotional space I occupy with her? But we also may not fool ourselves into imagining that their problems are not our problems, that their physical and psychological safety is not our concern. When you sign up to be an educator, you are enlisting in a complex ecosystem that demands we bring our entire selves into schools and classrooms every day. As the sociologist and author Bene Brown puts it, "schools should be places where children can hang up their backpacks, coats and armour,"[17] when they walk in the door, finding solace and support, at least for a good portion of their day, with the educators and professionals that surround them during such critical junctures of their lives. Those who suffer from mental health issues are already prone to distrust and isolation, putting them in a vicious cycle of going deeper and deeper into their static emotions and feelings. A school community that demonstrates care can help break that pattern by making children who suffer feel as if there are adults who have them in their thoughts and hearts in a caring and loving way. There is an advocate for them who is present even when the school day has ended. The entire school culture and its norms must reflect this reality.

I know that I am not here to save students like Sam from suffering that can inflict damage for a lifetime. What I also know is that presence and attentiveness matter. Students who are in my class need to line up, before the bell rings, right outside the door to my classroom. I do not do this to control them, intimidate them, or to create some artificial sense of order. I want to eyeball and greet every student who comes into my learning space for the day. What version of my students is coming into class? Do they look a bit frazzled? Has there been a big joyful family event that needs recognition? Are they making eye contact with me? Do they look tired? I want them to feel seen and acknowledged before anything else happens. Guess who is typically at the front of the line? Sam. There is some part of her that knows she needs to be seen and acknowledged perhaps more than anyone else. If this truly helps, I'm all in.

Kyle has had enough. He is not angry or enraged. He has been expressing those feelings previously at various times to his close friends and adults he considers allies for almost a year and a half. To no avail. Today Kyle is in my office with the director of campus life, and he is flatly describing, again, comments which are being directed at him about his sexuality. Kyle joined his current class in the beginning of middle school. Most of the other students have known each other for many years. His voice sounds defeated and resigned. "I can't take it anymore," Kyle says, sending our radar WAY up. This could mean a lot of things, including some form of self-harm he is contemplating or even planning. Too immature to understand their own cruelty, his classmates have relentlessly bombarded him with name calling, note writing, text sending, and physical encounters which range from hatred to cruelty to demonstrations of support and love. This has left Kyle shaken, tired, lonely, isolated. "I want them to just pretend I'm not there," Kyle says to us adults. "They don't even have to say hello to me. I don't need their nasty words or even support. I just want to show up and go to school."

Kyle is effeminate, with a high-pitched voice and an affect that reinforces gay male stereotypes. The recess yard is a nightmare for him. He cannot play basketball with the boys because he is both uninterested and does not like the aggressive physicality and competitiveness. He stays away from the girls who want him to sit and talk or even dance with them because he knows what the rest of the afternoon will be like if he gives in. Often, he finds a girl who wants to throw a frisbee with him.

We, the school, have gone through all our bag of tricks regarding this situation. We have tried to turn this into a "teachable moment," brought in outside speakers and experts to advise us and the students, spoken to students individually and in small groups, run educational sessions around tolerance, suspended students and ultimately expelled a student for calling Kyle a "dirty fag" on a school trip. The real question is, what are we combating and why is this issue so impervious to school interventions?

Another problem is that Kyle will not tell his parents anymore what is occurring at school. We have had school meetings with Kyle's parents about the harassment he is facing. Highly conservative, Kyle's father wants the harassment to stop but he does not want to face what the harassment is about. The mother is convinced that, once he gets to high school, this will all go away. And, while girls and boys both report harassment, it seems that the impact on women is much more severe. At least from student narratives, boys who are taunted retract less from school life, miss less days, and still participate in class. The type of sexual identity issues that are being played out through Kyle is heightened and less muted, more openly communicated in the middle school years.[18] But his mother should not fool herself. Students have been permanently scarred to the point of suicide in heavily misogynistic and homophobic high school environments, impacting psychological and physical health for years to come. They are what John Jay Professor of Psychology Kevin Nagal has coined "microaggressive trauma" developed over sustained periods of encountering relentless attacks on gender identity.[19] These can take the form of what Kyle experiences with other students, but they also manifest themselves in extracurricular exclusion or when institutions frame his struggles as an individual instance rather than a school culture issue.

LGBTQIA+ identifying students might find themselves in a much more gender aware world than twenty-five years ago, but that does not mean the *response* to their sexual identity by homophobic and bigoted individuals and groups in schools is any improved. In fact, a litany of states has passed restrictive laws regarding trans kids, giving doctors the right to refuse treatment and limiting their access to sports activities in schools based on their gender/sex identity. Several states have gone so far as to make giving certain hormonal treatments associated with the process of transition and recommended by The American College of Obstetricians and Gynecologists (hormone blockers) a criminal offense for medical professionals with up to ten years in jail.[20] All of these anti-trans efforts will only translate into further bullying, alienation, and violence for those students who do not identify in the false and dehumanizing framework of heteronormativity. We should not kid ourselves about that reality and what is occurring on our campuses, and we should not be fooling ourselves about the impact, how trauma inducing it can be. Schools should be honest that an ACE can be the direct product of repeated school experiences; it is not just something that happens in the big bad world "out there."

The other challenge to addressing these issues is how schools perceive themselves. As I have mentioned several times, many people go into education because they wish to spend their working hours in places that are defined by human warmth and nurturing attitudes and that provide a sense of safety and positive experiences where students can grow and develop. Teachers, by nature, are sensitive, not strong. This is what makes them good at their jobs but there are also drawbacks to having these masses of sensitive people in a single institution or profession. But the bigger issue is that school people tend to imagine that the default reality in schools, in *their* school, is that they are safe places, that there are good people in the building making sure that everything is going well for its students. They also tend to believe that the problems that are manifesting themselves during the day are a result of what is happening out there and elsewhere, in homes, on the streets, in other institutions. It is challenging for us educators to both honestly evaluate whether our schools are places of true safety and stability and, more importantly, whether the issues we are experiencing with children are a product of what is going on in the school as a result of the climate we have created. In other words, are we partially or largely responsible for the trauma students experience?

Faculty also experience gendered situations which can trigger mental health issues. Just one example would be the male adults who go into early childhood and elementary education who experience bias specifically related to gender, often with conflicting messages. Male students who struggle with behavioral issues are often placed into these male teachers' classrooms under the assumption that they need a "male presence" to get through their days. The assumption is that male teachers are perceived as the real deliverers of tough discipline while the female teachers are the nurturers and warm ones. Male teachers communicate great resentment at being placed in this role, having gone into the field of education exactly to be as nurturing and loving of their students as female colleagues. The flip side of this narrative is that men who go into the field of early childhood or elementary education must be gay (often perceived as problematic by parents) or even, and this is highly problematic, pedophiles. Steve, an elementary teacher, puts it this way:

> Had I not been married and begun teaching, there would be questions. When I started teaching, I carefully placed a picture of my wife on my desk. What difference does it make? When I was single and interning, the parents came to check me out. I think they were afraid that I was gay... [and] that if someone is gay, they're a molester.[21]

Steve's professional credentials were questioned, even his morality, because of the common understanding that what makes an elementary school teacher great are the "feminine" attributes such as nurturing and warmth, not if they can teach a child how to read well. The assumption is that the affect makes the teacher, not training or expertise. While male teachers talk about wanting to be in environments where women's "ways of knowing and being" are primary, the reality is that the culture pushes back hard on such desires. They can feel excluded and pushed out of and marginalized from the culture of the school.[22]

Considering the concepts of "feminine" and "masculine" that are so embedded in the cultures of schools and in the minds of parents, how immediately responsive are we to male students like Kyle who are under attack because they are LGBTQIA+ or exhibiting narrowly defined feminine qualities (non-athletic, quiet, etc.)? The answer to this question cannot be that we need to be more responsive. Yes, we need to be responsive, but without context, without everyone in a child's setting exploring their own explicit and implicit thoughts and feeling about a young male experiencing sexual harassment, responding to the individual student's needs is merely throwing a penny into a pond watching it make ripples for a moment and then the pond goes back to its original form. Institutional structures and cultural norms must be challenged regularly and persistently, with the entire school community, until new ways of being are established.

In general, males find themselves needing to define their masculinity by what they are not. It is an ongoing process of negation. The irony of being the default position of a hegemonic system is that there does not feel like a pressing need to define who you are in relation to that power structure to be heard or understood. When students are asked to define the feminine, both boys and girls give complex answers that vary, overlap, and contradict. When males are asked to define masculinity there is a uniformity of answers which align with "machismo, athleticism and heterosexual statuses." One of the great victories of the feminist movement is that women are more readily allowed to embrace aspects of themselves which align with traditional male archetypes, but for men, their understandings of themselves are staunchly anti-feminist.[23] This rigid posturing can both maintain positions of masculine "rightness" and power while being confusing and dehumanizing. What appears to be a vague definition of masculinity, which most boys suffer from, is instead propped up as some stable and standard measure, in both explicit and implicit ways.[24] Schools participate in maintaining these constructs and then, we are shocked and appalled when Kyle becomes a target of young males who are threatened by his emerging feelings and thoughts about sexuality and gender identity. Whatever Kyle feels about his identity and when and how he decides to communicate about it is up to him. The problem lies with those who wish to impose their own thoughts and feelings on him, whether positive or negative. He is one hundred percent correct when he asks for his privacy and sense of emotional and physical safety. We have not actively provided these boys who would make Kyle's life miserable with a different vision for their sense of identity (or anyone else's for that matter). The rejection of emotions and feelings associated with the feminine leaves boys with few options than to detach from potentially empathic feelings and fall into patterns of desensitization. Simply put, insensitivity, arrogance, bravado, and self-righteousness become badges of honor in their struggle over sexual identity. Unfortunately, schools would rather sacrifice Kyle's future mental health and well-being rather than challenge the disturbing misogynistic frameworks so embedded in how our schools are constructed.

Before my sixth-grade year, I was lucky and blessed to be accepted to the right school at the right time. My brother was already attending the warm, rich-in-values environment of Friends Seminary, a Quaker-run K-12 school in downtown Manhattan. Even after it was clear that my mother, a single parent raising two boys, could no longer afford to send my brother to Friends, the school not only made it work for him but accepted me as well. It is a school that took care of its families which I experienced in my years at Friends.

They had no school psychologists, no learning support. This was the late seventies. However, the culture was so devoted to each member of its community that it was a haven for me. Everyone knew each other. Everyone cared for each other. I cherished the relative calm and emotional safety of school in relation to what was often going on in my home and rough neighborhood of Alphabet City, New York.

Part of the Friends' tradition was for students to sit in silence several times a week in deep introspection. "Deep introspection" might sound like an almost fatal disease for a middle school or a high school student, but for me, particularly as I became older, it became a place of healing. It was a place where I learned to breathe. Long before schools recently began integrating meditation, yoga, and mindfulness practices, I felt tightly wrapped in the warmth and almost therapeutic nature of my school community. What I learned from my Friends education went far beyond content and curriculum. I learned to need others, to be there for others, and about the critical role a school community can play in supporting children and families. In other words, I learned something very countercultural to the typical masculine frame-work, that vulnerability and need do not define me as less of a man. Was gender and its crippling biases and implicit discrimi-nations a part of my school experience? I can't remember. I was too busy feeling like Jason most of the time.

I was lucky. For many children, their schools do not have the small feel of a private school, 200 years of embedded and prac-ticed culture of non-violence and pacifism, and the resources to focus on every child. Sustaining mental health issues and trauma burn relentlessly inside of those it affects. It has a measurable im-pact on children's ability to function, emotionally, and socially. As we have seen, a child's ability to learn becomes affected de-monstratively. By making our schools more gender and trauma aware and clearly seeing the relationship between the two can only help our schools become safe and healing environments for all students.

A potential solution to this issue (and others outlined in the book) should be no less than a complete restructuring of the middle years of education to focus on a whole other set of skills and abilities which will serve all of us and allow our children to be their best selves at school and in the world. Instead of being so hyper concerned and obsessed about what content students learn, ten- to fourteen-year-olds should be taught much more about how to learn and how to interrelate, how to interact. I am not saying that the early years (or the latter) should be devoid of ridding our schools of gender biases and their implications. But the middle years should be seen as a golden opportunity to teach them where they are, to define it for the unique experience which it is and lay the foundation for their human success in the future.

This entire period should be utilized to develop what I call "Developing the Self-Aware Learner." Students would develop the following: Build confidence and a high level of self-regulation, empathy, and human connection. The cultural barriers to this ap-proach are also buried inside of gender expectations. Most people would label these areas of student development as "soft skills." Really? Just listen to the gendered assumptions we imply by using such language to describe critical human areas of social development. The defining terminology aligns itself with the feminine and therefore in our highly binary world, they must be of lesser value. I would say that most people use these tools a lot more in life to find success and happiness after school than learning the weight of magnesium on the periodic table. And these areas should no longer be left up to happenstance on some roulette wheel of educational experience. The four levels of student and cultural development are what I call Orientational Awareness, Procedural Awareness, Expectational Awareness, and Inter-relational Awareness.

Orientational Awareness teaches students the basic skills of consistency. Showing up on time, understanding where you are at any given moment and knowing how to express what it means to be in that experience. Being ready to learn.

Procedural Awareness is about understanding processes. That a series of steps need to occur to be successful in a given place and time. Understanding sequences and following through on those steps need to be mastered.

Expectational Awareness means you are supported to become aware of who you are as a learner. When you transition into high school, that awareness informs your learning decisions at the highest level. Here, you are taught that communicating vulnerability and self-honesty are a strength.

Inter-relational Awareness allows students the room and the modeling to see themselves and others as subjects, not objects. How do I communicate my needs, rely on others, trust others, and reach out to others who need my support? How do I develop those deep relationships with others so that we all have value? In the words of the German philosopher, Martin Buber, as an educator I am helping students to see that world, not as an I-it relationship but as I-thou.

(See Appendix F for a more fully realized explanation of this middle school model.)

An incomplete list of resources for schools interested in learning about trauma and schools include:

◆ National Center for School Mental Health http://www.schoolmentalhealth.org

- ◆ Child Traumatic Stress Networks https://www.nctsn.org
- ◆ The School Based Health Alliance https://www.sbh4all.org
- ◆ The Collaborative for Social and Emotional Learning https://casel.org

Resources for schools, both nationally and locally, that help schools support students across the gender spectrum include:

- ◆ The Trevor Project https://www.thetrevorproject.org
- ◆ The Gay and Lesbian Alliance Against Defamation https://www.glaad.org
- ◆ The Gay, Lesbian and Straight Educational Network https://www.glsen.org
- ◆ Human Rights Campaign Foundation https://www.thehrcfoundation.org
- ◆ Teaching LGBTQ History https://www.lgbtqhistory.org

Conclusion

Reconstructing Schools and Celebrating Gender Diversity

In 2017, I attended a conference in Los Angeles of educators and lay leaders regarding student well-being. The wide range of discussions about all ages included sessions on mindfulness training for three-year-olds and student support for first-year undergraduates at universities. For many reasons, college can often be a time when young adults fall apart. An accumulation of

DOI: 10.4324/9781003217022-10

issues, compounded over time, hit our students, manifesting in depression, severe eating disorders, and drug and alcohol abuse. Many are unable to complete even their freshman year. Colleges and universities have become the number one provider of mental health support in the United States.

The workshop I was drawn to the most was where we got to break stuff.

I headed directly to the session that offered hammers, ceramic bowls, gold paint, and glue. The course description intrigued me: I was going to learn how to repair myself.

The instructor was a tall, calm woman with a commanding presence and cadence to her voice. She asked the twenty-five participants to come in and find a place at a long bench. Roughly half were women and half men. In front of us were the supplies, with the understanding that we were not to touch them until she gave the word.

She told us about the personal journey that brought her to the Japanese art of *Kintsugi* in her work with struggling teens. I immediately perked up; the idea was that students are at their learning best when holistically engaged with their hands, hearts, and minds.

Kintsugi, translated as the "golden rejoining" is a form of Japanese repair process for ceramics, often used when the vessels for the traditional tea service are broken. Originating in the Fifteenth Century, the practice suggests that cracks or shards are not damaged but part of the life cycle of the object. The ceramic not only retains its importance, but the gold paint used to repair it reaffirms its value in rituals. The breaks become an important part of the object's history and its story. So different in the United States, where the minute something is damaged, we throw it away and look for its replacement, "Kintsugi actually draws attention to the chips and perceives these marks of wear and tear as a valuable addition to the story of the piece."[1]

With a clear verbal gesture, the instructor told us to start by picking up our hammers and prepare to smash our bowls. We each took a cloth, covered the Costco ceramic bowls, and then smashed them with hammers. I immediately noticed two things.

Without hesitation, the men in the room took their hammers and with swift, clear determination (and a bit of naughty glee) came down on their bowls with force. Between the moment she tells us to do it and the act itself, there was little hesitation.

The women, in contrast, acted with greater caution, even trepidation. All dozen of them covered their bowls, lifted the cloth to look underneath them one more time, and lined up the hammers at various points on the bowl. They laughed nervously wondering aloud where to strike. Some put their hammers back down or lightly tapped the bowls with the hammer head but not causing any damage. Finally, one woman lifted her hand with a grimace, eyes shut, and gasped as she struck and felt the pottery shatter under her power. The other women followed suit, some lifting the cloth to see what had occurred, as though apologizing to the bowl.

Once everyone had inflicted damage on their bowls, the instructor directed us to uncover the cloth. She asked everyone to spend some time examining the pieces before gluing them back together. This time the men struggled with the task. They fidgeted and looked around the room. Some buried their faces in their phones or even got up and walked out.

In contrast, the women turned the shards over in their hands, examining the shapes and making analogies to episodes in real life. One woman told her neighbor a story about a vase that she broke as a child in her aunt's house; this exercise made her remember the event for the first time in a long time. She recalled how she retrieved the broken pottery after her aunt threw it into the trash and then started to look at them. She remembered thinking, even as a child, why is my aunt throwing these pieces away? They're beautiful even if they're no longer a vase.

The men begin struggling when asked to repair their bowls. I'm surprised. I thought they would love this part – tools, glue, a puzzle. And then one man looks at me from across the table and says, "This bowl is done. Can't use it for much."

The parallels to the work of educating children became clear to me. We need to shatter the system that exists, putting it back together into a new form.

Children are, thankfully, not the same people at three as they are at eleven or fifteen. They transform and change shape and morph over time. Schools play a vital role in this process. We would love to believe that this process of maturation is a gradual, step-by-step experience but in fact it can be jarring not just for the kids but also for their teachers and parents. Students have both been put together by the fire of the kiln, their molecules strung together, forging them, and they are also constantly transforming and developing in ways which leave unique, beautiful – revealing contours and golden scars, creating a narrative history of how we were ultimately shaped.

Schools were initially created in this country for a certain purpose. As I have mentioned, some of those objectives were noble and even radical, changing the entire world for the better, while others hold back our children from becoming their truest selves.

Our educational system needs to be shattered and reconstituted to better address the developmental needs of children and how we perceive gender. Schools need to create the language and practices that celebrate gender multiculturalism. We can remake schools so that they focus primarily on the developmental needs of young people; we are so much better able to do so given how much more we know about human growth and attainment. The question of gender is so critical because it creates a base line of equality, fairness, and dignity at the very heart of schooling. We need to make our schools places where the cracks, distinctions, accidents, and inevitably flawed process of child development and growth are not viewed as some preordained fate, but as markers of a unique and celebrated self, capable of great contributions to society.

Acknowledgments and Gratitude

When I began writing this book over four years ago, I thought it would be a lonely process. Not so. I learned quickly when taking on a project like this how much you need people.

You need the generations of thinkers, researchers, and practitioners before you who have brought their wisdom to the art and craft of education. You also need those living who are immersed in the same questions and considerations as you. Just as we regularly communicate to our students, needing others and being needed gives substance and value to your learning and to life.

A special level of appreciation goes out to Dr. Rachel Lerner who encouraged (and sort of demanded) that I take my ideas regarding gender and education and turn my graduate school classes into a sandbox for experimentation, discussion, and refinement. That permission to play was invaluable in sculpting and clarifying the ideas in these pages. You modeled the best of leadership in education. And, by extension, to my graduate students and my trainees in the mentor teacher certification program at the Fingerhut School of Education of American Jewish University who tolerated my annoying habit of inserting gender into our learning at every chance I could get. Your excitement and engagement regarding this critical issue kept me pushing forward and reminding me of the ultimate mission of this book.

To the professionals who took the time to read this work and give me their blessing and honesty regarding lots of words, your contributions are all over the book and rightly so. That would be: Dr. Stephanie Mihalas, master educator Samantha Pack, Dr. Rachel Lerner, head of school Dr. Hannah Bennett, and Dr. Elliott Rabin.

The journalists Anya Kamenetz and Judith Matloff proved incredibly patient and tolerant and caring when it came to my fragile writer ego. Anya, for teaching me how to write a coherent sentence, and to Judith for teaching me how to write a book. And to Gary Belsky (Hedley Popper) who knew when to push and pull just at the right time.

Lauren Davis and the good people at Routledge Eye on Education saw the vision for this book, tested the vision with the people who matter, namely teachers, and then committed to the vision. I could not ask for more thoughtful partnership.

My mother, Hanka Ablin, and extended Neiger family taught me, from generation to generation, how to continue to commit myself to the fight for justice and fairness. And to my extended Bellows family for making my life richer and full of unconditional love. To Joan and Shael Bellows. How many son-in-laws can say that he had parents who constantly reminded him of the vital and critical work of being an educator. I am beyond blessed.

I have been in education so long that I have seen the children of the children I taught walk through the classrooms and schools in which I have had the privilege to work. I am humbled to have been part of your journey. Every time you reach out to me to reconnect by email, text, or when we just bump into each other in some random place, the decision to dedicate my career to education proves wise and endlessly rewarding. By becoming your best selves, you make all the hard work, commitment, and love worth it.

TOOLS
-FOR-
TEACHERS
-AND-
SCHOOLS

Addressing Gender Equity Through Teaching and Learning

APPENDIX (A)

Four Faculty Conversations Regarding Gender

PURPOSE AND OUTCOMES FOR THESE CONVERSATIONS

Every school community is different with varying cultures depending on geography, socio-economic profile, racial, ethnic, and religious backgrounds...etc. I purposefully provide several different versions of these conversations as options in both approach and language choices. The main purpose, whether you decide to do one of these activities or all of them, is to have teachers and staff see themselves as central to this conversation - how powerful their own attitudes and thinking are in influencing what their classrooms and ultimately the entire school culture looks like.

Outcomes should include:

1. Growing awareness of the diversity of thoughts, feelings, and sensitivities regarding gender among your educators.

2. Begin the process of shaping a common, respectful language so that the staff can discuss these issues together and help shape, collectively, school culture.

3. Begin building knowledge about gender issues and identities. Let's not assume that professional educators have a broad range of experience or background in this area. You need to start somewhere!

Any conversations we have around gender should be done with the utmost sensitivity. School leaders doing professional development with staff around these issues should realize that: 1. Everyone has gender stories to share and 2. Many people's stories are quite painful and can stir difficult responses. Here are some ground rules that can help with this important work.

1. Preview the professional development, *before* people enter the professional development space, through your trusted methods of faculty communication.

2. If you are running these sessions, leave your proverbial or actual door open for faculty who may be uncomfortable with this conversation. Find a comfortable way for everyone to participate in a positive way. For some individuals, this may not be possible.

3. Make sure that everyone knows up front that they can share exactly what they want to share. The expectations are theirs to define.

4. Nothing leaves the room, no video or audio will be recorded. These conversations are a critical way to encourage faculty to care for each other and trust the people who run these sessions. We build a stronger school culture when we respect other people's feelings and experiences.

FIRST CONVERSATION:
(Approximately 45 minutes)

In small groups (no more than six people in a group), ask faculty to share the ways that they define gender. If this is truly an open respectful conversation people will bring LOTS to the table. (10min.)

On block paper, have each group create a brainstorm map of their thoughts and feelings. They can use words, symbols, illustrations...etc. Post them around the room. (10min.)

Do a faculty gallery walk. Each teacher takes a marker and puts a check next to items that resonate with them on other groups' block paper. (10min.)

Put the following definition of Gender up on a screen or board and have your faculty respond as an entire faculty. Have the conversation. (15min.)

> Sexuality is who you go to bed with, and gender identity is who you go to bed as.

SECOND CONVERSATION:
(Approximately 30 minutes)

From *The Gender Equation*: Chapter 2. In small groups (no more than six people in a group)

What do the terms Precious Eggs and Kept Princes mean to you? Do we recognize Toby? Adam?

To what extent do we perpetuate these two stereotypes in our classrooms and throughout our schools?

Do we, in our own memories of school, remember if our behaviors mirrored either of these stereotypes?

Do we remember teachers who either maintained the idea of natural versus acquired aptitude or actively worked to push against it? What did this look like?

What can we do to notice this behavior in ourselves or how can we push against the natural inclination to fall back on these stereotypes?

THIRD CONVERSATION:
(Approximately 30 minutes)

Gender Experimentation and Identity: In small groups (no more than six people in a group)

Students are experimenting with their gender identity throughout their school days and years. Often, we adults do not notice these experimentations occurring as we can be busy constructing learning experiences and spaces that narrowly define gender expectations.

What do you notice that students and children do that could be classified as gender identity experimentation?

How do you see them using their relationships, words, writing, and general engagement with learning as forms of gender identity experimentation?

As an educator, how do you respond when you see student gender experimentation? How can you respond? When is it developmentally appropriate? Are there harmful and dangerous expressions that take place that we do not address?

FOURTH CONVERSATION:
(30-40 minutes)

Faculty Gender Stories: In small groups (no more than four people in a group)

Share a story from your professional or personal life that helps you make sense of gender. A story from your own schooling. A story from learning a particular subject area. From your community. A news story you read. An experience with a stranger you met.

What are the stories that help you make sense of gender? We all have them. Some are incredibly private and painful. Some are funny. Some are inspiring and enlightening. All of them are very human.

These stories should be ones that you feel comfortable with sharing. They can help others understand you as a colleague and a human being.

Here is an example of a story that was shared with me in one faculty training. (I was given permission to include this in the book.)

Terry: "I grew up in a very strict religious community where I was expected to follow many norms, one of them was extreme discretion with interactions with women. I had six brothers and by the time I reached my wedding day (20 years old), I realized that the only real contact and relationship I had had with a woman was with my mother.

It took me years to learn how to interact with my wife, to listen to her, to not be scared to say the wrong thing to her. Then we were blessed with five children. All of them, daughters!! I spent the next twenty years learning how to support them, how to see them as individuals, how to have conversations where we could connect and be respectful. I realized after many years that saying or thinking that they "were sometimes too emotional" was my issue. They were giving me the gift of learning how to be open and vulnerable about my own feelings. Instead of it being a weakness, I began to see it as an enormous strength".

APPENDIX (B)

Intrinsic Versus Acquired Aptitude:

School Research
and
Gendered Attitudes
Toward Learning:
Student
Assessments

Creating teacher inquiry or research teams around student attitudes toward learning. Gathering gender learning information and data about your school.

Purpose: Students are much more self-aware than we give them credit for. We can begin surveying students about their thoughts and feelings about learning as early as ten years old. These surveys should be given on a regular basis to check for changes in attitudes over time. They can be critical snapshots that can give you a gender geography of your school which then informs the professional development and pedagogy work that you focus on with your faculty.

Sample form and questions: Middle School Version

1. Name

2. Age

3. What subject in school are you most successful?

4. Is this also your favorite subject? If not, what is your favorite?

5. What makes you so successful in this subject?

6. What is your least successful?

7. Is this also your LEAST favorite subject? If not, what do you NOT like the most?

8. What makes this subject more challenging?

9. Of the following six words, which two describe you the best. Smart, Caring, Hard-working, Capable, Advanced, Cooperative or Well-behaved.

10. Do you think you work hard in school and put in a great deal of effort?

Sample form and questions: High School Version

1. Name

2. Age

3. In what subject do you excel?

4. What do you think is the reason for your success in this subject?

5. What subject would you not take if you had the choice?

6. What is the reason that you would opt out?

7. Do you not have the ability to do well?

8. In what class do you participate the most?

9. The reason for your high level of participation is:
   a. The teacher encourages/demands it.
   b. I am interested in the subject.
   c. I feel comfortable participating.
   d. I feel that I learn better when I participate.

10. Do you think your success in school is due to hard work or ability?

II. What do you think is the reason to get a strong education? Pick the top three.
   a. To be successful in life.
   b. To get a good job.
   c. To be a better person.
   d. To live a meaningful life.
   e. To be a good citizen.

APPENDIX (C)

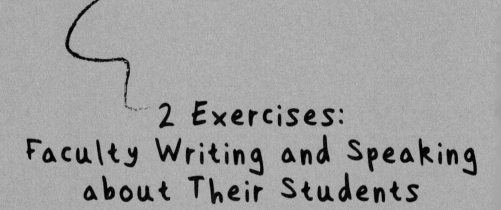

2 Exercises: Faculty Writing and Speaking about Their Students

Whether you work in a school that requires written evaluations of students during grading periods or one that just calls for numbers and data, it is vital that teachers learn how to write about students and talk about students in ways which reduce the binaries of gender and the assumed bias. This exercise is not just about preferred pronouns!! This is about making sure you know your students well enough where common gender bias, which seeps into all our language and contextualizing of students, begins to matter less and becomes minimized. In general, how can we make our comments more about observation and reduce inference.

FACULTY EXERCISE I:
(45 minutes)

Have the faculty (by grade level) think of two of their students.

Have them write a "learning report" on each of these students addressing the following questions:
- How does this student learn best?
- How is she aware of herself as a learner?
- How does she demonstrate curiosity and interest?
- How would you describe the ways in which she interacts with others?

Teachers have a "hit list" of words they are not allowed to use in their narratives. They include:

Sweet, Energetic, Clever, Caring, Careless, Collaborative, Gifted, Hardworking, Kind, Active, Capable, Smart, Intelligent, Cooperative, Talkative, Advanced, Neat, Physical, Inattentive, Silly.

Faculty share their narratives with each group. (If the teachers really know their students, these narratives should be filled with examples and stories which demonstrate and do not label.)

FACULTY EXERCISE II:
(45 minutes)

Give the teachers an extensive profile of a mock student with many examples of both successes and challenges. The profile does indicate a particular learning issue or behavior that needs to be addressed.

Allow faculty the chance to read it.

A team leader leads the group in a discussion. In the discussion the teachers may not talk about the student using the above list of adjectives. If someone does, the team leader needs to point it out as part of their role.

The goals of this exercise are the following:
- To come up with an action plan to meet the learning and social needs of the student.
- To determine if how the student is interacting from a gender standpoint is influencing their issues.
- To reflect on whether the faculty conversation was shaped in any way by gender bias. Was the faculty plan negatively influenced by perceived gender norms?

APPENDIX (D)

Rethinking Space

The construction and design of space inside of classrooms and the school community has all types of well-researched implications for student learning. Signs and signifiers tell students, in an ongoing rush of daily reminders, how to think about their learning and themselves. This process below is for administrators, mentor teachers, or cohorts of teachers to use during the first six weeks of school.

Process:

1. Share with teachers the observation and evaluation form before school starts.

2. Get out of their way as they design their spaces.

3. After three weeks of school beginning, come in and use the form as an observation tool.

4. As a team leader or administrator, first ask questions and listen carefully to their answers. Then review the results of your observations with the teachers.

5. Make a game plan for any revisions that need to be made or the ways in which administrators can acquire resources that will enhance the teachers' spaces.

6. After six weeks, devote a faculty meeting to teachers doing a visit of the different classrooms in the building.

7. Have them take notes on what ideas they captured from visiting each other's classrooms.

8. Share how classrooms provide for equity and are spaces that can make all students feel safe and confident that they can learn anything!

CLASSROOM/SPACE
OBSERVATIONS
-AND-
REFLECTIONS

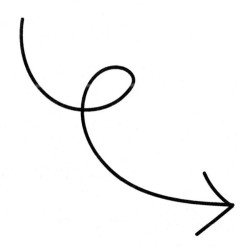

```
┌─────────────────────────────────────────────────────┐
│ INSTRUCTOR(S): _____          │
│ ROOM: _____          │
│ DATE: _____          │
└─────────────────────────────────────────────────────┘
```

AREA OF FOCUS:	NOTES AND SUGGESTIONS:
ORDER: (See Legend below: Questions 1-6)	
WALLS: (Questions 7-13)	
SPACE: (Questions 14-17)	
LEARNING AND CURRICULUM: (Questions 18-25)	

ORDER:

1. What is the process for keeping the room orderly and organized?

2. Are the students being taught (in an age-appropriate way) to partner and/or be in charge of that process?

3. What is the process for keeping the space clean and sanitary? (Access to tissue boxes, hand sanitizers, etc.)

4. Is the room safe? Enough room for student movement?

5. Is everything clearly marked, coherent? Would a stranger know where everything is?

6. Is student work organized, accessible and given honor in the room?

WALLS:

7. What do they reflect and why? What do students see from their physical vantage point?

8. Are the walls organic and flexible? Will the students see in April what they saw in September?

9. Are they under-stimulating?

10. Are they over-stimulating?

11. How do they represent student growth?

12. Are the walls decorated or a vehicle for student learning?

13. How do students play a role with what the walls look like and represent?

SPACE:

14. Given class size, is the room's space being maximized?

15. Are there flexible learning spaces for independent learning projects, space choice, co-teaching, etc?

16. Do they have tools to execute alternative space options for learning? (Clipboards, soft spaces, rugs, pillows, etc)

17. Does your space facilitate critical thinking?

LEARNING AND CURRICULUM:

18. Does the space indicate/make clear when, where, and how learning will take place? (i.e., routine, schedule)

19. Does the room make clear our fundamental core programs? (Math, Literacy, Science…?)

20. Is there a clear sense that all these programs are equally emphasized?

21. Is there a Writing Center?

22. Are libraries clearly marked and accessible?

23. How is space used to facilitate math education?

24. Have students "practiced" the space? Have you toured students through the class? Introduced them to changes in the space?

25. How will the space evolve to promote growth in student autonomy and independence over the course of the year?

Measuring Student Engagement and Bombing Rate

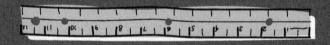

Teachers are interrupting students all day long. It happens in administrators' offices, it happens in the hallways, and predominantly it happens in classrooms where students should be learning to assert themselves respectfully. The reasons are often benign. School days move like lightning, and we need to get to the point and move on. Teachers become enthusiastic when a class discussion is going the right way, so they jump in when a student is in mid-sentence...etc. But this can mean that students may be discouraged from learning how to formulate their thoughts and articulate them carefully. Teachers' own skill and acumen for spoken language can work against them if we do not give our students the space and time to fill the room with their voices.

In addition, as I mentioned in chapter four, interrupting female students more often can imply that their voices are less valuable than males.

As many seasoned educators already know, calling on students to answer questions during direct instruction (as opposed to picking someone with a raised hand) can have extremely positive results for meeting engagement goals.

- Students feel seen and heard.
- Students begin to be more comfortable with participation.
- More students hear other student voices.
- Opting out is not an option!
- Students begin to feel comfortable with taking risks with possible answers and students feel more comfortable articulating that they "do not know."
- The anticipation of being called on raises levels of attentiveness and preparation.

Many different techniques are used to guarantee total student participation. Popsicle sticks, poker chips that need to be spent by the student...etc. I believe teachers need to be more strategic and planned to make sure of two major factors.

1. Teachers need to direct specific types of questions to specific students.

2. Teachers need to guarantee that the level and sophistication of questioning is distributed fairly, particularly regarding gender.

Administrators: When you are performing these observations, mark down every question asked in class. Do not mark just the questions which seem connected to content acquisition or direct instruction. Questions regarding classroom norms, objectives, and agenda (asking a student to read the objectives is a type of question), even questions regarding student behavior are still questions.

BOMBING RATE
ANALYSIS
PART I:

Purpose: This form creates an inquiry map of the teacher's classroom. By including all students, it will also immediately identify gendered patterns as well as quantity and quality of talk time by individual students.

(This should be conducted several times in the same classroom before moving on to Part II)

INSTRUCTOR(S): _____

INSTRUCTIONAL TIME: _____
(Day and time of Day) date:

LESSON MODALITY: _____
(Ex: Direct Instruction,
Collaborative, PBL...etc.) _____

STUDENT NAME (Every student in class should be listed)	TEACHER QUESTION OR STUDENT QUESTION (Please script exact language)	WAIT TIME (Did interruption occur to student response and how long did it take?)

FRAMING INQUIRY
BY GENDER:
PART II:

Purpose: Once you have created an inquiry map of your classroom, pick apart gender bias through directed teacher practice. Once the lesson plan has been written, you will pick students who need certain forms of inquiry, rather than doing it merely by hands raised or by someone who has or has not spoken.

Process:

1. Take six to eight students in your class, evenly divided between male and female.

2. Take the data on these students from your inquiry maps and answer the following questions.
   - What type of questions did I ask to whom?
   - Was I directing higher order thinking inquiry for the student who needed this challenge?
   - Was I directing attentiveness/presence questions at the students who needed it?

3. As part of your lesson planning, include the following form. Teachers need to fill out the first two columns before the lesson.

STUDENT NAME	TYPE OF QUESTION	STUDENT RESPONSE	REDIRECTED TO WHOM?

There are many ways of framing types of questions. I like the following framework.

1. Procedural: E.g. What page are we currently on in the book/textbook? e.g., What are we supposed to be doing in class right now? Please read the learning objectives.

2. Conceptual or Interpretive: e.g. Can you compare this math concept to one we learned previously? What is the main idea the author is trying to communicate?

3. Relevance or Application: e.g. Where can we see this chemical principle applied in practice? Do we have examples of this cause and effect in our current historical realities?

4. Self-knowledge or Empathy: e.g. Does coding and algorithms make the world a fairer, more just place? How?

Other Types of Questions:

A. Questions that ask for more evidence, e.g. How do you know that?

B. Questions that ask for clarification, e.g. What's a good example of what you are talking about?

C. Open questions, e.g., Sauvage says that when facing moral crisis, people who agonize don't act, and people who act don't agonize. What does he mean by this?

D. Linking or extension questions, e.g. How does your observation relate to what the group decided last week?

E. Hypothetical questions, e.g. If Shakespeare had intended Iago to be a tragic or more sympathetic figure, how might he have changed the narrative of Othello?

F. Summary and synthesis questions, e.g. What remains unresolved or contentious about this topic?

Rethinking the Critical Learning Environments of Physical Education Classes to Create Safer Schools

We talk to students about gender way too late, often only in the high school years. There are critical conversations that need to happen with students as early as ten years old and should culminate in certain results and outcomes by the time they are fourteen. These conversations and practices concern gender but revolve around body awareness, safety, and the reduction of violence. If there is one area, I would advocate for single sex education it is in programing around empowerment self-defense where middle school children can gain the tools to be upstanders and first responders when it comes to violence reduction in their schools and communities. The goals both intra-gendered and inter-gendered require that, in our current binaries, we work with both males and females to undermine narratives of power and powerlessness.

GOALS FOR A SAMPLE MIDDLE SCHOOL BOY'S PROGRAM

Targets or Learning Outcomes -- The Empowerment Self Defense boys (ESDb) curriculum looks to help support boys create healthy masculine identities in often challenging situations. Boys must learn not just that there is a diversity of male gender identities but as R.W. Connell writes: "We must also recognize the relations between the different kinds of masculinity...There is a gender politics within masculinity."[1]

Participants will be able to identify their individual worth and value and the value of those they feel connected to.

Participants will learn to create a climate of support and strength which allows them to be their best selves.

Participants will have a clear sense of their own boundaries and limits and be able to articulate them.

Participants will feel confident to push back against uncomfortable and threatening situations with a variety of tools -- mental, verbal, and specific to the situation and circumstances in which they find themselves.

Participants will be able to discern the right level of response to any situation to de-escalate or minimize violent confrontations.

Participants will have more diverse ways of defining their masculinity.

The curriculum seeks to transform the culture of the school or youth group or institution to create a safer, more thriving culture. Males will see themselves as socially and culturally capable of being first responders to violent and threatening circumstances, with the tools to facilitate peaceful resolution and social justice.

Boys should address the following areas:
- Boundaries.
- Redirection.
- Posture/Position.
- Verbal de-escalation of conflict.
- Escape or prevent violent conflict when possible.
- Being an upstander and supporting friends.
- Reporting and finding allies.
- Self-worth.
- Defining what it means to be a man and what it does not mean.
- Interactions with girls and stages of consent.
- The danger and damage done through social media.

The instructors then work with boys when confronted with situations where physical force was necessary to repel an attack or assault. They do drills, games and scenarios to teach the boys:

- Scratch.
- Strike.
- Release and break holds.
- Biting.
- Finding targets "head, groin."
- Kicking from the ground.
- Improvising weapons.

They are also taught how to discern the difference between a stranger attacking and someone known to them, not feeling as if they are unable to defend themselves because of social circumstances within the school and the community. Parents are also brought in to hear about ESD and to ask any questions. They are given language to talk to their boys at home to support the program's goals.

Student Awareness

—

A New Set of Learning Goals for Middle School Students.

The middle school years, or ages ten to fourteen, are an excellent place to begin to reshape our educational institutions to tackle entrenched gender bias and hegemonies in our schooling systems. We need to raise the student's awareness of self and others and community to help students access their entire education. This model also helps teachers and administrators focus on what really matters during these volatile developmental years in schools. It also helps relegate content learning to where it belongs during middle school, as a means to developing learning dignity, joy, and mental health for our children.

Independence, self, and inter-reliance:

Real independence and intrinsic motivation are taught and nurtured in children. We create different experiences and paradigms in our classrooms so that we help develop internal mechanisms for their future academic success and sense of belonging to themselves, to fellow students and to networks of overlapping communities. These are often new concepts for students and, just with anything else we would introduce to our students, teachers need clarity in strategy, pedagogy, and consistency in approach in order to meet these goals.

There are four broad categories or types of awareness (listed on the next page). As you think about planning lessons, keep these types forefront in your mind. Identify in your classroom expectations and your daily lesson planning in your planning by labeling which type of awareness you are addressing in each segment/activity.

CATEGORY	DESCRIPTION	EXAMPLES
ORIENTATIONAL AWARENESS	The teacher has oriented her students to certain kinds of routines, which are consistent and automatic. Orientational independence maintains a level of consistency. Ownership – there is this community I, the student, am a part of. I'm going to own that and not walk into class somehow having a dependence on the teacher to constantly remind me of how class works. That's my role inside the classroom, I own that. What are indications of orientational independence? The teacher tells students that there are always reasons for why we do what we do in this classroom.	• Do Now – first five minutes of class • Modes of voices: when someone is speaking, we allow them the time and space to fully articulate themselves. • Cue patterns which everyone is responsible for recognizing. • Nonverbal communications. Students take out their pens, they don't need to say anything. • Agenda on the board for the day, written on the board –visual. • Visual prompts for expectations are everywhere and all members of the class should refer to them. • Your Example:
PROCEDURAL AWARENESS	There are a set of ways in which the class proceeds. Students take ownership and they apply those procedures, even though it might not look the same every day. Apply a way of being and doing in the class, with the learning and with each other.	• Homework is always passed out, but I didn't get the sheet. So, I figure out how to get the sheet – not show up to school and say I don't have the sheet. • Decorum and physical safety of room – beginning of class, middle of class, end of class • Permissions: only one person out of the room at a time. • Your Example:

CATEGORY	DESCRIPTION	EXAMPLES
INTER-RELATIONAL AWARENESS*	I-it is one type of relationship. A perfunctory relationship, a transactional relationship. I-thou: a more complicated relationship, and I am always aware of these relationships. Deep connections with other people where we see them not just as objects, but subjects. Caring, Vulnerability, Respect, Empathy, Collaboration.[2]	• Feedback moments: How do you give feedback to an adult? To your peers? • How do we express and practice loving rebuke? • Modes of communication: What is the appropriate way to write digital correspondence? Who is our audience? How do we dignify them? • Peer-editing is a vehicle to get to character development, and to a model of inter-relational awareness. • Your Example:
EXPECTATIONAL AWARENESS	Self-awareness about who I am as a learner. Validating and even celebrating other people's interests. The teacher is not the only person I can learn from. The classroom is a place I can explore my curiosities and interests without judgement and that is my responsibility to do so. What do I need to do to meet that benchmark/standard?	• Ask three then me: if a student doesn't know what to do, the expectation is that they can figure it out for themselves, so they will ask a friend, look at the resource. Not immediately resorting to "I'm lost." That's how you know you've won. • Teachers do not feel compelled to address all student questions – that's a signal to them that they need to figure it out themselves. • By the end of the year, you will know Algebra 1. So, the big question is: How do I get there? Where do I begin? • Study skills: Do I know how I like to study? Exploring creative ways to capture learning. • Time management: do I know how to use my time? Students share their schedules and approaches with each other. • Your Example:

*Teachers and school leaders must exhibit these skills and human practices throughout the day in their school buildings and environments. Every day is a day to be humbled by a child's progress, growth, humor, struggles, fears, and trauma. We must stay in a relationship of awe and wonder when we walk into our schools every morning.

NOTES:

Endnotes

Introduction

1. Tocqueville, A.D., Heffner, R.D. & Gregorian, V. (2010). *Democracy in America* (Signet Classics) (Reissue ed.). Signet. 47.
2. Goldin, C. & Katz, L.F. (2010). *The Race between Education and Technology* (Illustrated ed.). Belknap Press: An Imprint of Harvard University Press. 24.
3. Goldin, C. & Katz, L.F. 154.
4. Goldin, C. & Katz, L.F. 154.
5. Rosin, H. (2013). *The End of Men: and the Rise of Women* (Reprint ed.). Riverhead Books.
6. Gumbel, A. (2020, April 16). California schools were once the nation's envy. What went wrong? *The Guardian*. https://www.theguardian.com/education/2019/jan/19/california-school-funding-los-angeles-strike-what-went-wrong.
7. Naureckas, J. (2019, August 1). Ronald Reagan's racism should come as no surprise. *Nation of Change*. https://www.nationofchange.org/2019/08/01/ronald-reagans-racism-should-come-as-no-surprise/.
8. Tanner, B.L. (2021, March 26). Column: New Hampshire system of public education on the auction block. Valley News. https://www.vnews.com/Column-The-voucher-system-will-dismantle-our-public-schools-39664351.
9. McGee, K. (2021, May 22). Texas' critical race theory bill OK'd by Senate over teachers' objections. The Texas Tribune. https://www.texastribune.org/2021/05/22/texas-critical-race-theory-legislature/.
10. Greene, P. (2021, May 6). Arizona GOP hopes to clamp down on teachers. Forbes. https://www.forbes.com/sites/petergreene/2021/05/06/arizona-gop-hopes-to-clamp-down-on-teachers/?sh=700378335aca.
11. Pomerantz, S. & Raby, R. (2017). *Smart Girls: Success, School, and the Myth of Post-Feminism* (1st ed.). University of California Press. 12–13.
12. National Center for Labor Statistics, Table 268.

13. Trends in High School Dropout and Completion Rates in the United States Compendium Report: 2018. National Center for Educational Statistics. US Department of Education. 2019.

14. Crime rates linked to educational attainment; 2013 alliance report finds. (2013). Alliance for Excellent Education. https://all4ed.org/press/crime-rates-linked-to-educational-attainment-new-alliance-report-finds/.

15. Lochner, L. & Moretti, E. (2004). The effect of education on crime: Evidence from prison inmates, arrests, and self-reports. *American Economic Review*, *94*(1), 155–189.

16. Farrow, R. (2018, July 27). Les Moonves and CBS Face Allegations of Sexual Misconduct. *The New Yorker*. https://www.newyorker.com/magazine/2018/08/06/les-moonves-and-cbs-face-allegations-of-sexual-misconduct.

17. Scope of the Problem: Statistics | RAINN. (2020). https://www.rainn.org/statistics/scope-problem.

18. Dewey, J. (1997). *Experience and Education* (Reprint ed.). Free Press.

19. Butler, J. (2006). *Gender Trouble: Feminism and the Subversion of Identity* (Routledge Classics) (1st ed.). Routledge.

20. Thorne, B. (1993). *Gender Play: Girls and Boys in School*. Rutgers University Press. 12.

Chapter 1: Who's Teaching Whom: Math, Literacy, and Making School for Everyone

1. Tsang, J.M., Dougherty, R.F., Deutsch, G.K., Wandell, B.A. & Ben-Shachar, M. (2009). Frontoparietal white matter diffusion properties predict mental arithmetic skills in children. *Proceedings of the National Academy of Sciences*, *106*(52), 22546–22551.

2. Dehaene, S. (2011). *The Number Sense: How the Mind Creates Mathematics* (Revised, Updated ed.). Oxford University Press. 273.

3. Reed, D. & Fox, L.H. (2007). Gender equity in testing and assessment. In: Klein, S.S. Ed. *Handbook for Achieving Equity through Education*. Routledge. 155–169.

4. U.S. Department of Labor, Bureau of Labor Statistics. Employment status of the civilian population by sex and age, January 2001–2018. www.dol.gov.

5. Reed, D. & Fox, L.H. 155–169.

6. Byrnes, J.P. (2005). Gender differences in math: Cognitive processes in an expanded framework. In: Gallagher, A.M. & Kaufman, J.C. Eds. *Gender Differences in Mathematics: An Integrative Psychological Approach.* Cambridge University Press. 73–98.

7. Royer, J.M. & Garofoli, L.M. (2005). Cognitive contributions to sex differences in math performance. In: Gallagher, A.M. & Kaufman, J.C. Eds. *Gender Differences in Mathematics: An Integrative Psychological Approach.* Cambridge University Press. 99–120.

8. 1,675+ Accredited, four-Year Colleges & Universities with ACT/SAT-Optional Testing Policies for Fall, 2021 Admissions In: www.fairtest.org/university/optional.

9. Sadker, D., Sadker, M. & Zittleman, K.R. (2009). *Still Failing at Fairness: How Gender Bias Cheats Girls and Boys in School and What We Can Do About It.* Scribner. 24.

10. Kimura, D. (2000). *Sex and Cognition* (A Bradford Book). Bradford Books. 7.

11. Klass, P. (2017, May 15). No such thing as a math person. *The New York Times.* https://www.nytimes.com/2017/05/15/well/family/trying-to-add-up-girls-and-math.html.

12. Halpern, D.F., Wai, J. & Saw, A. (2005). A psychobiosocial model: Why females are sometimes greater and sometimes less than males in math achievement. In: Gallagher, A.M. & Kaufman, J.C. Eds. *Gender Differences in Mathematics: An Integrative Psychological Approach.* Cambridge University Press. 72.

13. Reardon, S.F., Fahle, E.M., Kalogrides, D., Podolsky, A. & Zárate, R.C. (2018). Gender achievement gaps in U.S. school districts. *Stanford Center Education Policy Analysis Working Paper.* No. 18-13.

Chapter 2: Natural versus Acquired Aptitude: Of Precious Eggs and Kept Princes

1. Byrnes, J.P. 90.

2. Kloosterman, P. (1990). Attributions, performance following failure, and motivation in mathematics. In: Fennema, E. & Leder, G. Eds. *Mathematics and Gender.* Teachers College Press. 115.

3. Fausto-Sterling, A. (2021). A dynamic systems framework for gender/sex development: From sensory input in infancy to subjective certainty in toddlerhood. *Frontiers in Human Neuroscience, 15,* 150.

4. Fausto-Sterling, A. (2019). Gender/sex, sexual orientation, and identity are in the body: How did they get there? *The Journal of Sex Research*, *56*(4–5), 529–555.

5. Spencer, S.J., Steele, C.M. & Quinn, D.M. (1999). Stereotype threat and women's math performance. *Journal of Experimental Social Psychology*, *35*, 4–28.

6. Pomerantz, S. & Raby, R. 62

7. Duckworth, A.L., Peterson, C., Matthews, M.D. & Kelly, D.R. (2007). Grit: Perseverance and passion for long-term goals. *Journal of Personality and Social Psychology*, *92*(6), 1087–1101.

8. Character Lab. (https://www.characterlab.org/character).

9. Yeager, D.S., Henderson, M.D., Paunesku, D., Walton, G.M., D'Mello, S., Spitzer, B.J. & Duckworth, A.L. (2014). Boring but important: A self-transcendent purpose for learning fosters academic self-regulation. *Journal of Personality and Social Psychology*, *107*(4), 559–580.

10. Duckworth, A.L., Peterson, C., Matthews, M.D. & Kelly, D.R. 1087–1011.

11. Character Lab. (https://www.characterlab.org/research-network).

12. Connell, R.W. (1987). *Gender and Power: Society, the Person and Sexual Politics*. Polity Press. 84.

13. Kimmel, M. (2018). *Manhood in America: A Cultural History*. Oxford University Press. 22.

14. Sadker, M. & Sadker, D. (1986). Sexism in the classroom: From grade school to graduate school. *Phi Delta Kappan*, *67*(7), 512–515.

15. Feldhusen, J.F. & Willard-Holt, C. (1993). Gender differences in classroom interactions and career aspirations of gifted students. *Contemporary Educational Psychology*, *18*(3), 355–362. Fox, L. & Soller, J. (2007). Gender equity for gifted students. In: Klein, S. Ed. *Handbook for Achieving Gender Equity through Education* (2nd ed.). Routledge. 573–582.

16. Dweck, C.S. (2007). *Mindset: The New Psychology of Success* (Updated edition). Ballantine Books.

17. Dweck, C.S. (2002). Messages that motivate: How praise molds students' beliefs, motivation, and performance (in surprising ways). In: Aronson, J. Ed. *Improving Academic Achievement: Impact of Psychological Factors on Education (Educational Psychology)* (1st ed.). Emerald Publishing Limited.

18. Kimmel, M.S. (1994). Masculinity as homophobia: Fear, shame, and silence in the construction of gender identity. In: Brod, H.W. & Kaufman, M. Eds. *Theorizing Masculinities (SAGE Series on Men and Masculinity)* (1st ed.). SAGE Publications, Inc. 103.

19. Vandello, J.A., Bosson, J.K., Cohen, D., Burnaford, R.M. & Weaver, J.R. (2008). Precarious manhood. *Journal of Personality and Social Psychology, 95*(6), 1325–1339. https://doi.org/10.1037/a0012453.

Chapter 3: Learning from the Anomalies

1. Solnit, R. (2015). *Men Explain Things to Me* (Updated ed.). Haymarket Books. 71.

2. Tamnes, C.K., Herting, M.M., Goddings, A.L., Meuwese, R., Blakemore, S.J., Dahl, R.E., Güroğlu, B., Raznahan, A., Sowell, E.R., Crone, E.A. & Mills, K.L. (2017). Development of the cerebral cortex across adolescence: A multisample study of inter-related longitudinal changes in cortical volume, surface area, and thickness. *The Journal of Neuroscience, 37*(12), 3402–3412.

3. Hyde, S.J. & Lindberg, J.S. (2007). Facts and assumptions about the nature of gender differences and the implications for equity. In: Klein, S.S. Ed. *Handbook for Achieving Equity through Education.* Routledge. 19–32.

4. Sadker, D. Sadker, M. & Ziittleman, K.R. 190–191.

5. Spelke, E.S. (2005). Sex differences in intrinsic aptitude for mathematics and science? A critical review. *American Psychologist, 60*(9), 950–958.

6. Kimura, D. 5.

7. Gardner, H. (1983). *Frames of Mind: The Theory of Multiple Intelligences.* Basic Books.

8. Damasio, A.R. (2021). *Descartes' Error: Emotion, Reason and the Human Brain.* Vintage Books.

9. Ramachandran, V.S. (1998). *Phantoms in the Brain: Probing the Mysteries of the Human Mind.* William Morrow and Company, Inc.

10. Kandel, E.R., Schwartz, J.H. & Jessell, T.M. (2000). *Principles of Neural Science* (4th ed.). McGraw-Hill Medical.

11. Dehaene, S. 278.

12. Shakeshaft, C., Brown, G., Irby, B.J., Grogan, M. & Ballenger, J. (2007). Increasing gender equity in educational leadership. In: Klein, S.S. Ed. *Handbook for Achieving Equity through Education*. Routledge. 103–129.

13. Arms, E. (2007). Gender equity in coeducational and single-sex environments. In: Klein, S.S. Ed. *Handbook for Achieving Equity through Education*. Routledge. 171–190.

14. Caplan, J.B. & Caplan, P.J. (2005). The perseverative search for sex differences in mathematical ability. In: Gallagher, A.M. & Kaufman, J.C. Eds. *Gender Differences in Mathematics: An Integrative Psychological Approach*. Cambridge University Press. 25–47.

15. Battro, A.M. (2010). The teaching brain. *Mind, Brain, and Education*, 4(1), 28–33.

16. Frautschi, M. (1999). Culture, gender, leadership and the year 2000 problem. *Infrastructure – Sustaining Systems*, 1, 45–73.

Chapter 4: The Writing on the Wall: The Gender Influence of Student-Teacher Interactions

1. Immordino-Yang, M.H. (2008). All smoke and mirror neurons: Goals as sociocultural and emotional organizers of perception and action in learning. *Mind, Brain, and Education*, 2(2), 67–72.

2. Damasio, A. 83–113.

3. Immordino-Yang, M.H. 67–72.

4. Heller, F. Ed. Frustration in the schools: Teachers speak out on pay, funding and feeling valued. Kappan Magazine Supplement, September, 2019 PDK Poll.

5. Allegretto, S. & Mishel, L. (April 24, 2019). The teacher weekly wage penalty hit 21.4% in 2018, A record high: Trends in the teacher wage and compensation penalties through 2018. *Economic Policy Institute*.

6. Heller, F.. Greenberg, M.T., Brown, J.L. & Abenavoli, R.M. (2016). *Teacher Stress and Health Effects on Teachers, Students, and Schools*. Edna Bennett Pierce Prevention Research Center, Pennsylvania State University.

7. National Board Certification | NEA. (2021). National Education Association. https://www.nea.org/professional-excellence/professional-learning/teacher-licensure/national-board-certification.

8. National Board Certification – NBPTS | Shaping the profession that shapes America's future. (2021). National Board for Professional Teaching Standards. https://www.nbpts.org/national-board-certification/.

9. Gonzalez, J. (2013). Conquering national board certification (and why it's totally worth it). *Cult of Pedagogy*. https://www.cultofpedagogy.com/nbct/.

10. Dehaene, S. 4–6.

11. Ramirez, G., Hooper, S.Y., Kersting, N.B., Ferguson, R. & Yeager, D. (2018). Teacher math anxiety relates to adolescent students' math achievement. *AERA Open*, 4(1), 233285841875605.

12. Arms, E. 173.

13. Gilbert, P. & Gilbert, P. (2017). *Masculinity Goes to School*. Taylor & Francis. 205.

14. Gilbert, R. & Gilbert, P. 206.

15. PISA (2015) Results in Focus. OECD.

16. Halpern, D.F., Wai, J. & Saw, A. 49.

17. Sadker, D., Sadker, M. & Zittleman, K.R. 73.

18. Beilock, S.L., Gunderson, E.A., Ramirez, G. & Levine, S.C. (2010). Female teachers' math anxiety affects girls' math achievement. *Proceedings of the National Academy of Sciences*, 107(5), 1860–1863.

19. Baron-Cohen, S. (2004). *The Essential Difference: Male and Female Brains and The Truth about Autism* (Reprint ed.). Basic Books. 73.

20. Kimura, D. 67.

21. Catsambis, S. (2005). The gender gap in mathematics: Merely a step function? In: Gallagher, A.M. & Kaufman, J.C. Eds. *Gender Differences in Mathematics: An Integrative Psychological Approach*. Cambridge University Press. 232.

22. Fennema, E. (1990). Teachers' beliefs and gender differences in mathematics. In: Fennema, E. & Leder, G. Eds. *Mathematics and Gender*. Teachers College Press. 115.

23. McCambridge, T.R. (1997). Liberal Education and American Schooling. Unpublished dissertation. University of California, Los Angeles. 75.

24. National Education Association (NEA). (1911). Report of the Committee of Nine on the Articulation of School and College in Proceedings.

25. Cubberley, E.P. (1916). *Public School Administration: A Statement of the Fundamental Principles Underlying the Organization and Administration of Public Education*. Boston, MA: Houghton Mifflin Co.

26. NEA Report (1911).

27. Goldin, C. & Katz, L.F. (2008). *The Race between Education and Technology*. Belknap Press of Harvard University Press. 100–101.

28. Faludi, S. (1991). *Backlash: The Undeclared War against American Women*. Three Rivers Press. 81.

29. The 51st Annual PDK Poll of the Public's Attitudes toward the Public Schools. (2019). *Phi Delta Kappan, 100*(1), NP1–NP24.

30. 120 Years of American Education: A Statistical Portrait. (1993). *National Center for Education Statistics*. Ed: Snyder, T.S.

31. Faludi, S. 247.

32. England, P. (2010). The gender revolution: Uneven and stalled. *Gender & Society, 24*(2), 149–166.

33. Ingersoll, R.M., et al. (2018: Updated). Seven trends: The transformation of the teaching force. *Consortium for Policy Research in Education*. CPRE Research Reports. University of Pennsylvania. 3–25.

34. Dolton, P., et al. (2018). *Global Teacher Status Index*. Varkey Foundation.

Chapter 5: Learning Liberation and Integration: It's Not about the Math!

1. Nuttall, R.L., Casey, M.B. & Pezaris, E. (2005). Spatial ability as a mediator of gender differences on mathematical tests. In: Gallagher, A.M. & Kaufman, J.C. Eds. *Gender Differences in Mathematics: An Integrative Psychological Approach*. Cambridge University Press. 122.

2. Royer, J.M. & Garofoli, L.M. 113.

3. Royer, J.M. & Garofoli, L.M. 113.

4. Baron-Cohen, S. 119.

5. Baron-Cohen, S. 119.

6. Lerner, G. (1986). *The Creation of Patriarchy*. Oxford University Press. 22.

7. Smith-Lyttleton, J. (2017). Objects of conflict: (Re) configuring early childhood experiences of gender in the preschool classroom. *Gender and Education, 31*(6), 655–672.

8. Byrnes, J. 87.

9. Dehaene, S. 30.
10. Dehaene, S. 113.
11. Dehaene, S. 200.
12. Willcutt, E.G., Betjemann, R.S., Pennington, B.F., Olson, R.K., DeFries, J.C. & Wadsworth, S.J. (2007). Longitudinal study of reading disability and attention-deficit/hyperactivity disorder: Implications for education. *Mind, Brain, and Education*, *1*(4), 181–192.
13. Taylor, E. (2007). Gender equity in communication skill. In: Klein, S.S. Ed. *Handbook for Achieving Equity Through Education*. NY: Routledge. 281–303.
14. Davis, P. & Spencer, S. (2005). The gender gap artifact: Women's underperformance in quantitative domains through the lens of stereotype threat. In: Gallagher, A.M. & Kaufman, J.C. Eds. *Gender Differences in Mathematics: An Integrative Psychological Approach*. Cambridge University Press. 172–188.
15. Dehaene, S. 119.

Chapter 6: It *Is* about the Math: Gendered Mediators and Executive Functioning Skills

1. Reed, D. & Fox, L. 166.
2. Reed, D. & Fox, L. 166.
3. Brower, T. (2021, April 21). Women and the pandemic: Serious damage to work, health and home demands response. *Forbes*. https://www.forbes.com/sites/tracybrower/2021/04/18/women-and-the-pandemic-serious-damage-to-work-health-and-home-demands-response/?sh=7b064aec1f49.
4. Riley, K. & Stamm, S. (2021, April 27). Nearly 1.5 million mothers are still missing from the workforce. *WSJ*. https://www.wsj.com/articles/nearly-1-5-million-mothers-are-still-missing-from-the-workforce-11619472229.
5. Carrazana, C. (2021, April 29). The women's recession isn't over — especially for moms. *The 19th*. https://19thnews.org/2021/04/womens-recession-moms-covid-19/.
6. Society, G.B.P.A.V. (2021, March 23). Gender division of labor during COVID: Can remote work improve gender equality at home?

Gender & Society. https://gendersociety.wordpress.com/2021/03/22/gender-division-of-labor-during-covid-can-remote-work-improve-gender-equality-at-home/.

7. Grose, J. (2021, June 2). Why women do the household worrying. *The New York Times.* https://www.nytimes.com/2021/04/21/parenting/women-gender-gap-domestic-work.html.

8. Caplan, J.B. & Caplan, P.J. 40.

9. Sadker, D., Sadker, M. & Zittleman, K.R. 125.

10. Catsambis, S. 226.

11. Blair, C., Knipe, H. & Gamson, D. (2008). Is there a role for executive functions in the development of mathematics ability? *Mind, Brain, and Education, 2*(2), 80–89.

12. Blair, C., Knipe, H. & Gamson, D. 80–89.

13. Dehaene, S. 113.

14. Dehaene, S. 269.

15. Baron-Cohen, S. 67.

16. Davis, P. & Spencer, S. 172–188.

17. Inzlicht, M. & Ben-Zeev, T. (2000). A threatening intellectual environment: Why females are susceptible to experiencing problem-solving deficits in the presence of males. *Psychological Science, 11*(5), 365–371.

18. Reed, D. & Fox, L. 166.

19. Caplan, J.B. & Caplan, P.J. 37.

20. Bandura, A. (1997). *Self-Efficacy: The Exercise of Control* (1st ed.). Worth Publishers.

21. Hong, E., O'Neil, H.F. & Feldon, D. (2005). Gender effects on mathematics achievement: Mediating role of state and trait regulation. In: Gallagher, A.M. & Kaufman, J.C. Eds. *Gender Differences in Mathematics: An Integrative Psychological Approach.* Cambridge University Press. 264–293.

22. Hong, E. 297.

23. Hong, C. 268.

24. Blair, C. Knipe, H. & Gamson, D. 80–89.

25. Pajares, F. & Graham, L. (1999). Self-efficacy, motivation constructs, and mathematics performance of entering middle school students. *Contemporary Educational Psychology, 24*(2), 124–139.

26. Rosenthal, R. & Jacobson, L. (1968). *Pygmalion in the Classroom: Teacher Expectation and Pupils' Intellectual Development.* Crown House Publishing.

Chapter 7: Rage On! Gender/Sex, Emotional, and Physical Expression in Schools

1. Simmons, R. (2011). *Odd Girls Out: The Hidden Culture of Aggression in Girls.* Houghton Mifflin Harcourt. 21.
2. Lunneblad, J. & Johansson, T. (2019). Violence and gender thresholds: A study of the gender coding of violent behaviour in schools. *Gender and Education, 33*(1), 1–16.
3. Simmons, R. 118.
4. Reay, D. (2001). "Spice Girls", "Nice Girls", "Girlies", and "Tomboys": Gender discourses, girls' cultures and femininities in the primary classroom. *Gender and Education, 13*(2), 153–166.
5. Lunneblad, J. & Johansson, T. 7.
6. Lyttleton-Smith, J. (2017). Objects of conflict: (Re) configuring early childhood experiences of gender in the preschool classroom. *Gender and Education, 31*(6), 655–672.
7. Thorne, B. 92.
8. Solnit, R. 4.
9. James, W. & McDermott, J.J. (1978). *The Writings of William James: A Comprehensive Edition* (Phoenix Book). University of Chicago Press. 17 and 79.
10. Kandel, E.R., Schwartz, J.H. & Jessell, T.M. (2000). *Principles of Neural Science.* McGraw Hill. 492.
11. Connell, R.W. (2000). *The Men and the Boys.* University of California Press. 29.
12. Gilbert, R. & Gilbert, P. (1998). *Masculinity Goes to School.* Routledge. 205.
13. Miedzian, M. (2002). *Boys Will be Boys: Breaking the Link between Masculinity and Violence.* Lantern Books. 42.
14. Sapolsky, R. (1997, March). Testosterone rules. *Discover.*
15. Miedzian, M. 3.
16. Center for Disease Control – Violence Prevention. https://www.cdc.gov/violenceprevention/datasources/nvdrs/index.html.
17. Sadker, D., Sadker, M. & Zittleman, K.R. 69.

Chapter 8: The Crippling Impact of Mental Health Issues and Trauma: Gender Informed Responses

1. Braff, D. (2019, May 20). Don't leap into buying a home based on school district alone — Dig into these details first. Chicagotribune. Com. https://www.chicagotribune.com/real-estate/ct-re-0813-buying-for-school-district-20170809-story.html.
2. Gorman, L. (2003). School spending raises property values. *National Bureau of Economic Research*, *1*(1).
3. The condition of education: Characteristics of children's families. National Center for Education Statistics. Updated: May 2020. https://nces.ed.gov/programs/coe/indicator_cce.asp.
4. Center for Disease Control. https://www.cdc.gov/violenceprevention/aces/about.html.
5. Felitti, V.J., Anda, R.F., Nordenberg, D., Williamson, D.F., Spitz, A.M., Edwards, V., Koss, M.P. & Marks, J.S. (1998). Relationship of childhood abuse and household dysfunction to many of the leading causes of death in adults. *American Journal of Preventive Medicine*, *14*(4), 245–258.
6. Warning Signs of Traumatic Stress. Table 1. School Crisis Prevention and Intervention Curriculum, National Association of School Psychologists.
7. Arundel, K. & Arundel, K. (2020, September 23). Updated school psychology standards aim to curb shortages, create cohesive support systems. K-12 Dive. https://www.k12dive.com/news/school-psychology-standards-to-curb-shortages/585748/.
8. PTSD is More Likely in Women than Men | NAMI: National Alliance on Mental Illness. (2019). NAMI.Org.
9. Rhodes, A.E. (2014). Antecedents and sex/gender differences in youth suicidal behavior. *World Journal of Psychiatry*, *4*(4), 120.
10. der Kolk, V.B. (2015). *The Body Keeps the Score: Brain, Mind, and Body in the Healing of Trauma* (Reprint ed.). Penguin Books. 72.
11. der Kolk, V.B. 72.
12. der Kolk, V.B. 73.
13. der Kolk, V.B. 73.
14. Perry, B.D. & Szalavitz, M. (2017). *The Boy Who Was Raised as a Dog: And Other Stories from a Child Psychiatrist's Notebook – What*

Traumatized Children Can Teach Us about Loss, Love, and Healing (3rd ed.). Basic Books.

15. Friedrich, A.A., Mendez, L.M.R. & Mihalas, S.T. (2010). Gender as a factor in school-based mental health service delivery. *School Psychology Review, 39*(1), 122–136.

16. Damour, L. (2017). *Untangled: Guiding Teenage Girls through the Seven Transitions into Adulthood* (Reprint ed.). Ballantine Books. 11 and 102.

17. "The Courage to Be Vulnerable." Interview with Bene Brown. On Being Podcast. January 29, 2015.

18. Paludi, M.A. (2007). Sexual harassment: The hidden gender equity problem. In: Klein, S.S. Ed. *Handbook for Achieving Equity through Education*. NY: Routledge. 216–217.

19. Nadal, K. (2018). *Microaggressions and Traumatic Stress: Theory, Research, and Clinical Treatment*. American Psychological Association.

20. López, C. (2021, May 11). Every anti-trans bill US lawmakers introduced this year, from banning medication to jail time for doctors. Insider. https://www.insider.com/over-half-of-us-states-tried-passing-anti-trans-bills-2021-3.

21. King, J.R. (2000). The problem(s) of men in early education. In: Lesko, N. Ed. *Masculinities at School*. Sage Publications. 13–21.

22. King, J.R. 13–21.

23. Mandel, L. & Shakeshaft, C. (2000). Heterosexism in middle schools. In: Lesko, N. Ed. *Masculinities at School*. Sage Publications. 75–103.

24. Mac An Ghaill, M. (2000). "New times" in an old country: Emerging black gay identities and (hetero) sexual discontents. In: Lesko, N. Ed. *Masculinities at School*. Sage Publications. 163–185.

Conclusion: Reconstructing Schools and Celebrating Gender Diversity

1. Making peace with broken pieces. (2018, November 17). Golden rejoining. https://www.goldenrejoining.com/post/making-peace-with-broken-pieces.

Appendix G

1. Connell, R. W. (2005). *Masculinities*. University of California Press. 37.
2. Noddings, N. (1984). *Caring: A Feminine Approach to Ethics and Moral Education*. University of California Press.

Printed in the United States
by Baker & Taylor Publisher Services